Race, Education and Educational Leadership in England

Also available from Bloomsbury

Education Towards Race Equality, Lillian R. Klein
Ethnicity, Race and Education: An Introduction, Sue Walters
Eugenics, Race and Intelligence in Education, Clyde Chitty

Race, Education and Educational Leadership in England

An Integrated Analysis

Edited by
Paul Miller and Christine Callender

BLOOMSBURY ACADEMIC
LONDON · NEW YORK · OXFORD · NEW DELHI · SYDNEY

Bloomsbury Academic
Bloomsbury Publishing Plc
50 Bedford Square, London, WC1B 3DP, UK
1385 Broadway, New York, NY 10018, USA
29 Earlsfort Terrace, Dublin 2, Ireland

Bloomsbury, Bloomsbury Academic and the Diana logo are trademarks of
Bloomsbury Publishing Plc

First published in Great Britain 2019
Reprinted 2021

A catalogue record for this book is available from the British Library.

A catalog record for this book is available from the Library of Congress.

ISBN: HB: 978-1-3500-6859-9
ePDF: 978-1-3500-6860-5
eBook: 978-1-3500-6861-2

Typeset by Newgen KnowledgeWorks Pvt. Ltd., Chennai, India
Printed and bound in Great Britain

To find out more about our authors and books visit www.bloomsbury.com
and sign up for our newsletters.

Contents

Notes on contributors

Jason Arday, PhD, is a senior lecturer in education at Roehampton University and a Trustee of the Runnymede Trust. Jason's research focuses on race, education, culture and social justice. He is the author of three forthcoming books entitled *Considering Racialised Contexts in Education: Using Reflective Practice and Peer-Mentoring to Support Black and Ethnic Minority Educators* (Routledge); *Being Young, Black and Male: Challenging the Dominant Discourse* (Palgrave); *Exploring Cool Britannia and Multi-Ethnic Britain: Uncorking the Champagne Supernova* (Routledge) and an edited collection with Professor Heidi Mirza entitled *Dismantling Race in Higher Education: Racism, Whiteness and Decolonising the Academy* (Palgrave).

Claudette Bailey-Morrissey, PhD, is an independent consultant and careers leader. She began her career as a teacher in the secondary school sector. Throughout the nineteen years of her career she held senior and middle leadership roles including that of assistant headteacher, leadership coach and head of faculty, working with teachers and middle leaders to develop their leadership skills and capabilities. Claudette is an advocate for women school leaders and is a coach on the Women Leading in Education programme. She completed her doctorate in education in December 2015 (Bailey-Morrissey, 2015) and is passionate about sharing the findings from her research to empower others.

Adam Burns, PhD, spent several years teaching history and politics in secondary schools across the south of England before taking up his current role as senior lecturer in history at the University of Wolverhampton. In 2017, he completed an EdD at the University of Leicester, with a thesis exploring the place of British imperialism in English schools in the twenty-first century. His education-based research has appeared in *Teaching History*, the *International Journal of Historical Learning, Teaching and Research* and the *Journal of Learning Development in Higher Education,* and he is currently on the editorial board of the journal *Management in Education.*

Tony Bush, PhD, is Professor of educational leadership at the University of Nottingham, and previously held similar positions at the universities of Leicester, Reading, Lincoln and Warwick. He is a vice president of the British Educational Leadership, Management and Administration Society (BELMAS) and editor of the Society's academic journal, *Educational Management, Administration and Leadership* (EMAL). His extensive international work includes research, consultancy, external examining and invited keynote presentations in twenty-two countries on all six continents.

Christine Callender, PhD, is a lecturer in education at the University College of London (UCL) Institute of Education, London, and a senior fellow of the Higher Education Academy. She has worked in schools, colleges and in the higher education sector for over twenty years and has undertaken consultancies nationally and internationally. Christine is the co-convenor of the British Educational Leadership Administration Society (BELMAS) Race and Leadership Research Interest Group, and her research interests are in the areas of race, equality and diversity in teacher education; the experiences of black and minority ethnic males in teaching, race and leadership; and the use of critical race theory as a theoretical, methodological and analytic lens for examining race in education.

Sharon Curtis, PhD, has a background in a combination of nursing, teaching and counselling. She has worked in a number of educational establishments and at Sheffield Relate counselling services. She has both a diploma and an MA in counselling. Sharon has worked in the early years sector for over twenty years. She has gained her National Professional Qualification in Integrated Centre Leadership, as well as her Early Years Professional Status, and is also aware of the benefits of multi-diverse leadership. She is well networked both locally and nationally. Sharon completed her doctorate at Leeds Beckett University. Her research was based upon black women leaders in early years education. She currently sits on the national board of the Training Advancement and Co-operation in Teaching Young Children and recently worked as an external validator for a new degree course in Leeds and has been a member of the team from Sheffield University, who were successful in receiving a recent Froebel Fund award.

Helen Deane, EdD, is a qualified teacher with twenty plus years experience of teaching, training and assessing in schools, colleges and universities. She manages her own business, has held senior education management roles and has experience inspecting further education teacher training. Helen is a researcher, practitioner and writer with a research interest in leadership, management and diversity. Her professional expertise is in leadership, management, education and training, and equality and diversity. As a qualified and practising coach, she engages coaching in her work as a method of empowering others to face their challenges and reach their goals.

Jan Fook, PhD (BSW, MSW, PhD, FAcSS), was born and raised in Australia, and originally trained as a social worker. She has spent most of her career as an academic and has held professorial positions (in social work and education) at nine universities in Australia, Canada, Norway and the United Kingdom. She is currently visiting professor at Royal Holloway, University of London, but from 2019 will be professor and head of social work at the University of Vermont. She is most known for her work on critical social work and critical reflection. She has published 16 books and over 100 book chapters and articles.

Dennis Francis is a PhD candidate at the UCL Institute of Education. He has a vast amount of experience in the field of education and is a former college assistant principal. He earned a BA (Hons) in French language with government from the University of Essex and an MBA in Educational Leadership (International) from the Institute of Education, University of London (2011). Dennis spent a year at Morehouse College, Atlanta (2013–2014) as a scholar-in-residence where he undertook research on race, racism, critical race theory and their link to educational leadership and achievement: this research informs his current work

Asima Iqbal, PhD, has a doctorate in education with a particular focus on Muslim school leaders. Following from her PhD research, she is interested in doing further research on Muslim professionals working in the field of education. By collecting narratives of Muslim professionals, she intends to further explore the multiple concerns faced by Asian Muslims living in England. Considering the numerous national and international events which portray Muslims as problematic, Asima Iqbal is keen to pursue further research to understand the lived experiences of Muslim professionals since it is crucial to have a healthy debate about the place and perception of Islam in British public sphere.

Alice Johns, BA (Hons), was programme manager for the Leadership Foundation's funded work. This included maintaining oversight of all equality, diversity and inclusion (EDI) funded outputs. During her tenure in the role she helped launch the initiatives detailed within the chapter: the Diversifying Leadership programme, Sponsor Toolkit, BME Leadership in Higher Education Summit and the Senior Leaders EDI retreat. Previously, she worked within the international schools sector and the Canadian and British Houses of Parliament. Due in December 2018 to complete an MSc in education, power and social change at Birkbeck, University of London, she specializes in peace education and the use of storytelling pedagogies to promote cultural reconciliation.

Deborah Jones, PhD, is Reader in Education at Brunel University where she has undertaken a variety of management roles and taught across a range of programmes including EdD, MA, PGCE and BA. She started her career as a primary teacher and subsequently joined an inspectorate and advisory service in a London borough. Deborah's current research interests include the perceptions and experiences of British South Asian primary head teachers and also oracy in primary education.

Geeta Ludhra, PhD, is a freelance consultant working in a variety of educational contexts. She was a Senior Lecturer in Education at Brunel University lecturing on the PGCE, masters and doctoral programmes. Her teaching experiences span diverse primary schools in challenging areas of West London, where she held various management positions. She has undertaken research into children's cultural and bilingual identities, and how teachers and schools nurture these. Her doctoral study explored the narratives and identities of academically 'successful' South Asian girls, which has led to her current focus with minority ethnic student teachers.

Paul Miller, PhD, PFHEA, FAcSS, is Professor of educational leadership and management, in the School of Education and Professional Development at the University of Huddersfield. He is President of the Commonwealth Council for Educational Administration and Management (CCEAM), and a member of Council of the British Educational Leadership Management Administration Society (BELMAS) where he is co-convenes the Race & Educational Leadership Research Interest Group. He has written widely on equity and discrimination issues in leadership/career progression related to black, Asian and minority ethnic (BAME) and overseas trained teachers in England. His theory of 'White sanction', used to examine and explain practices and patterns among BAME staff in education in England, has assisted the UK Cabinet Office in the development of policies aimed at tackling race equality in education in England.

Vijaya Nath, BA (Hons), MA (Hons), was the recent past director of Leadership Development at Leadership Foundation for Higher Education. She has over twenty-six years of experience in developing leaders in the private and not-for-profit sectors. Previous director of leadership development at The King's Fund, London, she contributed to thought leadership in medical leadership. Vijaya has published and written a number of papers on leadership development and continues to write on areas of medical engagement, quality improvement in health, equality and diversity, including the importance of advancing women in leadership. She is a visiting professor at Milan's SDA Bocconi School of Management and was appointed trustee of Windsor Leadership in 2017.

Richard Race, PhD, is a senior lecturer in education in the School of Education at Roehampton University and visiting professor in education at Sapienza University of Rome, Italy. As well as being editor of *Advancing Multicultural Dialogues in Education* (Palgrave Macmillan), he is also author of the monograph *Multiculturalism and Education* (Bloomsbury) and co-editor with Professor Vini Lander of *Advancing Race and Ethnicity in Education* (Palgrave Macmillan). Richard is currently working on his next monograph: *Integration and Education Policy-Making* (contracted with Palgrave Macmillan) and a special edition of the *London Review of Education* entitled *Multiculturalism and Interculturalism in Education*.

Victoria Showunmi, EdD, is a senior lecturer at Maynooth University and currently holds a fractional lecturing post at the University College of London (UCL) Institute of Education. Her interests are gender, class, identity and race. She uses such interests to interrupt areas such as educational leadership and gender policies. She has local, national and international experience in the area of gender and education and the wellbeing of young black women.

Introduction: Race, education and educational leadership in England

Christine Callender and Paul Miller

Introduction and context

Despite the implementation of policies aimed at curtailing the negative consequences of race discrimination and racial inequality, their permanence in the educational landscape of England is long-standing. At the time of writing, many pupils from black, Asian and minority ethnic (BAME) groups are failing to thrive in the schooling system, and the number of teachers and leaders in schools, further education colleges and universities in leadership positions are stubbornly low and/or are diminishing over time. That there has been a plethora of research that has aimed to find causes and solutions to the permanence of differential racialized outcomes and experiences is not without doubt. Several volumes have been published on the topic in addition to numerous journal articles, dissertations and theses. One area that has attracted less attention in England, however, is the intersection of race and leadership and research that examines these issues within macro-, meso- and micro dimensions of educational institutions.

Coleman (2012: 597) argues that leadership 'tends to be equated with being white (in Western countries), male, heterosexual, middle class and middle aged. This means that those who diverge in any way from this ideal are seen as "outsiders" if they aspire to become leaders'. This salient stereotypical notion of who inhabits leadership roles has consequences for those who ultimately aspire to *and* attain leadership. Qualitative studies have shown that homosociability – a bias which results in recruitment panels appointing in their own image – is prevalent; thus, it is less likely that a leader in any educational establishment is likely to diverge from this norm (Grummell et al., 2009; Blackmore et al., 2006). Coleman (2012: 597) also points to the ways in which studies examining 'diversity' conceptualized diversity largely in terms of gender, more specifically the lack of representation of women in leadership roles. In the United Kingdom studies of educational leadership up until this time largely ignored the specificity of minoritized groups and their lived experiences as leaders. In the case of minoritized women, for example, who represent a minority (gender) within a minority (race/ethnicity), Coleman contends that where research has privileged race or ethnicity it has 'broadly focused on 'how difference impacts on becoming a leader and how that difference impacts on the practice of leadership' (2012).

A recent report on BAME teachers in the educational system in England highlights the extent of disproportionality at the level of school leadership, noting that racial inequality represents

> an almost endemic problem at the leadership levels of teaching. In November 2014, the School Workforce Census showed that just 3% (435 out of 14,500) of the headteachers from local authority maintained primary schools and 3.6% (47 out of 1,300 headteachers) from local authority maintained secondary schools were from BME backgrounds. The racial disparity in leadership roles is exacerbated when gender is taken into account, as there are greater disparities between male BME and male white teachers, compared to their female counterparts. Twice the proportion of white males (18.3%) are in senior roles compared to BME males (8.7%); whereas 12.3% of white female teachers are in senior roles compared to 8.1% of BME female teachers. (Runnymede/NASUWT, 2017)

The systemic barriers and school-based mechanisms through which inequality persists are indeed complex and are perhaps neatly summed up in a quotation taken from an National Union of Teachers-commissioned report entitled *Visible and Invisible Barriers: The Impact of Racism on BME Teachers* (2017):

> BME teachers spoke about an invisible glass-ceiling and widespread perception among senior leadership teams (SLTs) that BME teachers 'have a certain level and don't go beyond it'. (6)

Similar patterns are found in other educational institutions such as the university sector, where leadership at all levels, that is, academic and senior administrative staff, senior leadership and governance, is occupied by a preponderance of white, middle-class men. In contrast, BME staff in the sector encounter 'gatekeeping' and 'blocking'. Singh and Kwhali (2015: 9) place the slow progress of equality in higher education firmly at the feet of the institutions:

to claim a public image of diversity and equality – in the knowledge that HEIs remain dominated by white men, and where serious concerns about BME student attainment levels and BME academic employment rates pertain – is ethically questionable. By adopting what Gilroy termed a 'coat of paint' theory of institutional racism, what arguably emerges across the sector is a passive, superficial institutional response to issues of race equality that appears dislocated from the lived realities of BME academics and their experiences within the academy. It is the reluctance to acknowledge the prevalence of staff inequality, discrimination and racism within universities and the variable ways in which these might manifest, that arguably restricts progress.

More recently, Bhopal (2018: 103) has noted that universities are bastions in the reproduction of racial inequality, and that they are complicit in maintaining an unjust racial and class hierarchy. She describes the sector as representative of 'white privilege which fail[s] to cater for the experiences of black and minority ethnic groups', often employing a 'rhetoric of inclusion, but one that is rarely evidenced in practice or outcomes'. The situation in the further education sector is similarly inequitable, illustrating that not only is the proportion of BME staff in post-16 education small, but that they experience bullying and barriers to career progression, feel that they will not progress in their current careers, are excluded from decision-making and experience cultural insensitivity. Similar to the university sector, there is significant under-representation at leadership levels, especially when one considers that the demographic of further education settings is well represented by students from minoritized backgrounds (University College Union, 2016).

In schools, the work of Bush, Glover and Sood (2006) and Bush et al. (2005), highlights the many obstacles that BME staff encounter on the journey to school leadership and concludes that a number of factors are at play, including personal experience, context, facilitating factors and support, barriers to career progression and notions of exceptionality. These factors individually and in combination impact on the potential pool of available BME leaders and their ascendency to leadership positions. Bush et al. (2005), for instance, note that

> research makes an important contribution to understanding the position of BME teachers and leaders in English schools. The 'voices' of the participants paint a clear picture of their lived experience of leadership. It is evident that they face a number of problems in advancing their careers, including direct and indirect racism and discrimination. (72)

They go on to underscore the consequences of a lack of representation, arguing that 'the presence of these leaders at all levels is needed to provide the role models that will encourage BME people and children to enter the profession, progress to leadership positions and remain as leaders to become the role models of the future' (ibid.). There are compelling reasons for greater racialized and ethnic representation in leadership that go beyond representation. Miller (2018) agrees, arguing that 'educational leaders have a moral duty to create, promote, facilitate and embed race equality within and throughout their institutions' as this is necessary to avoid the invisibilization of BME groups in leadership and further their marginalization in educational institutions.

In an attempt to address the lack of race and ethnic diversity in leadership, the creation of bespoke programmes aimed at preparing aspirant BME leaders for leadership roles has been promoted. Whilst such programmes are positively reviewed and valued by BME staff, they cannot on their own redress the long-standing imbalances that exist. McKenley and Gordon (2002: 19), for example, report that school leaders question the value of sending senior staff on generic training, and that BME staff felt that 'the most important leadership development cited was the experience of being managed by effective headteachers'. Later, Coleman and Campbell-Stephens (2010: 48) examined the views of participants on a bespoke BME leadership programme, Investing in Diversity, which concurs with the findings of Bush et al. (2005, 2006) and reports that access to the lower echelons of leadership was 'relatively straightforward, but it was in the development and acquisition stages of their career that [BME] staff met difficulties'. They describe how, despite being selected for fast-track progression into leadership, promotion was often stymied and that 'most had found it hard to reach the acquisition stage or had stalled at a point just short of acquisition (cf. the findings of the NUT/Runnymede report cited earlier). Ogunbawo's (2012: 173) review of a number of customized programmes for BME staff concludes:

> Customized BME programmes need to be unpacked further, the components and the value added evaluated and the participants' progress tracked over a period of time. There is definitely urgent need for extensive research in this area. The value of such studies would not only be in ascertaining the short- and long-term benefits of customized BME development programmes, it will be of tremendous value in revealing the essential elements required to be present and available within all generic, mainstream leadership development programmes to make them fit for all leaders (regardless of ethnicity, colour or race) working in a multicultural society, delivering a culturally diverse curriculum and leading a diverse workforce.

What is clear is that the educational leadership literature in England is replete with studies on 'diversity'. These tend to focus on gender but without examining 'race' or the intersections of 'race' and gender. This volume aims to add to the existing literature, taking the discussion of 'race' outside of a more general conversation of 'diversity' in education and educational leadership in order to provide a more nuanced, explicit focus on race *and* educational leadership. This is critical to understanding not just the experiences but also the perspectives of BAME individuals. Citing the work of Benhabib (2002), Blackmore (2006: 192) reinforces this point, noting that it is important to examine questions of privilege, particularly in order to ascertain,

> how does privilege work in and through schools and school systems around the inextricable intersections between race, gender, class, ethnicity in ways that focus on the relations of power, hybridity and fluidity of multiple identities that arise from cross membership in different groups?

This book draws together a number of empirical and conceptual studies of race, education and educational leadership. In doing so it provides a vista which examines 'race' within the context of curriculum and of a range of education settings. The cross-cutting theme of intersectionality is threaded through many of the chapters, illustrating the complex and dynamic operationalization of race, gender, class and religion within the micro-organizational structures and processes of schools, further and higher education. It positions questions of access, opportunity, support and success at the nexus of BAME leadership experiences and highlights how these are experienced and lived. The present volume, *Race, Education and Educational Leadership in England*, provides a snapshot of the current state of play in the hope that it both stimulates and continues discussion of these very important and pressing issues. In Part One of this volume, 'Curriculum, attainment and diversity', Callender, Francis and Burns (i) examine the perspectives of leaders and the ways in which they enact racial knowledge and (ii) illustrate how the History curriculum in secondary schools, especially its historical antecedents of Empire, is multifaceted and complex. Burns examines the importance of teaching British imperial history from varied stakeholder perspectives, especially its role in providing a much-needed and invaluable context for young people in understanding the nature of cosmopolitan, multicultural Britain today. All of the chapters in this section centre on race and, as Alston (2012: 128), opines,

> When race is placed at the center of discourse – in this particular case, the field of educational leadership – the human experience will be grounded in the realities

of the lived experience of racism and will embrace the subjectivity of individual perspectives, while also openly acknowledging that perceptions of truth, fairness and justice reflect the mindset, status, and experience of the knower.

The chapters in this volume point to the significance of how race is understood, enacted and practised. In Part One, the chapters draw attention to the significance of connectedness and racial knowledge. Callender, for example, highlights how race is understood and conceptualized by leaders in teacher education, noting that 'where teacher educators' views are sought, research has concluded that, although teacher educators are well versed in race equality issues, they may not be well placed to bring about change within their institutions'. She refers to the presence of a bipolar narrative where racial knowledge is known yet unacknowledged and where race is understood by its inscription on the bodies of BAME students and understood in terms of racialized othering. Callender reports that 'race is a distant out of body experience, disconnected from and unrelated to their [teacher educators'] own white racialized identities – and privilege – yet, at the same time race is hypervisible, valued and problematic when it enters the white space of ITE'. Callender asserts that they (teacher educators) are 'implicated in forms of racialized myopia – recognizing race whilst simultaneously engaging colour-blind or colour-neutral practices and that teacher educators are intricately bound up in these processes'.

Francis, in contrast, foregrounds the lived experiences of black male leaders and students, illustrating how leading with justice and care is integral to achievement. In his chapter he reports that 'the race of the leader and their praxis cannot be placed in the margins of the leadership–student achievement discourse. Moreover, the praxis of leadership-based justice and care can contribute to strengthening student achievement'. Francis reminds us that 'leadership based on justice and care is a sine qua non for improving the students' achievements. The leaders routinely enact this leadership based on a genuine care and love for the students and a connection with them: they want the students to succeed. In turn, the students valued the leaders' positive attitude toward them and they recognized that the leaders expected and pushed them to realize their potential and gain the qualifications they required. Indeed, race in leadership does matter.'

Last, Burns contends that 'a wider definition of curriculum – as a process, rather than a body of knowledge to be transmitted – is crucial to understanding the equally contentious role of diversity in a curriculum'. Burns argues that not only is the History curriculum, and in particular British imperial history, a body of knowledge that is to be taught, but that it is mediated through the understandings and experiences of both teachers and students. He notes that young people's conceptions of 'race' and ethnicity owe a great deal to perceptions gathered from outside the classroom, and that both students and teachers 'bring a variety of social identities into a classroom, ranging from identities forged through frequent encounters with racism to those living in bubbles of unexamined white privilege'. In his study he underscores the importance of an informed and contextualized knowledge of British history, claiming that 'now, more than ever, additional curriculum time needs to be given to studying topics that could serve to better educate our young people on the diverse roots of British society'. More importantly, Burns encourages us to see its benefits in producing critical and informed citizens.

In Part Two, 'Talent management and career progression', Bush, Miller, Bailey-Morrissey and Race, Deane, Arday and Johns, Fook and Nath examine the experiences and untapped potential of aspirant and existing BAME teachers and leaders as well as the barriers and enablers to their success in a range of educational settings. The importance of an intersectional lens and the need for more intentional and proactive strategies is evident in the chapters which comprise this section. Bush's chapter, for example, maps research on BAME leaders in schools and disrupts normative explanations for the low numbers of BAME leaders, arguing that 'there is some evidence that BAME teachers and leaders are likely to be better qualified than white leaders, often educated to master's level, suggesting that their under-representation is not due to a qualifications "gap"'. Bush outlines a number of systemic issues facing access to and enactment of BAME teachers and leaders, describing these as 'barriers to equity and social justice'. Bush contends that grit, tenacity, determination and resilience are key factors in leadership success, and that 'BAME teachers and leaders do experience barriers and either direct or hidden discrimination. Under-representation has some cultural dimensions but also arises from the "invisible" criteria used by selection panels, a form of covert racism. Most of these leaders have progressed despite these barriers rather than as a result of positive discrimination or any other systematic support'.

Miller's chapter continues with an examination of the experiences of overseas trained teachers (OTTs), highlighting how the lack of recognition of overseas qualifications has led to 'a politics of knowledge which stems from epistemological and ontological misunderstandings of difference that combines to advantage the career progression of OTTs from white, industrialized countries, whilst simultaneously limiting the career progression of OTTs from non-industrialized, non-white countries'. Miller highlights that OTTs have been negatively impacted as a result of the existence of a 'hostile' race and immigration context. Consequently, 'OTTs from white, industrialized countries are given a head start to promotion, progression to leadership roles due to being exempt from additional training and assessment for UK QTS, whereas OTTs trained in non-white, non-industrialized countries are disadvantaged', leading to a situation where 'OTTs from non-white, non-industrialized countries must undergo additional training and assessment, since their qualifications, the educational systems that trained them, and their experiences are not considered "equivalent" to British standards'. Miller underscores the importance of OTTs to the sustainability of schooling in England, especially in the context of acute teacher shortages, but reminds us of OTTs' precarious position as they are 'caught in this "double jeopardy" where race discrimination and stereotyping delivered through hostile migration and education policies in Britain dictate how quickly, and how far, they are likely to progress and not their qualifications, skills and work experiences'.

Bailey-Morrissey and Race examine the intersections of race, gender and class in the lived experiences of black women senior leaders, arguing that 'for black women senior leaders the complex intersectionality of race; gender and social class raise important issues in enabling them to recognize stereotyping and, therefore, work to socially construct a positive perception of black women as senior leaders'. They point to the fact that 'for black women senior leaders, where their race and gender intersect, they can experience intersecting oppressions, or the convergence of being both black and female, and often they come from a lower socio-economic social class than whites'. The theme of resilience is threaded through the narratives of the black women senior leaders, and the chapter acknowledges that 'the journey into senior leadership is largely shaped by black women's personal and professional experiences'. The question of *who* is a senior leader was evident in their study, and the way in which the study participants were 'challenged in some way, either through racism and stereotyping, unspoken rules or by creating barriers by promoting others who fit a certain profile. Their narratives demonstrate a refusal to comply and "play the game" to get ahead at the expense of compromising their values.'

Next, Deane shifts the focus to staff progression and succession planning in the further education (FE) sector. Deane points to the paucity of BAME leaders in FE and the ways in which previous successful attempts at increasing the number of senior leaders in FE has diminished in recent times. Deane identifies succession planning, BME staff attrition rates, attitudes and micropolitical behaviour as integral to the discussion and reviews the success of initiatives such as positive action, asserting that 'the interests of BME staff were advanced when they converged with the interests of white staff, the advances made became given up as the impact and effect of austerity and the cutbacks started to threaten the leadership status of white staff. "Demand-led" and "customer-driven" approaches to funding, austerity and political expediency have spurred decision-makers to abandon positive action and some would argue, revert to the old ways of doing things.' Deane cites the Education Training Foundation's (ETF) stated commitment to ensuring 'that the senior leadership of the sector reflects the student population in its diversity by 2020. There are, however, no clear documented plans on how this is to be achieved'. Deane concludes that it is crucial to change the 'internal organizational cultures, [. . .] in order to truly deal with BME staff progression and succession planning in the FE sector.

The theme of opportunity and access to leadership is continued in Arday's chapter on race and educational leadership in higher education where he contributes to the 'ongoing debate within higher education, which situates racial inequality and discrimination as a barrier to greater diversification within the sector'. Arday elucidates the view that 'racial discrimination within the academy remains problematic and continues to be a persistent barrier for BME individuals attempting to progress in academia. Paradoxically, universities continue to contradict egalitarian ideals associated with developing processes, which endorse access and inclusion for all.' He too points to the complex and multifaceted BAME academic experience characterized by racism, oppression and silencing, arguing that a 'tectonic shift is required regarding the landscape of higher education and this needs to be driven by university senior administrators that must be held accountable for not actively prioritizing and advancing the diversification of staff particularly at leadership levels'. He concludes that 'disrupting patterns of inequality within the academy is difficult, particularly when we consider the dearth of BME leaders, but the terrain of academia as it presently exists, ensures that collectively much effort is still required if we are to continue to advance progressive change which ultimately dismantles pop shoes racial inequality within higher education'.

Johns, Fook and Nath, evaluate programmes and measures undertaken by the Leadership Foundation for Higher Education (LFHE) to increase the numbers and representation of BAME leaders in higher education. They argue that the work undertaken by the LFHE mirrors existing approaches to diversifying the leadership pool in higher education (HE), but that in addition, the 'pressing work is to establish and embed BME equality as an organizational priority across the sector and that Advance HE continues to employ, alongside institutions and other sector bodies, a range of strategies to support progress in different ways and at different levels'. They highlight the fact that an integrated and 'joined up' approach is required that takes 'into account how the personal experiences of BME staff in seeking leadership roles can be supported and enhanced by systemic policies and practice that enable success'. Moreover, they emphasize 'that to really expedite change and show commitment, there is an essential need to obtain senior staff buy-in, for them to be visible advocates for change and that their vision for change needs to be communicated and championed across the whole organization'.

In Part Three, 'Race and intersectionality', Iqbal, Jones and Ludhra, and Curtis and Showunmi apply the analytic tool of intersectionality to the experiences of Muslim, British South East Asian and black women leaders through the lenses of race, gender, class and religion. Iqbal's cross-cultural study of school leaders in England and Pakistan compares 'the manifestation of religion in a professional role in two religiously and culturally diverse countries', illustrating the impact of religion as an aspect of culture on educational leadership. Iqbal's study highlights a duality in head teachers' identity that is 'played out differently in relation to pupils, parents, community and the media'. The study illuminates the ways in which, 'while dealing with Muslim pupils and parents, the selected head teachers were flexible in using their religious faith in a professional role'. They experienced what Iqbal refers to as a form of 'cultural racism' where they felt discriminated against by people of their own kind, that is, Asian Muslim parents. 'Remaining alert to their sense of belonging to a religious as well as a racial group, these head teachers valued their professional identity as much (or more) as their religious identity'. Iqbal concludes that 'the strategic way in which the head teachers separated aspects of religion from culture reflected their intention to remain true to their faith while simultaneously conforming to the expectations of the Western school system'. Thus, at the same time Pakistani Muslims want to defend the basic elements of their religion and culture. The findings of the current study evidence that Muslim professionals do not necessarily have to face a conflict between abiding by the rule of law and the basic tenets of Islam.'

Following this, Jones and Ludhra explore the lived experiences of academically and professionally successful British South Asian adolescent girls and women. They posit the view that 'the notion of "success" is a contested one, being interpreted and experienced in various ways beyond academic and professional achievements. It can include practical intelligences, personality traits, a demanding work ethic, and may take account of ways in which family, culture, and emotional support, can facilitate "success" journeys'. Albeit that success was performed in different ways, the study participants 'employed discipline and drew on sophisticated mechanisms to cope with stress, in order to maintain the "Superwoman" status that they embodied and performed'. Jones and Ludhra assert that 'success is complex as women move in and out of comfort zones. For a successful British South Asian head teacher or head girl, being "in the minority" brings visibility, weight of responsibility and a sense that failure will impact on their entire community. "Holistic" success is difficult, if not impossible, to achieve, but through psychological resilience and moral commitment, the girls and women in this study were nevertheless, resolute in striving for it'.

In the final chapter of this volume, Curtis and Showunmi draw together the findings from two studies on black women leaders and the silence that surrounds their experiences in educational settings, noting that 'for those who live on the margins, the discussion within academia must move research forward by exploring the multiple dimensions of the effects of race and gender rather than presenting a reductionist view'. They note that 'in order for women leaders to fulfil their full potential, it is crucial the culture of the organization is one in which race and gender are recognized and supported. The study indicates the need for further work to be carried out in organizations to unlock the barriers that potentially stop women leaders moving ahead as fast as their male counterparts'. Fundamentally, Curtis and Showunmi's chapter underlines that 'the organizational structure, working environment, mentoring activities and leadership styles are all factors which can promote success'. Moreover, 'black women can indeed define their own world views and realities through voicing their own experiences. We need to ensure that we no longer remain echoes of our silentious presence'.

References

Alston, J. A. (2012), 'Standing on the Promises: A New Generation of Black Women Scholars in Educational Leadership and Beyond', *International Journal of Qualitative Studies in Education*, 25 (1): 127–29.

Benhabib, S. (2000), *The Claims of Culture: Equality and Diversity in the Global Era*, Princeton, NJ: Princeton University Press

Bhopal, K. (2018), *White Privilege: The Myth of a Post-Racial Society*, University of Bristol: Policy Press.

Blackmore, J. (2006), 'Deconstructing Diversity Discourse in the Field of Educational Management and Leadership', *Educational Leadership and Management*, 34 (2): 181–99.

Blackmore, J., P. Thomson and K. Barty (2006), 'Principal Selection: Homosociability, the Search for Security and the Production of Normalized Principal Identities', *Educational Leadership and Management*, 34 (3): 297–317.

Bush, T., D. Glover and K. Sood (2006), 'Black and Minority Ethnic Leaders in England: A Portrait', *School Leadership & Management*, 26 (3): 289–305.

Bush, T., D. Glover, K. Sood, C. Cardno, G. Potgeiter and K. Tangle (2005), *Black and Minority Ethnic Leaders: Final Report to the National College for School Leadership*. Last accessed 3 August 2018: http://citeseerx.ist.psu.edu/viewdoc/download?doi=10.1.1.550.244&rep=rep1&type=pdf.

Coleman, M. (2012), 'Leadership and Diversity', *Educational Leadership and Management*, 40 (5): 592–609.

Coleman, M. and R. Campbell-Stephens (2010), 'Perceptions of Career Progress: The Experience of Black and Minority Ethnic School Leaders', *School Leadership & Management*, 30 (1): 35–49.

Grummell, B., D. Devine and K. Lynch (2009), 'Appointing Senior Managers in Education: Homosociability, Local Logics and Authenticity in the Selection Process', *Educational Leadership and Management*, 37 (3): 329–49.

McKenley, J. and G. Gordon (2002), *Challenge Plus: The Experience of Black and Minority Ethnic School Leaders*. National College of School Leaders (NCSL). Last accessed 3 August 2018: http://dera.ioe.ac.uk/5192/7/download_id=17115&filename=challenge-plus-experience-of-bme-leaders-full-report_Redacted.pdf.

Miller, P. (forthcoming), 'Race and Ethnicity in Educational Leadership', in T. Bush, L. Bell and D. Middlewood (eds), *The Principles of Educational Leadership and Management*, 3rd edn, London: SAGE.

Ogunbawo, D. (2012), 'Developing Black and Minority Ethnic Leaders: The Case for Customized Programmes', *Educational Leadership and Management*, 40 (2): 158–74.

Runnymede/NASUWT (2017), *Visible Minorities, Invisible Teachers*. Last accessed 3 August 2018: https://www.nasuwt.org.uk/uploads/assets/uploaded/6576a736-87d3-4a21-837fd1a1ea4aa2c5.pdf.

University College Union (UCU) (2016), *The Experiences of Black Minority Ethnic Staff in Further and Higher Education*. Last accessed 3 August 2018: https://www.ucu.org.uk/media/7861/The-experiences-of-black-and-minority-ethnic-staff-in-further-and-higher-education-Feb-16/pdf/BME_survey_report_Feb161.pdf.

Part One

Curriculum, attainment and diversity

1

Race and race equality: Whiteness in initial teacher education

Christine Callender

Introduction

There is a paucity of research concerned with teacher educators' perspectives and understandings of race and race equality in initial teacher education (ITE) in England. This issue is particularly significant given the current shift towards a school-led workforce development model in which schools are increasingly responsible for training newly qualified teachers (NQTs), through, for example, School Centred Initial Teacher Education (SCITT), Teaching Schools, Schools' Direct and under the auspices of designated powers to award Qualified Teacher Status (QTS). By focusing on the 'gatekeepers of the profession' (Wilkins and Lall, 2011) – those with responsibility for strategically leading and managing teacher education courses – this chapter aims to disrupt the gaze of the extant literature to illuminate how initial teacher education is implicated in the production and maintenance of Whiteness and white privilege resulting in the perpetuation of hegemonic discourses about the participation of black, Asian and minority ethnic (BAME) students in ITE. Specifically, whiteness is considered in the context of ITE by focusing on how senior leaders understand and practice race equality during a period of race salience.

A qualitative methodology utilizing semi-structured interviews with university-based ITE course leaders across England was adopted and asks two main questions: (1) What do teacher educators understand by race and race equality; (2) How do these understandings influence the ways in which they work with and for race and race equality? Drawing on data collected in 2006, the chapter illuminates how, despite the legal requirement to promote race equality, institutional practices did not achieve their intended aims. This has significance not just for BAME students in ITE but also for the ways in which discussions of race are erased and/or censured from the early training experiences of beginner teachers. By locating the research in its historical moment and through making connections to its contemporary context, the chapter illustrates that, in the midst of a national efforts in the ITE sector to increase the number of BAME students, the underlying ideological perspectives of teacher educators were nonetheless imbued with the 'Tools of Whiteness' (Picower, 2009). It highlights how in a period of heightened race awareness, where there was a national focus on greater representation of BAME teachers in the form of diversity targets, teacher educators maintained dominant racial hierarchies through the deployment of these tools. At the historical point of relative convergence, teacher educators, whilst sensitized to race equality, espoused a commitment whilst systematically resisting notions of privilege and power. Contemporarily, the chapter points to the recent marketization of ITE and the proliferation of teacher training routes which emphasized 'teacher quality', with the inevitable, concomitant effect being that those entering the profession often do so without the opportunity to examine their own prejudices or assumptions. Fundamentally, the chapter argues that there has been little change.

In the current moment race has been erased and silenced, replaced instead by a discourse of meritocracy where only 'the brightest and the best' are selected for ITE programmes. Moreover, changes to race equality legislation which now combine race equality under the broader remit of equalities has, in effect, diluted the focus on race overall. An emphasis on teacher quality under the guise of meritocracy has led to fewer BAME entrants to ITE overall in recent years and the creating of what can be described as a 'mirrortocracy'. In the post-racial era, race is seemingly historicized, a non-existent factor in contemporary discourse where its relevance is questioned despite the racial disparities that exist at various levels of society.

The issue in context

Despite research into the experience of BAME students entering education, there is little critical analysis of the work of teacher educators related to race and racism in England. This is not just a feature of teacher education. In fact, it can be argued that the higher education sector has struggled to get to grips with the differential degree outcomes of BAME students and the small proportion of students gaining access to Russell Group institutions (Boliver, 2016). These concerns are long-standing, operating as the metaphorical elephant in the room:

> Higher education has a dirty little secret: white students get more firsts and 2:1s than black students – and no one even talks about it [. . .] we don't know why this is but we should certainly talk and disagree about it. (Cited in Reisz, 2012)

Several writers report that universities have failed to deliver on race equality (Curtis, 2000; John, 2003; Pilkington, 2009, 2011; Reisz, 2011), despite the legal duty to promote it. According to Back (2004), the higher education sector in England remains 'hideously white' both in terms of its student body and its staff. Writing later, Pilkington (2011) reports that higher education institutions (HEIs) are 'oblivious to inequalities in our midst and the need to ensure that our policies and procedures are evidence based'. Whilst Miller (2016) draws attention to the ways in which racial inequality has impacted upon the recruitment, selection and promotion of BME staff in HEIs and other education settings.

More recently, Bhopal (2018: 93) has argued that 'racism and racist practices dominate the experiences of black and minority students in higher education'. In an analysis of white privilege in the United Kingdom and United States, Bhopal asserts that:

> elite universities are the epitome of the legitimation and reproduction of institutional racism. They continue to play their part in the reproduction and reinforcement of racial and class inequalities. In this system of exclusion, black and minority ethnic students remain marginalised and excluded. Higher education institutions are spaces of white privilege which fail to cater for the experiences of black and minority groups. They employ a rhetoric of inclusion, but one that is rarely evidenced in practice or outcomes. (103)

Bhopal makes an important distinction between acceptable and non-acceptable forms of whiteness, and in so doing illuminates the ways in which class, whiteness and white privilege intersect in powerful ways:

> Acceptable forms are those which are marked at the intersection of class, whiteness and white privilege whereas unacceptable forms can be located in the identities of Gypsy and Traveller groups, expressed through 'a racism that is acceptable towards an unacceptable form of whiteness'. (157)

The performance of whiteness speaks the rhetoric of inclusion whilst simultaneously practising exclusion. Applebaum (2010: 9) asserts that while the definition of whiteness is difficult to pin down, there is widespread agreement that whiteness is a socially constructed category that is normalized within a system of privilege.

She cites the work of Ruth Frankenberg, who defines whiteness as:

a location of structural advantage, of race privilege. Second it is a 'standpoint', a place from which White people look at ourselves, at others, and at society. Third, 'Whiteness' refers to a set of cultural practices that are usually unmarked and unnamed. (9)

Whiteness thus operates in different ways. It is unmarked, unrecognized and not consciously acknowledged. At one level whiteness, as Penny McKintosh argues, is the sum of an invisible knapsack of privilege – unearned and unseen by its beneficiaries. Leonardo (2004: 148), on the other hand, states,

whites enjoy privileges largely because they have created a system of domination under which they can thrive as a group. The volumes of writing on the issue of domination testify that the process is complex and multi-causal. But the enactment is quite simple: set up a system that benefits the group, mystify the system, remove the agents of actions from discourse, and when interrogated about it, stifle the discussion with inane comments about the 'reality' of the charges being made.

For Hick et al. (2011: 18), ITE is a key starting point for examining race, noting that there 'remains the need to recognize the reality and persistence of racism in education'. It is important to acknowledge that a number of studies examine the experiences of BAME students in ITE and in teaching in the United Kingdom (McNamara et al., 2010; Carrington et al., 2001; Osler, 1997; Showunmi and Constantine-Simms, 1995). Themes to emerge from this literature include BAME student experience, strategies to improve participation through recruitment and retention and experiences of racism. It is not the purpose to examine these here but instead to use these to emphasize the invisibility of teacher educators' perspectives and understandings of race in ITE – teacher educators are largely seen in relation to work undertaken in the pedagogical areas of equality and diversity, whilst conversations about race are projected upon BAME bodies or narrated in relation to student experiences.

Few studies in the United Kingdom have explored the perspective of teacher educators, particularly those with responsibility for leadership and management of ITE courses and curricula. Where teacher educators' views are sought, research has concluded that, although teacher educators are well versed in race equality issues, they may not be well placed to bring about change within their institutions, suggesting 'there is a need for greater knowledge of teacher educators' understanding of issues of race; and how race and race equality are embedded into teacher education' (Hick et al., 2011: 6). Hick et al. make an important observation that not only speaks to the application of knowledge of race but also to teacher educators' personal understanding/experience of race – a factor that has had little empirical coverage in the literature. Bhopal, Harris and Rhamie (2009) make a similar point, albeit more explicitly, noting that teacher educators play a pivotal role in disrupting normative assumptions of race but may lack knowledge and expertise in these issues (see also Galman, Pica-Smith and Rosenberger, 2010). The significance of teacher educators is highlighted by Ryan and Dixson (2006: 181), who also refer to the critical role of teacher educators' pedagogy in shaping their own and their student's understanding of race in the United States. Similarly, Bhopal and Rhamie (2013) point to the need for increased practical support and training for beginner teachers in order to improve understanding of and responses to issues of race in the classroom.

Maylor (2014: 178) has also commented on the role of teacher educators and the critical role they play in ensuring that beginner teachers develop an understanding of race and racism, arguing that they should be afforded opportunities to examine their own attitudes and assumptions:

> If pre-service teachers are to become more critically aware of the limited parameters of their thinking Johnson, Lachuk and Mosley suggest that teacher educators should engage pre-service teachers in 'continual opportunities for dialogue and storytelling' (2012: 327, cited in Maylor 2014) about themselves, their internalised ideologies, the influence of White privilege and power and issues concerning 'race' and racism (including their own; King, 2007).

The practical task of engaging in critical conversations about race, however, is far more complex. Discussions of race in ITE are often regarded as 'scary' and met with a deafening silence or are derailed (Lander, 2011). Picower (2009), describing the strategies used by predominantly white students to avoid (or evade) engagement in conversations and/or explorations about race and racism, refers to this practice as the 'tools of whiteness'. In her study of pre-service teachers, she states that

> participants responded to challenges to these understandings by relying on a set of 'tools of Whiteness' designed to protect and maintain dominant and stereotypical understandings of race – tools that were emotional, ideological, and performative. (197)

The 'tools' support the maintenance of hegemonic stories and are comprised of three types. Picower describes these as emotional tools, which are based on feelings and function so as to 'obfuscate the concepts being introduced'; ideological tools, which represent beliefs that protect hegemonic stories; and performative tools of whiteness, which relate to behaviours that are consistent with hegemonic understandings.

The study (methodology and design)

The present study draws on interviews which examine race from the perspective of the 'gatekeepers of the profession' (Wilkins and Lall, 2011) – those with responsibility for strategically managing teacher education courses. By focusing on teacher educators' practice, it disrupts the gaze of the extant literature in the United Kingdom on race/race equality in ITE and illuminates how Whiteness is deployed to perpetuate hegemonic (and often negatively oriented) discourses about race/racism. In the words of Leonardo (2009: 107), this chapter attempts to 'make race visible' by 'making whiteness visible'.

The original study (Callender, Robinson and Robertson, 2006) set out to understand teacher educators' understandings of race and the ways in which this influenced their approach to the programmatic functions of ITE. It was particularly interested in how these actions impacted upon the outcomes of BAME students. The study evaluated the extent to which the institutions explicitly undertook monitoring and tracking of various aspects of ITE provision (e.g. recruitment and retention, academic performance, practice-based aspects of training and appointment to a teaching post) but also drew on interview data with programme and course leaders. It is the latter which is the focus of this chapter. The research is conducted within an interpretative paradigm and employs critical race theory (CRT) as an analytical lens. Participating institutions were drawn from universities across England. Collectively, the institutions differed greatly in terms of demography. Initially, twenty HEIs were invited to participate, of these ten were included in phase one of the study. In phase two this was reduced to six as four of the institutions withdrew due to Office for Standards in Education, Children Services and Skills (Ofsted) inspections. In each institution the key members of staff with strategic responsibility for leading the ITE provision were interviewed (comprising a total of nine participants altogether as in some institutions more than one person was present for interview). Data from a sample of three institutions and three participants are reported here to contextualize the discussion and to illuminate the issues as they perceived and experienced in the institutional setting. Whilst there is a level of selection in the presentation of findings, the institutions have been chosen due to their profiles (Russell Group and post-1992 universities) and different geographical locations (one in an inner city, another in an affluent university town and the other in a shire community). The names of institutions have been changed to assure their anonymity and that of staff. A brief outline of each institution is presented below:

Yewtree University is on the outskirts of a vibrant multi-ethnic city. It prides itself on its reputation for widening the participation agenda and has a history of attracting higher than average numbers of minority students. Acorn University is located in an affluent, predominantly white university town. It has a national and international reputation of academic excellence. Oak University is located in a former industrial city which has undergone extensive regeneration. The student body is mainly white and drawn from a wide geographical area. In recent years it has seen growth in its international student cohort. The university has several outreach projects aimed at local communities. All geographical references which might identify the locations of the institutions have been altered.

Data were collected in two phases. First, questionnaires which elicited contextual information such as ethnicity and achievement data, student profiles, retention, withdrawal, failure and success rates, achievements and challenges and any actions to support equality and diversity work were completed. Second, face-to-face semi-structured interviews of senior ITE staff with leadership and/ or management responsibilities were conducted. Interviews were digitally recorded and verbatim transcripts were returned to participants to check for accuracy prior to analysis. Thematic analysis (Braun and Clarke, 2006) was used to organize data into themes. Additionally data triangulation supported the identification of similarities and differences in the practices of teacher educators.

CRT is used as a lens through which to examine the ways in which teacher educators understand and practice race equality. The antecedents of CRT can be located in the field of critical legal studies in the United States. Its use, however, has subsequently been applied to education in the United Kingdom (Chakrabarty, Roberts and Preston, 2012; Gillborn, 2005, 2006, 2013, 2014, 2015; Hylton, 2012; Rollock, 2012; Warmington, 2012). Underlying CRT is the premise that racism is not an anomaly but a historical legacy and continuing process of the subordination of people of colour. In this sense racism is normal and mundane within society. CRT is deployed here to foreground the salience of race in teacher educators' practice. At its core is the contention that racism is endemic, institutional and systemic – it is normal, ordinary, not abhorrent and integral to the way in which society works (Bell, 1992; Solórzano and Delgado Bernal, 2001). CRT analysis provides a framework for a race-conscious examination of structural racism. It does not set out to find answers but instead exposes issues, revealing the overt and covert ways that racist ideology, structures and institutions create and maintain racial inequality. As such, it is a helpful tool with which to examine questions of epistemology, knowledge production and dissemination. CRT critically examines master (or dominant) narratives that are reproduced and the counter-narratives that are silenced. Based on five key tenets, CRT focuses upon the centrality and intersectionality of race and racism; the challenge to dominant ideology; a commitment to social justice; the centrality of experiential knowledge and the interdisciplinary perspective. It is not my intention to rehearse the details of CRT here as these are examined elsewhere (Bell, 1992; Crenshaw et al., 1995; Taylor, Gillborn and Ladson-Billings, 2009; Gillborn and Ladson-Billings, 2010). Rather, it is my intention to reveal 'interest convergence', one of the tenets of CRT which highlights that teacher educators are central to maintaining the ways in which discussions of race and racism take place within ITE, and which illuminates whiteness and white privilege as a lens through which race and racism are understood and practised. The underlying premise of interest convergence is that race equality is only advanced when the interests, expectations and ideologies of Whites converge with those from minoritized groups. A key aspect is the notion of loss and gain, where one group (usually the dominant one) has to give up something or negotiate for the interests of both groups to converge. In this case, the research was undertaken in the period after publication of the *McPherson Report* and where changes to legislation impacted upon the race equality practice of all public bodies, including universities, and where the requirement to promote race equality and to take active steps to reduce racial discrimination were codified in law. The duties under the Race Relations (Amendment Act) also meant that institutional data had to be publicly available for scrutiny. With regard to ITE, an additional accountability measure in the form of diversity targets from the then-Training and Development Agency[1] (TDA) meant that all universities were expected to take proactive steps to recruit BAME students, all of which would contribute to a national target. In short, if universities recruited at or above target and/ or could demonstrate that they were engaged in activities designed to improve the recruitment and retention of BAME students, this information was used to benchmark race equality practice and used to improve a university's institutional capital.

The chapter thus illuminates how race is *done* by teacher educators and the slow pace at which change in practice takes place. In this sense, the use of CRT and interest convergence, in particular, exposes whiteness as a system of meaning about race, ethnicity, class and gender (Leonardo, 2009; Bonilla-Silva, 2010).

The evidence

All institutions involved in the study expressed a commitment to race equality. This was regarded as highly prized and as a measure of good standing within the audit and accountability framework within which teacher education in the United Kingdom took place at the time (i.e. the post-MacPherson era). At this time externally set diversity targets aimed to increase the number of BAME students and played an integral role in either building upon or maintaining a commitment to widening participation and by implication reputational capital – the profit gained from engaging in 'diversity' work.

'We've met our target'

It was not uncommon during interviews for the phrase 'we've met our target' to be invoked as evidence of good race equality outcomes or indeed practice. In many senses it was considered to have contributed to the reputational capital of institutions. Despite this, however, race equality was perceived as problematic and difficult – with the potential to lead to institutional losses (e.g. non-completions or high dropout and withdrawal rates). It was apparent that recruitment targets were seen as an external driver leading to institutional success and esteem. Universities had a vested interest in meeting diversity targets as it conferred enhanced status in the ITE sector and by implication (the universities) were more appealing to BAME student groups. HEIs who met the target were judged (and judged themselves) as not only being 'good' at recruitment and retention but also 'good' at race equality (Ahmed, 2007).

Acorn University, a prestigious pre-1992 university with a global reputation for academic excellence, draws its student cohort from a monocultural, wealthy, mainly white student body. Due to its reputation of academic excellence and the fact that it attracts high-calibre students nationally and internationally, it does not regard diversity targets as integral to its ITE work. Its courses were often oversubscribed. Unlike Yewtree, its reputational capital is not based on its image as a diverse institution. It has struggled to recruit BAME students. Those who study at Acorn are academic high-flyers, most of whom go on to teach in the independent school sector. Acorn has focused efforts on supporting those of exceptional ability who may not possess the financial resources to support their course of study. Class is a determining factor at Acorn, and it is vocal about its commitment to widening participation and recruiting the brightest students from schools in the state sector. Pilkington (2009: 17) notes, 'there is little doubt that widening participation is primarily concerned with class'. Race has been a lesser concern amongst most institutions. Acorn's commitment was evidenced in the provision for students without the financial means to study. In terms of its ITE provision, it had undertaken a range of additional activities to raise aspirations and encourage applications from under-represented groups and had implemented initiatives with regard to race equality. For example, it worked with BAME alumni to promote teaching as a career; developed an information management system to monitor BAME student progress; and consulted with/ revised its schools partnership agreement to ensure a consistent approach to dealing with racist incidents. In response to a question about the low application rate of BAME students, the course leader commented,

> I just feel it's the image we have. Also we don't want to recruit more [BAME students] in some senses until we get sorted out. There's no point saying 'Oh great, we've met the target', that's the wrong way around. I mean targets are important because they are expressing a commitment [. . .] but you get everyone on, they have a horrible experience and they never go into teaching.

BAME students are perceived as somewhat problematic. They are bodies out of place, disorienting and disrupting the equilibrium of whiteness, or, as Puwar (2004) puts it, they present dissonant bodies that take the form of 'space invaders' and 'aliens' in white spaces. The statement above additionally raises important questions about how a commitment to race equality is expressed. In this case it is by not recruiting BAME students until the institution is able to sort itself out or, in other words, through the production and maintenance of normative whiteness.

'Good' diversity practice was concealed within hidden institutional practices, attitudes and assumptions about race and race equality. For example, at Yewtree School of Education, although the number of BAME students is low, their completion rates are high – leading the course director to report, 'although recruitment of BAME students can be a challenge, we are pleased that we do meet the targets for recruitment of BAME students to ITT programmes'. The 'challenge' for Yewtree is worthy of continued investment as this is seen to lead to good retention rates – a tool to measure institutional performance and an indicator of 'good' race equality practice. It also provides Yewtree with an opportunity to promote itself as a mainly white university committed to and proactive about race equality and to use this as a marketing strategy for future recruitment. Like other institutions in the study, Yewtree's race equality policy set out how it aimed to achieve its goals. These documents were a key barometer of an institution's 'race' work and were often referenced during interviews. According to Prior (2003) cited in Ahmed (2007: 591), documents may have a significant function in that 'the University is its documents rather than its buildings'. Documents can work in unique ways, moulding organizational structures and deciding what, how something gets done and why something gets done, or, as Ahmed notes, 'the politics of diversity has become what we call "image management": diversity work is about generating the "right image", and correcting the wrong one'. Thus, with respect to race equality, it is concerned with 'changing perceptions of whiteness rather than changing the whiteness of organizations' (605). Deem and Morley (2006: 196) make a similar point with regard to senior managers' views of diversity and equality being couched in 'well told stories' and that 'senior managers are institutionally placed to provide positive stories about institutional policies'. These, they argue, play a pivotal role articulating and enacting key messages about institutional ethos and position:

> We're meeting the targets that we set for our ethnic minority numbers and are actually over them and our year one students are up as well in terms of that. It's not to be complacent. My focus is on keeping them here once we've got them and ensuring what we are doing is valid and relevant to them. (Course Leader, Oak University)

Thus, in those institutions where there were high levels of student diversity, this was invoked as an indicator of success – doing well in race equality was inextricably tied to having a 'diverse' student body. Hey, Dunne and Aynsley (2011: 4) observe that 'where student diversity has a strong marketing appeal there is a sense that diversity and equality has been achieved'. This would appear to be the case at Yewtree University, which prides itself on achieving success in recruiting significant numbers of students from diverse backgrounds:

> For the last three years our retention, our recruitment has been very, very strong. We have had no problems this year. We didn't go into clearing this year, we didn't go into clearing the year before and we didn't take any borderline students this year. So obviously we'll see how things go. (Course Leader, Yewtree University)

It is interesting to note the initial confusion between recruitment and retention and its uncoupling from race. The strong recruitment process is, in effect, deracialized and bound up in notions of 'quality'. On the one hand, it is instructive to note that ethnic minority student numbers are presented as being outside of, separate from and an adjunct, fulfilling a diversity tick box exercise. In this instance, race takes on an ephemeral quality. It is a metaphor for success. In this education space, BAME students signify a form of reputational capital, strengthening Oak's position in the ITE marketplace and provides proof of its success in race equality – reaching the target is demonstrative of institutional success and of being good at 'doing' race equality (Ahmed, 2007).

(Un)doing race

Diversity targets presented both a tangible way of demonstrating and a measurable way of *doing* race equality. Institutions were not always clear of the ways in which targets masked a different narrative of race or the student reality. For example, data provided prior to interview revealed a significantly higher attrition rate for some categories of BAME students at Oak University. Clarity was sought about one such group during interview:

> **Author:** Please tell me if I've got this right. Three students that passed, four who failed, three that withdrew and four that transferred?
> **Course Leader:** Something like that [. . .] Yes.
> **Course Leader:** We've only recently had Ofsted [. . .] I was looking at those success rates and the Black Caribbean 21% you know and you look at it as numbers. It maybe doesn't [. . .] well it does. It's a disaster and clearly something we have to focus on in terms of understanding what is contributing to that. It's all well getting people in if you can't keep them. It seemed to us that there were a greater proportion of them who were failing to succeed.

The recent positive Ofsted outcome is seen as analogous to confirmation of good race equality practice despite the fact that the data at Oak revealed significant underlying issues with completion rates of particular BAME groups, especially those who were African Caribbean. Initial uncertainty (something like that, it maybe doesn't [. . .] well it does) is replaced by the disaster that has evaded the gaze of the university itself and seemingly Ofsted too. It has remained quietly sleeping in Oak's institutional structures as the headline data indicates that recruitment and retention is good overall. Race, whilst visible in institutional diversity discourse, is, at the same time, silent, unacknowledged and untroubling. In explaining the data a bipolar narrative emerges in the way that Oak understands and practices race equality. On the one hand, the course leader draws attention to good race equality practice (we are doing well in BAME recruitment) and on the other creates institutional stories about why some groups of students do not do as well as others:

> I think a number of these students are Access students who have come through the Access to Teaching route. They're coming through as mature students who have other issues so the intensity of the course is contributing to the difficulties that they are having. Some of them are perhaps not adequately prepared for that jump from the Access course onto the undergraduate course.

BAME students are presented in the form of problematic stories whose function explains (and in some cases justifies) BAME student outcomes. These narratives, like the discussion of recruitment and retention above, position BAME students as the arbiters of their own demise. BAME students comprised an undifferentiated homogenized mass with similar educational histories and associated 'problems'. Students were commodified, measured and benchmarked as steps toward race equality, yet race is simultaneously valourized as a positive institutional quality but also lamented upon as displayed by the disastrous consequences of a disproportionately high failure rate. The term 'Access student' acts as a synonym for all BAME bodies and is utilized to maintain an ideological assumption of student deficit. Picower's (2009) notion of the ideological tools of Whiteness are apposite here as a way of understanding how race and race equality are constructed and reconstructed, and of the operationalization of normative whiteness. Moreover, these tools further enable the course leader (and by implication the university) to reproduce hegemonic stories of BAME attainment and race, in addition to dominant ideologies that negate, ignore or tiptoe around the issues raised.

Acorn University, in contrast, is aware that it is perceived as elitist and somewhat out of reach for many BAME students. Its reputation as a white, privileged world-leading institution unaccustomed to difference is captured by the course director:

> Obviously we are very white and we come over as being very middle class and if you look at our institution White English, White English, White English. White English everywhere.

The repetition of the phrase White English underscores the overwhelming weight of whiteness. It is omniscient and pervasive – it is everywhere, surrounding and engulfing the institution. Its global reputation in some ways protects it from the racialized other and discourses of race equality. It is a bastion of excellence with only the brightest and the best being afforded the opportunity to study there. At Acorn the pursuit of race equality is viewed as an external imposition, a mechanism for central government to ultimately make claims about the diversification of the teaching force:

> It's all about government ministers being able to stand up and say we've got so many black and ethnic minority students in recruitment then nobody is actually looking at what is actually happening.

This is evidence that the ideological tools of whiteness can be identified in the way that the course leader at Acorn perceives race and race equality as problematic, indicating that the education system more broadly is the reason why many BAME applicants do not apply:

> In Asian Pakistani groups you don't get many coming through because we know how the system disadvantages them so they never feel they could apply to Acorn for a start and then apply to a PGCE course here. Yes, that's one of the problems I think with minority ethnic recruitment that our education system disadvantages many minority ethnic students so they underachieve in the education system so they never get to degree level and then, you know [. . .] become teachers.

As indicated earlier, the number of BAME students attending Russell Group institutions remains stubbornly low in England, whilst a preponderance of BAME students attend post-1992 institutions. Furthermore, recent research has shown that BAME students are more likely to have their application to university scrutinized as part of university admissions processes (Busby, 2018). The extract highlights an uncoupling from race – the presence of racialized bodies disrupts the whiteness of the institution and in so doing stymies discussions of race equality. On the one hand Acorn University wants to better prepare itself for minoritized students, but on the other hand it was attempting to manage the presence of a few BAME students on its courses. An area which appeared to cause concern was in the placement of students in local schools for school-based professional learning:

> We are never really sure about this [. . .] to resist the temptation of they are Muslim and we'll send them to School X. They speak Urdu and Urdu is a subject at School X. But that's not what we should be doing. We should be making every

single school that we send our students to an acceptable placement and not ghettoize if you like.

It was intriguing that the matching of beginner students to schools on the basis of cultural or religious affiliation was considered a viable option for school placement. Acorn is aware of the need to engage its partner schools so that the placement of a BAME student is not regarded as out of the ordinary or problematic but appeared at a loss as to how this was to be achieved. It became clear that matching was indeed considered an option when schools 'reacted' to the placement of minority students:

> There is lots of poverty in XXXX, the schools are quite demographically different in terms of social class but not in terms of ethnicity at all. If you take one of the schools in XXXX you would think that you are in Tory land. It's nice. You've got XXXX, the school itself is a very interesting school because its predominately white students but there is a lot of poverty – farming, urban problems, very poor children go to that school. So it is very bipolar, very middle class and very poor agricultural working class. Schools are very interesting in this area, In some cases very white actually. If you send an Asian or black or minority ethnic teacher to one of those schools it does get commented upon and you will see from the comments [one the student report] [. . .] although everyone has seen the report and we would have discussed it. But at the end of the day the students don't tell you. That's the issue they don't tell you. They don't rock the boat.

The extract above draws attention to the practice of normative whiteness and negative perceptions of race *and* class. The accepted forms of whiteness can be found in the schools in Tory land, whilst unacceptable whiteness is related to poverty, urban problems and very poor children. The racialized bodies of students, in contrast, interrupt the whiteness of both types of schools to the extent that it gets 'commented upon'. At Acorn University, race (and by implication race equality) is the responsibility of and belongs to the bodies of BAME students. Race *is* apparent when BAME students are placed in 'Tory land' or indeed 'interesting schools' that serve the urban poor. However, responsibility for dealing with racism is placed upon the BAME students themselves as 'they don't tell you' for fear of rocking the boat. The university is knowing yet unknowing, complicit and silent – engaging in what Leonardo (2009: 113) refers to as white racial knowledge: 'knowing *how* the world works in racially meaningful ways, but avoiding to name it in these terms'.

Implications and conclusion

The findings outlined above illustrate the ways in which race and racism are talked about, responded to and understood by course leaders at Yewtree, Oak and Acorn Universities. It is important to acknowledge here that this discussion set out to illuminate how a small number of course leaders at a specific point in time understood race and the ways in which they engaged in the *doing* of race. The findings therefore are intended to highlight practice and are not generalizable nor necessarily indicative of practices across all ITE provision. The deployment of CRT as an analytical lens has highlighted the ways in which race is ascribed as evidence of 'good' institutional race equality practice; inscribed on the bodies of BME students as other and problematic; used to reproduce ideological discourses of race and/or student experience of racism; and is significantly inextricably bound up with the ideological tools of whiteness. In addition to this it illustrates how the leaders of ITE provision understand and experience race as a distant out-of-body experience, disconnected from and unrelated to their own white racialized identities – and privilege – yet, at the same time, race is hypervisible, valued and problematic when it enters the white space of ITE. As Leonardo (2009: 107) reminds us, knowledge about race and racism is known, and 'whites do know a lot about race in both its everyday sense as a lived experience and its structural sense as a system of privilege. In other words, it is imperative to "make race visible," with the specific goal of "making whiteness visible"'.

The 'Tools of Whiteness' provide a useful lens through which to examine teacher educators' unexamined assumptions and taken-for-granted notions. The 'tools' are the critical elements that bolster dominant ideologies such as white supremacy. They are essential to the sophistication of whiteness and its durability as a significant force. Like the beginner teachers in Picower's study, when teacher educators are challenged to think beyond their white normative ideologies, they draw on these tools to avoid, subvert and obfuscate conversations of race and race equality, highlighting that it is not passive resistance that is significant here but the active protection of dominant ideologies that pervade ITE.

At a time where there exists a range of ITE options in England, when the teacher workforce is becoming less reflective of the communities it serves and the student population is becoming more diverse, it is incumbent upon those with responsibility for leading and managing teacher education, regardless of the route to certification, to be far better equipped to understand how 'ordinary' everyday practice reinforces racism and reproduces whiteness. Hick et al.'s (2011) and Bhopal and Rhamie's (2013) observations are pertinent here as this study concurs with the view that teacher educators' personal racial biographies, awareness of race and racism as well as awareness of the ways in which normative whiteness is contingent to anti-racist practice and inclusive praxis are critical to attaining race equality. In short, as O'Brien (2009: 205) reminds us, 'the responsibility for tackling racism should not rest solely on the shoulders of teachers or "multicultural" teacher educators, it is quite simply the responsibility of every power player involved in all aspects of the system'.

The study also sheds light on how ITE institutions are implicated in forms of racialized myopia – recognizing race whilst simultaneously engaging colour-blind or colour-neutral practices – and that teacher educators are intricately bound up in these processes. BAME student cohort numbers provide some institutions with a rhetoric that enables them to laud their success of widening participation, which is also sometimes seen as being equivalent to a commitment to 'good' race equality practice. The day-to-day experience of BAME students, however, regardless of institution and school-based professional learning, is de-racialized. Race occurs and is worn on the bodies of BAME students. It is embedded in their academic credentials and problematic in their allocation to school placement as well as their experience of it. For the teacher educators at Oak, Acorn and Yewtree, race and racism are understood as stories of problematized others. As Leonardo argues, 'white educators' epistemological framework is not *determined* [author's emphasis] by their whiteness' (109); rather, they see race through a different lens, that of white racial knowledge. In the context of the study, it is important to recognize that the interviews were conducted at a time when there was a legal duty to promote race equality, and that the course leaders were therefore more sensitized to discussions of race and racism. In the same way that it is incumbent upon beginner teachers to engage with and understand their own racial identities, it is critically important that those who are responsible for educating beginner teachers subject themselves to similar levels of self-examination, not least because to do so is to subject one's unexamined assumptions to scrutiny. Yet the discussion above raises questions about the extent to which teacher educators proactively position themselves as change agents who advocate for race equality or whether they are compliant, collude with or are complicit in reproducing normative whiteness.

Note

1   The TDA was established in 2005 as a body responsible for the initial and in-service training of teachers and other school staff in England.

References

Ahmed, S. (2007), '"You End Up Doing the Document Rather Than the Doing": Diversity, Race Equality and the Politics of Documentation', *Ethnic and Racial Studies*, 30 (4): 590–609.

Ahmed, S. (2009), 'Embodying Diversity: Problems and Paradoxes for Black Feminists', *Race Ethnicity and Education*, 12 (1): 41–52.

Ahmed, S. (2012), *On Being Included: Racism and Diversity in Institutional Life*, Durham, NC: Duke University Press.

Back, L. (2004), 'Ivory Towers? The Academy and Racism', in I. Law, D. Phillips and L. Turney (eds), *Institutional Racism in Higher Education*, 1–13, Stoke-on-Trent: Trentham Books.

Bell, D. (1992), *Faces at the Bottom of the Well: The Permanence of Racism*, New York: Basic Books.

Bhopal, K. (2018), *White Privilege: The Myth of a Post-Racial Society*, Bristol: Policy Press.

Bhopal, K. and J. Rhamie (2013), 'Initial Teacher Training: Understanding "Race", Diversity and Inclusion', *Race Ethnicity and Education*, 17 (3): 304–25.

Bhopal, K., R. Harris and J. Rhamie (2009), *The Teaching of 'Race' Diversity and Inclusion on PGCE Courses: A Case Study Analysis of University of Southampton*, Report for Multiverse.

Boliver, V. (2016), 'Exploring Ethnic Inequalities in Admission to Russell Group Universities', *Sociology*, 50 (2): 247–66.

Bonilla-Silva, E. (2010), *Racism without Racists: Colour-Blind Racism & Racial Inequality in Contemporary America*, 3rd edn, Plymouth, UK: Rowman & Littlefield.

Braun, V. and V. Clarke (2008), 'Using Thematic Analysis in Psychology', *Qualitative Research in Psychology*, 3 (2): 77–101.

Busby, E. (2018), 'Black People in UK 21 Times More Likely to Have University Applications Investigated, Figures Show', *The Independent*, 23 April. Last accessed 1 May 2018: https://www.independent.co.uk/news/education/education-news/uk-black-students-university-applications-investigation-more-likely-ucas-figures-nus-labour-a8314496.html.

Carrington, B., A. Bonnet, J. Demaine, I. Hall, A. Nyak, G. Short and C. Skelton (2001), *Ethnicity and the Professionalisation of Teachers*. Report to the Training Agency, London: Teacher Training Agency.

Chakrabarty, N., L. Roberts and J. Preston (2012), 'Editorial: Critical Race Theory in England', *Race, Ethnicity and Education*, 15 (3): 1–3.

Crenshaw, K., N. Gotanda, G. Peller and K. Thomas, eds (1995), *Critical Race Theory: The Key Writings That Formed the Movement*, New York: The New Press.

Curtis, P. (2002), 'Universities "Panicking" over Race Act', *The Guardian*, 25 June.

Deem, R. and L. Morley (2006), 'Diversity in the Academy/Staff Perceptions of Equality Policies in Six Contemporary Higher Education Institutions', *Policy Futures in Education*, 4 (2): 185–202.

Department for Education (2016), School Workforce in England, November. Last accessed 25 July 2018: https://www.gov.uk/government/uploads/system/uploads/attachment_data/file/620825/SFR25_2017_MainText.pdf.

Galman, S., C. Pica-Smith and C. Rosenberger (2010), 'Aggressive and Tender Navigations: Teacher Educators Confront Whiteness in Their Practice', *Journal of Teacher Education*, 61 (3): 225–36.

Gillborn, D. (2005), 'Education Policy as an Act of White Supremacy: Whiteness, Critical Race Theory and Education Reform', *Journal of Education Policy*, 20 (4): 485–505.

Gillborn, D. (2006), 'Critical Race Theory and Education: Racism and Anti-Racism in Educational Theory and Praxis', *Discourse: Studies in the Cultural Politics of Education*, 27 (1): 11–32.

Gillborn, D. (2013), 'Interest-Divergence and the Colour of Cutbacks: Race, Recession and the Undeclared War on Black Children', *Discourse: Studies in the Cultural Politics of Education*, 34 (4): 477–91.

Gillborn, D. (2014), 'Racism as Policy: A Critical Race Analysis of Education Reforms in the United States and England', *The Educational Forum*, 78 (1): 26–41.

Gillborn, D. (2015), 'Intersectionality, Critical Race Theory, and the Primacy of Racism: Race, Class, Gender, and Disability in Education', *Qualitative Inquiry*, 21 (3): 277–87.

Gillborn, D. and G. Ladson-Billings (2010), 'Critical Race Theory', in P. Peterson, E. Baker and B. McGraw (eds), *International Encyclopedia of Education*, vol. 6: 341–47. Oxford: Elsevier.

Hey, V., M. Dunne and A. Aynsley (2011), *The Experience of Black and Minority Ethnic Staff in Higher Education in England*, London: Equality Challenge Unit.

Hick, P., R. Arshad, L. Mitchell, D. Watt and L. Roberts (2011), *Promoting Cohesion, Challenging Expectations: Educating the Teachers of Tomorrow for Race Equality and Diversity in 21st Century Schools*, Teacher Educators for the 21st century: Grant Project Final Report. Escalate, Manchester. http://www.esri.mmu.ac.uk/resstaff/Promoting%20Cohesion%20Challenging%20Expectations.pdf.

Hylton, K. (2012), 'Talk The Talk, Walk the Walk: Defining Critical Race Theory in Research', *Race Ethnicity and Education,* 15 (1): 23–41.

John, G. (2003), Review of Race Equality Action Plans in HEFCE funded Higher Education Institutions. Last accessed 1 May 2018: https://www.hefcw.ac.uk/documents/publications/circulars/circulars_2007/W0740HE%20circ.pdf.

Lander, V. (2011), 'Race, Culture and All That: An Exploration of the Perspectives Of White Secondary Student Teachers about Race Equality Issues in Their Initial Teacher Education', *Race Ethnicity and Education*, 14 (3): 351–64.

Leonardo, Z. (2004), 'The Color of Supremacy: Beyond the Discourse of "White Privilege"', *Educational Philosophy and Theory*, 36 (2): 137–52.

Leonardo, Z. (2009), *Race, Whiteness and Education*, Abingdon: Routledge.

Maylor, U. (2014), *Teacher Training and the Education of Black Children: Bringing Color into Difference*, Abingdon: Routledge.

McNamara, O., J. Howson, H. Gunter and A. Fryers (2010), *The Leadership Aspirations and Careers of Black and Minority Ethnic Teachers. NASUWT and the National College for Leadership of Schools and Children's Services*, Birmingham: NASUWT.

Miller, P. (2016), 'White Sanction', Institutional, Group and Individual Interaction in the Promotion and Progression of Black and Minority Ethnic Academics and Teachers in England', *Power and Education*, 8 (3): 205–21.

O'Brien, J. (2009), 'Institutional Racism and Anti-racism in Teacher Education: Perspectives of Teacher Educators', *Irish Educational Studies*, 28 (2): 193–207.

Osler, A. (1997), *The Education and Careers of Black Teachers: Changing Identities, Changing Lives*, Buckingham, UK: Open University Press.

Picower, B. (2009), 'The Unexamined Whiteness of Teaching: How White Teachers Maintain and Enact Dominant Racial Ideologies', *Race Ethnicity and Education*, 12 (2): 197–215.

Pilkington, A. (2009), 'The Impact of Government Initiatives in Promoting Racial Equality in Higher Education: A Case Study', *Ethnicity and Race in a Changing World*, 1 (2): 15–25.

Pilkington, A. (2011), *Institutional Racism in the Academy: A Case Study*, Stoke-on-Trent: Trentham Books.

Prior, L. (2003), *Using Documents in Social Research: Introducing Qualitative Methods*, London: SAGE.

Puwar, N. (2004), *Space Invaders: Race, Gender and Bodies Out of Place*, Oxford: Berg.

Reisz, M. (2012), 'Racial Divide Is Higher Education's "Dirty Secret"'. Last accessed 30 April 2018: https://www.timeshighereducation.com/racial-divide-is-higher-educations-dirty-secret/422140.article.

Rollock, N. (2012), 'The Invisibility of Race: Intersectional Reflections on the Liminal Space of Alterity', *Race Ethnicity and Education*, Special Issue: Critical Race Theory in England, 15 (1): 65–84.

Ryan, C. and A. Dixson (2006), 'Rethinking Pedagogy to Re-Center Race: Some Reflections', *Language Arts*, 84 (2): 175–83.

Showunmi, V. and D. Constantine-Simms, eds (1995), *Teachers for the Future*, Stoke-on-Trent: Trentham Books.

Solórzano, D. and D. Delgado Bernal (2001), 'Critical Race Theory, Transformational Resistance and Social Justice: Chicana and Chicano students in an Urban Context', *Urban Education*, 36: 308–42.

Taylor, E., D. Gillborn and G. Ladson-Billings, eds (2009), *Foundations of Critical Race Theory in Education*, New York: Routledge.

Warmington, P. (2012), '"A Tradition in Ceaseless Motion": Critical Race Theory and Black British Intellectual Spaces', *Race Ethnicity and Education*, 15 (1): 5–21.

Wilkins, C. and R. Lall (2011), ' "You've Got to Be Tough and I'm Trying": Black and Minority Ethnic Student Teachers' Experiences of Initial Teacher Education', *Race, Ethnicity and Education*, 14 (3): 365–86.

2

Male leaders of African Caribbean heritage: Leading with justice and care to enhance black male student achievement

Dennis Francis

Introduction

A range of publications analysing the nexus of school leadership and achievement and the impact of the former on the latter traverses the educational leadership landscape (Ross and Gray, 2006; Gaziel, 2007; Leithwood et al., 2010; Louis, Dretzke and Wahltrom, 2010; Day, Gu and Sammons, 2016). However, analyses of the influence of the race of leaders and their leadership on student achievement remain a troubling gap in the literature. The purpose of this chapter is to address this gap, foreground and contest the notion of phenotypic blind leadership in the analysis of student achievement and ignite the production of scholarly works on this subject in the United Kingdom. As the subject of race is central to this chapter, it is important that we understand what we mean by the term. In short, white European men fabricated the notion of race, the categorization of people based on phenotypic differences, hierarchical racial ordering and placed themselves (their race) at the top of the race hierarchy (Rose, 1968; Painter, 2006). Given the social construction of race, Fields and Fields (2010) confirm that it is a 'phantom concept'; however, race remains a powerful fixture in society as particular groups of people reap socio-economic and cognitive benefits from it (Smedley and Smedley, 2012). In this chapter, race is understood as a value-free concept: simply, it describes groups of people with different phenotypic features (Webster's, 1993) and is used here interchangeably with words such as heritage, black or white to identify racialized individuals.

This chapter draws upon the literature from the United States pertaining to race and leadership, as there is a paucity of academic materials on this topic in the United Kingdom and especially with respect to black male leadership. Nonetheless, the chapter provides an opportunity for readers to listen to the perspectives of male students and leaders of African Caribbean heritage as all too often their voices are silenced or misrepresented.

Additionally, the chapter challenges the praxis of white leadership and explores the 'failure' of white leaders to enhance black male achievement. This chapter presents ways in which black male leaders may contribute to positive changes to black male student outcomes through the praxis of leadership based on justice and care. The contributors to the chapter expressed that they were comfortable to have a candid dialogue with someone who mirrored their heritage, and therefore the tone of the chapter reflects and honours their frankness.

Finally, to grasp the significance of the issues explored within this chapter, it is fitting to commence this chapter with a delineation of the presence of people of African Caribbean heritage in the United Kingdom and the educational trajectory of black children over the past five decades. After the aforementioned outline, the following sections of the chapter, namely the issue in context, the study, evidence, discussion, implications (for research, practice, policy) and conclusions are presented. It is important to note that this work emerges from research undertaken in 2011 and yet the academic materials on black leadership in the United Kingdom are wanting.

The issue in context

In the first forty years of the last century, 'West Indians,' primarily men, migrated to the United Kingdom to join the air force and work in the armament industry when called upon by the British government (Davison, 1962). Post-war labour shortages of the 1950s and white British Nationals' refusal to undertake certain jobs prompted the government to invite 'West Indian' women and men to England to fill vacant posts (Mason, 2000). However, the reception that 'West Indians' received from white British people was not welcoming but hostile: some white people routinely used the colour bar system to discriminate openly against black people (Sherwood, 2003).

Given the above delineation, it is noteworthy that the number of people of Caribbean heritage remains miniscule as percentage of the United Kingdom's overall population. According to Peach (1991), the Caribbean population was estimated to be 18,000 in 1951 and 200,000 by 1961 (of which 26,000 were British born), the latter representing 0.004 per cent of the 53 million people living in the United Kingdom. The 2011 census revealed that 594,525 people of African Caribbean heritage live in the United Kingdom, most of whom (344, 597) reside in London: they represent 4.2 per cent of the 8.3 million London population and 1 per cent of the UK population (Office of National Statistics [ONS], 2011).

Education of black people

The School Workforce data indicate that the teaching profession is white dominated, as 86 per cent of the teachers is recorded on its census as white British (DfE, 2017a). Even in a racially diverse city such as London, most of the teachers are white: in fact, the Greater London Authority figures in 2006 revealed that 70 per cent of all teachers were white. However, London's current teacher demographic does not appear in the 2017 *Annual London Education Report*.

Thus, black children in London, as in England, will typically have a white teacher. It is, therefore, woefully disturbing that the literature on black education spanning the past five decades is replete with examples of how 'teachers' and 'policymakers' stymied the children from receiving an education which would lead to successful outcomes (see Andrews, 2013; Warmington, 2014). Indeed, the seminal book by Bernard Coard in 1971, *How the West Indian Child Is Made Educationally Sub-Normal in the British School System*, exposed the ways in which white teachers and policymakers in the 1960s indiscriminately placed black British children in 'special needs schools'. The *Rampton Report* 1981 highlighted the insidious nature of racism inter alia in English schools, while Mac an Ghaill, 1988; Gillborn, 1995; Blair, 2001; and Gillborn, 2008 all document the discriminatory behaviour of white teachers towards black students, especially black boys and the detrimental effect this had on their achievement. White teachers' removal of black boys from classrooms at a disproportionately higher rate than other racialized groups of students is a recurrent theme in the literature (Coard, 1971; Troyna and Carrington, 1990; DfES, 2006; Gillborn and Rollock, 2010; DfE, 2017a, b) as is their preclusion from prestigious school examinations (Wright, 1987 and Gillborn, 2008). While head teachers are mentioned in passing in the literature on achievement, what most of these works fail to present is a considered exploration of the hegemony of leadership and the 'hue' of leadership on achievement.

Despite the above educational experiences endured by black male students, many of them do eventually achieve the national benchmark of passing General

Certificate in Secondary Education (GCSE) examinations in at least five subjects including English and Mathematics (Byfield, 2008). However, the students as a racialized group do not hit yearly national percentage benchmarks for achievement (Gillborn, 2008; GLA, 2017) set by the government. The distance from the national threshold crowds the literature pertaining to black male achievement. If there is an acknowledgement that leadership has an influence on achievement (Day et al., 2016), then part of the failure to ensure that black male students reach the aforementioned threshold can be attributed to the leaders, the overwhelming majority of whom are white British (DfE, 2017).

Justice, care and leadership

It is against the above context that the topics for this chapter are explored, starting with an outline of the terms 'justice' and 'social justice', continuing with care in leadership and then ending with the ways in which black male leadership based on justice and care can favourably affect the achievement of the students.

Justice is a contested term and a myriad of perspectives (religious, philosophical and judicial) blur its genesis and block any broad agreement on its meaning. Nevertheless, in prosaic terms, justice fosters evaluative discourses on how individuals are treated, the constitution of individual rights and encapsulates the notion of fairness (Noddings, 1999) and 'impartiality' (Alston, 2015). However, the concept of social justice has appeared increasingly in the field of education over the past twenty years or so and has been ensconced in the educational vernacular (Shoho, Merchant and Lugg, 2005). Thus, fairness towards one's fellow citizen underpins the concept of social justice (Shoho et al., 2005) with a recognition that we live in shared social spaces. The term justice was included in the title of the chapter to reflect its frequent usage by those who participated in the study and its association with the idea of fairness. An overview of the term social justice is presented below to reflect its extensive usage in the education literature.

There appears to be some latitude in the way in which the term social justice may be understood. As similar to the notion of justice, no single definition of the term exists (Fraser, 1997; Larson and Murthada, 2003; Shoho et al., 2005; Dantley and Tillman, 2006; Ryan, 2013). Nonetheless, core values and ideas such as equity, respect, care, fairness, opportunity, recognition and inclusion undergird the concept of social justice (Larson and Murtadha, 2003; Dantley and Tillman, 2006; Theoharis, 2007; Randall, Lindsey and Terrell, 2011; Ryan,

2013). Indeed, the lens of social justice is used to seek out and analyse iniquitous treatment of people, be it based on race, physical or cognitive ability; gender; sexual orientation; or any other personal marker used for exclusion from social participation (Shoho et al., 2005; Dantley and Tillman, 2006; Theoharis, 2007; Ryan, 2013).

In exploring a definition for social justice, Dantley and Tillman (2006: 24) bring together three areas of focus: 'leadership for social justice, moral transformative leadership and social justice praxis'. Under these keys areas, colleagues expound the critical need for an analysis of polices and power dynamics which replicate marginalization as well as dialectical and pedagogical interventions which promote leadership based on social justice. Indeed, the mark of leadership for social justice is the commitment to take action to remove any form of marginalized status (Shields, 2004; Dantley and Tillman, 2006; Theoharis, 2007; Randall et al., 2011 and Alston, 2015).

Shields (2004) reminds us of the importance of engaging in conversations about the circumstances and 'features' which demarcate groups and individuals: it is critical to be aware of how difference affects people, and this would include race. Shields usefully points out that race denialism gives permission to people to ignore and anaesthetize the needs of some students. In Shields' estimation, we become accomplices in the maintenance of injustice and human suffering when we fail to articulate knowledge of socially divisive situations: our 'silence' is tantamount to complicity. Indeed, Shields asserts that there is a need for 'moral dialogue' and transformative leadership to make social justice changes.

Care and love are interwoven into the concept of social justice, and Alston (2015) remarks that the two concepts are inextricably linked. With respect to the notion of care, a broadened view is shared here: care incorporates not only the idea of love but also the demonstration of commitment and a connection to students' historiography and the ability to patrol teachers' behaviour towards students. Starratt (1994) uses the term 'ethic of care' and opines that central to its practice is a demonstration of respect for students, their needs and a desire to promote 'self-actualization'.

Exemplifying the treatment of young African American males, Smith (1997) outlines how the act of caring towards these young people can positively affect motivation and self-esteem and equip them with ways to deal with a tide of negative forces which coalesce and create intractable circumstances within their lives. Similarly, Gay (2010) notes that care empowers students, 'boosts confidence' and also positively affects achievement.

Commenting on the significant role that care plays within leadership, and specifically black leadership, Tillman (2004: 186) noted that

> leadership based on interpersonal caring includes the principal's direct and purposeful attention to meeting the psychological, sociological, and academic needs of students.

Thus, caring serves to meet the holistic needs of students. Tillman (2004) explains that caring in leadership is deployed to counter both ad intra and extra school hegemonies which black students encounter: examples mentioned are 'low teacher expectations, racism and poverty'. Moreover, Newman (2006) advocates that leaders need to make sure that staff nurture compassion and care for their students, cultivate high expectations and have an affinity with them. Nevertheless, the underlying assumption expressed here is that staff form a moral-thinking monolithic group view students through the same prism and therefore will treat all students fairly. What is glossed over is how staff heterogeneity coupled with their alliances, based on race for example, can deny students' equitable treatment in school sites.

Whilst the demonstration of care is essential to educational leadership, Larson and Murtadha (2003) explain that incorporating the concept of love into discourses on leadership and social justice can provide the catalyst for others to become part of the social justice agenda and create new 'realities' for individuals. Larson and Murtadha (2003) note that Scheurich (1998) opines that love has a changing effect on children and families in terms of the education they receive and achievements gained: indeed, the love displayed by principals can change people's lives and therefore 'arm's- length' leadership should be substituted for immersive and communicative leadership. Further, Larson and Murtadha (2003: 144) assert that

> leaders must recognize communities that have been marginalized in our schools and build trusting relationships with them, committing themselves to act out of love rather than fear, and to make decisions based on principles of care, human dignity, love, justice, and equity.

Indeed, these two colleagues explain that both bell hooks and Freire in their writings stress the concept of love as an integral part of social justice and the starting point in activating life-changing possibilities for any disadvantaged group within society. Nonetheless, there is an acknowledgement that some leaders find it difficult to discuss the concept of love.

Connectivity with students and acknowledgement of African heritage

The idea of connectivity with students extends the premise of care in leadership and contributes to an understanding of leader-student affinity and the degree to which leaders take action through curriculum delivery to raise students' achievement. In the United Kingdom, Bush, Glovcoheer and Sood's (2005) report confirms the benefits that leaders from a culturally rich background bring to the leadership arena, namely, 'trust' having a knowledge of the students' cultural background, supporting their holistic needs and being able to contemplate issues through a culturally rich lens. Brooks and Jean-Marie's (2007) article on black and white leadership in the United States explores the divergent ways in which racialized leaders interact with and support black students and how leaders' practices impact on the students and subsequently their achievement. One interesting point which emerges from the article is that, unlike their white counterparts, black leaders recognized the ways in which students' racialized categorization was acquiesced to, to explain and justify differential achievement. This resulted in the leaders adopting the position of mentor in order to provide extra guidance to the students. Further, a focus on 'social uplift' and African American culture distinguished the black leaders' approach from their white peers in relation to supporting the students. In fact, black leaders' active pursuit of a rectifying social justice agenda based on care of the students was perceived to be instrumental in driving up student success.

Shockley (2008) advocates for a culturally relevant curriculum and the concept of 'cultural reattachment' as the basis for Afrocentric education and for improving achievement: Afrocentric leadership is viewed as instrumental to the implementation of this education (Shockley, 2008). In fact, through this education students become cognizant of their heritage, history, culture and the contributions made by their forebears, resulting in improvements in students' self-worth (Shockley, 2008; Hopson et al., 2010; Schneider and Turenne, 2010), learning and achievement (Shockley, 2008). Blair (2002) confirms that the introduction of 'Afrikan studies' had a positive impact on students of African Caribbean heritage in the United Kingdom. Indeed, Shockley (2008) remarks that achievement rates in schools with a 'full' African American student cohort and an African-based curriculum exceed district standards. Actual data on student outcomes are absent from these papers: such data would provide further evidence of the effectiveness of this leadership and how it contributes to the improved achievement rates through its emphasis on justice and care. What is disturbing, however, is the high level of hostility received at any endeavour to embed an African perspective into the curriculum: Shockley (2008) comments that there has always been opposition to providing support or giving black people the means to determine their 'destiny'.

Brooks and Jean-Marie (2007: 764) share the following comment from one leader of the expected reaction of white officialdom if black leaders were able to improve achievement,

> the district was likely to send out a 'lynch mob' that wod und their wor and/or 'fire us all'.

The point raised here is that white people in education and in leadership positions are fundamentally against the educational success of black children when black leaders are the catalyst of that success. While this is a shocking revelation, it would be interesting to be informed of the prevalence of feeling amongst leaders with respect to white officialdom behaviour.

Leading teachers and teaching and learning

Finally, Blair's paper (2002) draws attention to the need for strong transformational leadership to foster achievement for all students. A focus on teacher professional responsibility for students' outcomes is cited as an approach instigated by one head teacher who deployed the aforementioned leadership to improve student achievement: the head teacher was proactive and took steps to ensure that students had a fair chance of success by confronting the professionals charged to secure that success. Further, Gay (2010) asserts that expectations play a role in demonstrating care for students, but that such expectations also indicate how seriously teachers take their professional responsibility. Indeed, challenging students both academically and non-academically and the teachers' expectations of their students is also a demonstration of care and indeed underscores leadership based on justice and care.

The study

This research aimed to gather black students and leaders' perspectives on black and white leaders' practices and establish if there are any divergent ways that both sets of leaders enact leadership, which may affect students' achievement. Given the omission of research on this topic, I believed that direct engagement with black students and leaders to ascertain their personal perspectives on the research topics would bring a fresh dimension to the study. Consequently, a qualitative research methodology was adopted as it permitted me as the researcher to elicit information from participants regarding a particularized social situation (King and Horrocks, 2010; Cohen, Manion and Morrison, 2013).

The qualitative methodological approach influenced the design of the research. One of the major decisions to be made in the design process was the way in which the data were to be gathered. I considered a number of ways of collecting data (such as using a questionnaire or a case study). However, I selected to use qualitative interviews as they are the most appropriate method to obtain individuals' views, and moreover interviews correspond with the phenomenological underpinnings of the research (Kvale and Brinkmann, 2009). The other principal elements of the research design are delineated: the determination of the sample and data collection and how ethical integrity is observed.

In order to obtain individuals (the sample) for my research, I sent invitation letters to college principals and head teachers outlining the details of the research, the ethics of undertaking the research and how suitable individuals could participate in the study. The response was poor, and therefore I asked colleagues to assist with the research. Eventually, I was successful in sourcing participants from a college and a school which had both made improvements to the achievement of black male students.

The topic of my research and the individuals whom I wished to interview were the principal drivers in the selection of my sample. Sixteen people, eight leaders and eight students, participated in my research: these participants were London based, and they were representative of the wider group population of males of African 'Caribbean' heritage in the United Kingdom (Mason, 1996). I selected four leaders from the participating school and four from the college: the leaders had considerable leadership experience and had led and contributed to student retention and achievement. In terms of the students, they were aged between fifteen and nineteen, and were divided into two equal groups based on their institutional attendance (school or college): this facilitated a comparison of students' current and post-school experience.

I decided to collect the data for this research through one-to-one semi-structured interviews with leaders and group interviews with students (Dencombe, 2014) using open, descriptive and inferential questions (Creswell, 2013). Participants were asked questions about how black educators lead, any differences between white and black educators' leadership and whether the aforementioned black and white leaders affected student outcomes.

Further to the reasons previously highlighted, interviews were used as they have the additional advantage of enabling the researcher to gain clarification on information provided by participants (Denscombe, 2014). A key benefit of a group interview is that the range of responses to a particular question lend themselves to a form of internal triangulation (Robson, 2002; Denscombe, 2014). However, two main drawbacks of a group interview are the variable level of contribution by participants and the risk of 'group think' (Denscombe, 2014). To mitigate against this situation, I encouraged all participants to contribute to discussions and asked them for their point of view on specific points which were raised.

In undertaking research, it is important to be clear about the way in which the data are to be collected, and of parallel importance is having an awareness of research integrity: all researchers are expected to adhere to ethical guidelines for research. Participants must be made fully aware of the study and deemed suitable to participate in it. Therefore, I distributed the details of my research in advance to all participants to ensure transparency. In fact, the head teacher, principal and teachers at the college and school referred leaders and students who they believed would be comfortable to share their views candidly: I discussed all the students with the teachers to confirm this. Only leaders with appropriate knowledge and leadership expertise were identified for the research. There was no evidence that the research carried any risk or harm (O'Leary, 2010).

I needed to demonstrate that all participants (leaders and students) had voluntarily agreed to partake in the research and given informed consent (King and Horrocks, 2010); therefore, the participants were requested to complete and sign a consent form (O'Leary, 2010).

Further, I sent a letter to each participant informing them of their right to withdraw from the research process at any point, and before I started each interview I reminded participants of this right (Kvale and Brinkmann, 2009).

Another critical aspect of undertaking research which requires consideration is the interviewer effect. This refers to the possible influence that a researcher may have on his or her participant. Caution must be taken when conducting research as any researcher trait (e.g. race, gender, class) may affect the participants' responses to questions. Therefore, researchers are expected to exercise self-awareness and recognize that they may inadvertently lead participants to respond in a particular way. I shared an ancestral background with the participants and was fully aware of the notion of cross boundaries and the dichotomous role of 'insider' and 'outsider' (Rubin and Rubin, 2005). Being cognizant of the interview effect minimizes any skewing of data collection and analysis (Dencombe, 2007).

Therefore, I reviewed the data collected through critical analsys of my postionality nad possible partiality (King and Horrocks, 2010).

However, the presence of 'researcher linkage' to participants may result in more nuanced data being collected than would be gathered when such a linkage is absent. Indeed, Tillman (2002) confirms that acknowledgement of the historical, sociopolitical context of the participants and its alignment with that of the researcher through a culturally sensitive approach to research design may generate more accurate data. Moreover, Blair (1998) makes the cogent point that it is the researcher's professionalism which guides the integrity of the research undertaken, as 'researcher objectivity' is a misnomer.

Once the data were collected, I transcribed them manually and ascribed codes to the data to establish emergent themes or subthemes (Richards, 2009). I devised data analysis sheets to record the results from both sets of participants. It was from an analysis of the data (codes and from the sheets) that I drew up the findings.

My appreciation and consideration of the above-mentioned areas of research design contributed to the dependability of the findings and consequential conclusions (Robson, 2002). The following section provides an analytical summation of the views of the participants on the main topics of the research.

The evidence

The following evidence for this research is drawn from the leaders and students' responses to the interview questions pertaining to the topic of the study. The presentation of the participants' responses mirrors the order in which the main topics appear within the section, 'Issue in Context'. For ease of identification, the letters A–D are ascribed to college participants and E–H to those from the school. Due to space restrictions, it is not possible to include all participants' responses.

Justice, care and leadership

All leaders reported that justice and care influenced the way in which they led and interacted with students and staff. Indeed, the importance of respect, equity, care, fairness and inclusion was mentioned throughout the interviews. However, it was the use of the term 'fairness' linked to justice, which emerged most often in dialogue with the leaders. They expressed a deep desire to create a just society which would reflect the needs of all students regardless of their background. *'Just be fair'* was the prosaic comment made by Leader B, and this encapsulated the mood of the leaders generally. Leader A stated that 'their' leadership required a particular mindset, and that [it] is borne out of a sense of *'making things better and fairness'*

In highlighting the importance of the presence of black male leaders in schools, Leader E stipulated that these leaders were needed to *'change and transform the [leadership] landscape [...] to make things fair'*. This echoed the sentiment of Leader A, who stated that *'social justice [it] is what a school should be'*. Indeed, the role of the school was emphasized by a number of leaders as essential in creating the type of society in which one wished to live. Reflecting on this, the leaders articulated that they challenged practices that had a negative impact on the students.

Throughout the interviews, the leaders referred to care as an integral part of leadership and as a means of securing fairness and student achievement. Some of the leaders mentioned that white leaders lacked care for the students, and that, therefore, as black leaders it was their responsibility to make sure that staff (leaders as well as teachers) demonstrate care towards the students.

> You need to show you care, just as much as they care [...] show compassion for them and show you understand where they are coming from. (Leader A)

> Black leaders know how to support the child. (Leader E)

There was collective agreement amongst students that the leaders showed care towards them and this made them want to succeed.

> The black leaders always show us they care and they will talk to us in a certain way and you can tell that they don't judge you [...] they want us to do well. (Student A)

> They're like your father and they want the best for you. (Student F)

Though none of the students made specific reference to love in relation to leadership or as key to supporting them to succeed, they constantly mentioned that teachers and leaders showing care contributed to their doing well in school, The leaders, by contrast, emphasized that love for the students was vital as this informed the manner in which students are treated. Leader A made the following remark about the lack of love exhibited by white leaders towards the students, *'Without love in your heart, you cannot embrace the student.'* This comment epitomizes the general sentiment amongst the leaders that the absence of love for the students will affect leaders and their praxis.

Connectivity with students and acknowledgement of African heritage

All leaders spoke about the value of connecting to the students and demonstrating care for them: there was unequivocal agreement that race of the leaders played a key role in one's ability to connect with the students.

> I can talk to the child and key into their heritage [...] I genuinely want them [black students] to succeed. (Leader C)

Most students articulated the importance of seeing leaders who looked like them: they mentioned that it spurred them on to do well.

> It's nice to see someone from the Caribbean and someone like you doing well [...] it makes you want to do well too. (Student A)
>
> They understand because they went through the same thing. It's nice to see someone that thinks like you. (Student G).

The leaders remarked that it was extremely important that the students learn about the history of Africa. They believed that the inclusion of African history within the curriculum would have a positive influence on the students as they would gain knowledge of their ancestors' contributions to world history, which could increase their confidence and eventually improve achievement.

> You need to give the students a better framework and incorporate history into the curriculum [...] talk about their Kings and Queens. (Leader G)
>
> Bring students to the National History Museum [...] you need to show how great our people were. (Leader D)

Without exception, the students stated that learning about their history was key in boosting their confidence.

> History is important and we do not have the full history. they don't teach us this. If black children knew the full history it would make them more confident at school. (Student F)

Leading teachers and teaching and learning

The students confirmed that teachers were important in ensuring their *success*, *'If the teachers want you to achieve they will show an interest in you and you will show an interest.'* (Student B)

However, the students reported that black teachers, unlike white teachers, showed they cared and did not have negative feelings about them. Student F pointed out that black teachers had respect for them and high expectations.

> We had a black teacher and his name was Mr. X [. . .] he spoke to us like our father did [. . .] we respected him [. . .] he pushed us, motivated and inspired us to do well [. . .] he expected us to do well.

It is interesting that the leaders also mentioned that they had high expectations for the students and expected the same from staff. Leader A's following comment touches upon the top-down approach to challenging teacher expectations of the students,

> Your leadership affects the expectations you have for the students and this will translate into your expectations from all staff.

The leaders in both sectors believed that it was essential to ensure that white teachers take responsibility for students' achievement as these teachers had negative feelings towards the students. With a focus on success, Leader E stated,

> I have no problem in questioning staff about justifying their achievement rates for black students and getting the answers.

Discussion

There was unequivocal evidence that the praxis of the leaders was substantially influenced by the main components of justice, that is, respect, equity, fairness and recognition of difference, inclusion (Larson and Marthada, 2003; Shields, 2004; Shoho et al., 2005; Dantley and Tillman, 2006; Ryan, 2013). Indeed, leadership based social justice and care is predicated on a moral imperative to arrest the marginalization of the members of any group who are subjected to discrimination or exclusion (Dantley and Tillman, 2006; Randall et al., 2011): fostering transformative leadership was central to their leadership enactments (Shields, 2004; Dantley and Tillman, 2006).

The importance of exhibiting care specifically and love generally (Starratt, 1994; Smith, 1997, Noddings, 1999; Alston, 2015) within leadership was consistently emphasized as a combatant weapon against injustice (Larson and Murtadha, 2003; Alson, 2015). Resultantly, leaders organized their leadership to enable students' holistic needs to be met through 'interpersonal caring' (Tillman, 2004). The leaders openly expressed their care and love for the students as a way of inspiring success (Noddings, 1999).

Love, alongside and within care, was cited as forming an integral part in healing the lives of those touched by 'unfairness'. Unlike the students, leaders highlighted love as an important element of leadership (Larson and Murtadha, 2003; Alston, 2015). The lack of love for the students at the leadership level prevented its permeation throughout the school, and this had a detrimental effect on the students. The question of connectivity of the leader with the student emerged from the participants' conversations.

The leaders and students commented that leaders connecting with the students contributed to student success and confidence. There was evidence that the leaders having a connection to the students' heritage contributed to an augmentation of students' confidence and success. The leaders viewed providing additional support for the students as important (Brooks and Jean-Marie, 2007). While the students acknowledged this, they valued the presence of leaders who resembled themselves and understood their journey (Bush et al., 2005).

Both leaders and students concurred that history should be embedded within the curriculum as it assists students to reconnect to self (Shockley, 2008); buttresses confidence; reinforces an acknowledgement of forebears' contribution to world history (Hopson et al., 2010); promotes a sense of pride (Blair, 2002); and positively contributes to achievement (Blair, 2002; Shockley, 2008).

The leaders made it unequivocally clear about their stance on teaching. They stipulated that they expected high standards from teachers, who in turn needed to have such expectations for their students. The leaders stated that they would confront any teacher about their practice and achievement rates as it related to the students (Blair, 2002). The leaders, however, singled out white teachers as a group who particularly required examination in terms of their poor attitude to the students.

Leaders and students alike continually talked about the importance of factoring the race of the leader into the understanding of how leadership links to the students and their outcomes. Further, the leaders believed that white leaders did not have a vested interest in changing the current iniquitous landscape in schools or society. Thus, leadership based on justice and care is offered as way of creating the circumstances to improve the outcomes of students.

Implications (research, practice and policy)

Evidence from the study and the integrative literature review reveal that 'black male leadership' based on justice and care has a positive impact on students' confidence and as a consequence on their achievement. The following suggestions are offered to propel action for this leadership praxis.

Research

An extended research project could provide broader evidential data in relation to the correlation of the leader's race to student achievement. In fact, a mixed methods approach, combining elements of quantitative and qualitative methods, could widen the range of instrumentation; enable access to a larger sample and greater data collection opportunities; improve data reliability (statistical evidence); and address some of the weaknesses which occur with a single-strand methodological approach (Creswell, 2013; Dencombe, 2014).

The scope of the research could include black female leaders and students as well as white leaders. The inclusion of these groups into the research could add a new layer of triangulation. Intersecting the findings of the research from aforementioned groups with those that are already available may provide some powerful insights into the leader race-student correlation as it pertains to achievement.

Although London was the context for the study, there would be some value in conducting similar studies in other parts of the country, which have some concentration of the sample group. This would serve to establish whether emerging conclusions regarding the leadership practice of the leaders and their benefits to the students are confined to London.

Practice

Given the moral imperative to ensure all students are treated fairly (Shields, 2004; Alston, 2015), and in response to the evidence provided, a review of and changes to leadership practice and curriculum delivery in schools generally, and in particular in schools with a poor record of improving the outcomes of the students, should be seriously considered. Indeed, sharing good practice plays a critical role in heuristic opportunities for schools, and such practice may be deployed to support the fulfilment of the aforementioned moral imperative.

In 2017, the Department of Education earmarked £140m funding for school improvement (DfE, 2017c, d). The exact allocation to secondary schools was not mentioned. However, schools with white leadership teams, which have failed to ensure students' achievement rates exceed the national benchmark rates, could benefit from using school improvement funds if permissible. These schools could invite designated black male leaders to share their practice of enhancing student achievement through leadership based on justice and care.

Further, a shift to culturally responsive curricula and pedagogies would demonstrate a commitment not only to responding to students' learning but also to caring for the students. However, to allay concerns of misappropriation or miseducation, the development of an African history curriculum should be led by black academics, historians and institutions with knowledge of this silenced history. Moreover, the aforementioned group of specialists should be tasked with the delivery of the curriculum. This would counter accusations that black people are not permitted the opportunity to lead the change in their 'destiny' (Shockley, 2008).

Lastly, leaders could implement accountability measures for student success by examining student achievement based on census racial categorization. This would enable schools to track teachers who have a record of failing the students.

There are no normative national policy directives on the ways in which senior leaders should implement their leadership. Day and Sammons's (2014) report usefully highlights effective leadership praxes, yet leadership based on justice and care is omitted from the report.

Given the evidence provided, schools may wish to include leadership based on justice and care within its wider equality and diversity policy and specifically within its curriculum policy. Accountability tools such as review of schemes of work, student evaluations and teacher observation records could be used to determine the effectiveness of this leadership to bring about change to the curriculum and improve and achievement rates.

The Office for Standards in Education, Children's Services and Skills (Ofsted), as the body responsible for school inspections in England, could make more explicit reference to the importance and inclusion of leadership based on justice and care by monitoring its impact on student confidence and outcome in schools where this leadership is exercised. Further, an updated common inspection framework could highlight leadership based on justice and care as indicative of progressive and strong school leadership and penalize institutions which fail to draw upon this leleadership. . Such a failure could affect all judgement grades, in particular that of the effectiveness of leadership and management and overall effectiveness.

Conclusions

This chapter has provided an opportunity for black male leaders and students to share perspectives of their educational experiences. It demonstrates that the race of the leader and their praxis cannot be placed in the margins of the leadership-student achievement discourse. Moreover, the praxis of leadership-based justice and care can contribute to strengthening student achievement.

The leaders provided examples of how leadership based on justice and care informed their praxis and how its successful deployment can buttress the educational chances of the students and counter the leadership praxis of white leaders. Whilst confronting instances of marginalization, the leaders created a space for the consideration of the broad needs of the students (Tillman, 2004).

The leaders' treatment and conceptualization of the students was diametrically opposite to their white peers. White leaders distanced themselves from the students and neglected to exhibit care for them (Brooks and Jean-Marie, 2007), and they paid scant attention to the critical importance of African history, though the subject evinced the promotion of confidence and stimulation of student achievement (Shockley, 2008). Contrastingly, the leaders viewed the students in a positive way: they had high expectations of the students and a desire to secure positive outcomes. Some leaders' unrelenting focus on achievement drove them to confront staff about their examination results.

What has been singly telling and worth reiterating is that the leaders and students mentioned that this study afforded them the space and opportunity to articulate in a candid way their educational experiences. The study, therefore, permitted unbridled conversations, and this book chapter acknowledges the men and teenagers who kindly gave of their time to partake in the study.

This chapter does not purport that all leaders' praxes can be reduced to their racialized categorization. Nevertheless, it does highlight the divergent praxes and behaviours of racialized leaders and acknowledges that the former could be rooted in the latter's geo-historical experience as well as their emotional and racial connection to the student. Crucially, this chapter illustrates that the information that we gather about racialized groups may be impoverished if the participants are unwilling to speak freely with people they do not trust or have little connection with.

Leadership based on justice and care is a sine qua non for improving the students' achievement. The leaders routinely enact this leadership based on a genuine care and love for the students and a connection with them: they want the students to succeed. In turn, the students valued the leaders' positive attitude toward them and they recognized that the leaders expected and pushed them to realize their potential and gain the qualifications they required. Indeed, race in leadership does matter.

References

Alston, J. A. (2015), 'Leadership as Soul Work: Living, Leading and Loving the Work', in C. Bosket and A. E. Osanloo (eds), *Living the Work: Promoting Social Justice and Equity in Schools around the World*, 395–404, Bangley, UK: Emerald.

Andrews, K. (2013), *Resisting Racism: Race, Inequality, and the 'Black' Supplementary School Movement*, London: Institute of Education Press, University of London.

Blair, M. (1998), 'The Myth of Neutrality in Educational Research', in P. Connolly and B. Troyna (eds), *Researching Racism in Education*, 12–20, Buckingham: Open University Press.

Blair, M. (2001), *Why Pick on Me? School Exclusion and Black Youth*, Stoke-on-Trent, UK: Trentham Books.

Blair, M. (2002), 'Effective School Leadership: The Multi-Ethnic Context', *British Journal of Sociology of Education*, 23 (2): 179–91.

Brooks, J. S. and G. Jean-Marie (2007), 'Black Leadership, White Leadership; Race and Race Relations in an Urban High School', *Journal of Educational Administration*, 45 (6): 756–68.

Bush, T., T. Glovcoheer and K. Sood (2005), *Black and Ethnic Minority Final Report to the National College for School Leadership*, Lincoln: International Institute for Educational Leadership.

Coard, B. (1971), *How the West Indian Child Is Made Educationally Sub-Normal in the British School System*, London: New Beacon Books.

Cohen, L., L. Manion and K. Morrison (2013), *Research Methods in Education*, London: Routledge.

Cresswell, J. W. (2013), *Research Design – Qualitative, Quantitative and Mixed Methods Approaches,* 4th edn, Thousand Oaks, CA: SAGE.

Dantley, M. E. and L. C. Tillman (2006), 'Social Justice and Moral Transformative Leadership', in C. Marshall and M. Oliva (eds), *Leadership for Social Justice: Making Revolutions in Education*, 16–30, Boston, Cambridge: Pearson Publishing.

Davison, R. B. (1962), *West Indian Migrants*, London, Oxford: Oxford University Press.

Day, C. and P. Sammons (2014), *Successful School Leadership*, Reading, UK: Educational Development Trust.

Day, C., Q. Gu and P. Sammons (2016), 'The Impact of Leadership on Student Outcomes: How Successful School Leaders Use Transformational and Instructional Strategies to Make a Difference', *Educational Administration Quarterly*, 52 (2): 221–58.

Denscombe, M. (2014), *The Good Research Guide*, 5th edn, Maidenhead: McGraw Hill (Open University Press).

DfE (Department of Education) (2010), *The School Workforce in England*, London: Department of Education. Available at: https://www.gov.uk/government/statistics/school-workforce-in-england-november-2017.

DfE (Department of Education) (2017a), *The School Workforce in England,* London: Department of Education.

DfE (Department of Education) (2017b), *Permanent and Fixed-Period Exclusions in England: 2015–16,* London: Department of Education. Available at: https://www.gov.uk/government/statistics/permanent-and-fixed-period-exclusions-in-england-2015-to-2016.

DfE (Department of Education) (2017c), *New Funding for School Improvement,* London: Department of Education. Available at: https://www.gov.uk/government/news/new-funding-for-school-improvement--2.

DfE (Department of Education) (2017d), *Strategic School Improvement,* London: Department of Education. Available at: https://www.gov.uk/guidance/strategic-school-improvement-fund.

DfES (Department for Education and Skills) (2006), *Priority Review: Exclusion of Black Pupils' Getting It, Getting It Right!* London: Department for Education and Skills.

Fraser, N. (1997), *Justice Interruptus,* London: Routledge.

Gay, G. (2010), *Culturally Responsive Teaching,* New York: Teachers College Press.

Gaziel, H. H. (2007), 'Re-examining the Relationship between Principal's Instructional/Educational Leadership and Student Achievement', *Journal of Social Sciences,* 15 (1): 17–24.

Gillborn, D. (1995), *Racism and Antiracism in Real Schools,* Buckingham: Open University Press.

Gillborn, D. (2008), *Racism and Education: Conspiracy or Coincidence,* London: Routledge.

Gillborn, D. and N. Rollock (2010), 'Education', in A. Bloch and J. Solomos (eds), *Race and Ethnicity in the 21st Century,* 193–208, London: Palgrave Macmillan.

Greater London Authority (GLA) (2017), *Annual London Education Report,* London: Greater London Authority. Available at: https://goo.gl/Nw7ISn.

Hopson, R. K. M., U. Hotep, D. L. Schneider and I. G. Turenne (2010), 'What's Leadership without an African Centred Perspective? Explorations and Extrapolations', *Urban Education,* 45 (6): 777–96.

King, N. and C. Horrocks (2010), *Interviews in Qualitative Research,* London: SAGE.

Kvale, S. and K. Brinkmann (2009), *InterViews: Learning the Craft of Qualitative Research Interviewing,* London: SAGE.

Larson, C. and K. Murtadha (2003), 'Leadership for Social Justice', in J. Murphy (ed.), *The Educational Leadership Challenge: Redefining Leadership for the 21st Century,* 134–61, Chicago: University of Chicago Press.

Leithwood, K., K. Anderson, B. Mascall and T. Strauss (2010), 'School Leaders' Influence on Student Learning', in T. Bush, T. Bell and D. Middlewood (eds), *The Principles of Educational Leadership and Management,* 13–30, London: SAGE.

Louis, K. S., B. Dretzke and K. Wahlstrom (2010), 'How Does Leadership Affect Student Achievement? Results from a National US Survey', *School Effectiveness and School Improvement,* 21 (3): 315–36.

Mac an Ghaill, M. (1988), *Young, Gifted and Black*, Oxford: Oxford University Press.

Mason, D. (2000), *Race and Ethnicity in Modern Britain*, Oxford: Oxford University Press.

Mason, J. (1996), *Qualitative Research*, London: SAGE.

Newman, M. (2006), 'School Leadership and Social Justice', *Caribbean Journal of Education*, 27 (1): 3–21.

Noddings, N. (1999), 'Care, Justice and Equity', in M. S. Katz, N. Noddings and S. A. Strike (eds), *Justice and Caring: The Search for the Common Ground in Education*, 7–20, New York: Teachers College Press.

O'Leary, Z. (2010), *The Essential Guide to Doing Your Research Project*, London: SAGE.

Office of National Statistics (2011), *Census 2011*, National Office for Statistics. Available at: https://goo.gl/2RWJGN.

Painter, N. I. (2010), *The History of White People*, New York: W.W. Norton and Company.

Peach, C. (1991), *The Caribbean in Europe: Contrasting Patterns of Migration and Settlement in Britain, France and the Netherlands*, Coventry: Centre for Research in Ethnic Relations, University of Warwick.

Rampton, A. (1981), *West Indian Children in Our Schools*, London: HMSO.

Randall, B., D. B. Lindsey and R. D. Terrell (2011), 'Social Justice – Focussing on Assets to Overcome Barriers', in A. M. Blanstein and P. D. Houston (eds), *Leadership for Social Justice in Our Schools*, 25–44, Thousand Oaks, CA: Corwin.

Richards, L. (2009), Handling *Qualitative Data – A Practical Guide*, London: SAGE

Robson, C. (2002), *Real World Research*, Oxford: Blackwell Publishing.

Rose, P. I. (1968), *The Subject of Race*, Oxford: Oxford University Press.

Rubin, H. I. and I. S. Rubin (2005), *Qualitative Interviewing – The Art of Hearing Data*, London: SAGE.

Ryan, J. (2013), 'Promoting Inclusive Leadership Diverse Schools', in I. Bogotch and C. M. Shields (eds), *International Handbook of Educational Leadership and Social (In)Justice*, 359–380, London: Springer.

Sherwood, M. (2003), 'White Myths, Black Omissions: The Historical Origins of Racism in Britain', *International Journal of Historical Teaching, Learning and Research*, 3 (1): 49–59. Available at: http://centres.exeter.ac.uk/historyresource/journal5/jhltr5.pdf#page=49.

Shields, C. M. (2004), 'Dialogic Leadership for Social Justice: Overcoming Pathologies of Silence', *Educational Administration Quarterly*, 40 (1): 109–32.

Shockley, K. M. T. (2008), 'Africentric Educational Leadership: Theory and Practice', *International Journal of Education Policy and Leadership*, 3 (3): 1–11.

Shoho, A. R., B. M. Merchant and C. M. Lugg (2005), 'Social Justice – Seeking a Common Language', in F. W. English (ed.), *The Sage Handbook of Educational Leadership*, 35–42, Thousand Oaks, CA: SAGE.

Smedley, A. and B. D. Smedley (2012), *Race in North America*, Boulder, CO: Westview Press.

Smith,V. G. (1997), 'Caring: Motivation for African American Male Youth to Succeed', *Journal of African American Men*, 3 (2): 49–63.

Starratt, R. J. (1994), *Building on the Ethical School*, London: Falmer Press.

Theoharis, G. (2007), 'Social Justice Educational Leaders and Resistance: Toward a Theory of Social Justice Leadership', *Educational Administration Quarterly*, 43 (2): 221–58.

Tillman, L. C. (2002), 'Culturally Sensitive Research Approaches: An African-American Perspective', *American Research Association*, 31 (9): 3–12.

Tillman, L. C. (2004), 'African American Principals and the Legacy of Brown', *Review of Research in Education,* 28: 101–46.

Troyna, B. and B. Carrington (1990), *Education, Racism and Reform*, London: Routledge.

Warmington, P. (2014), *Black British Intellectuals and Education: Multiculturalism's Hidden History*, London: Routledge.

Webster's Third New International Dictionary of the English Language Unabridged (1993), Springfield, MA: Merriam-Webster, Inc., Publishers.

Wright, C. (1987), 'Black Students – White Teachers', in B. Troyna (ed.), *Racial Inequality in Education London*, 109–26, London: Tavistock Publications.

3

Race, ethnicity and diversity: British imperial history and the secondary school curriculum

Adam Burns

Introduction

Both 'curriculum' and 'diversity' are words open to a wide variety of interpretations. Curriculum is defined and understood here as a 'process': an 'interaction of teachers, students and knowledge' (Smith, 2000) that puts 'depth of understanding' ahead of 'the recitation of trivial facts' (McKernan, 2008: 94). This chapter will consider – first and foremost – the curriculum as it relates to secondary education and particularly History, though most of the arguments made can be applied far more widely than such narrow confines. Academics have long found it difficult to unite around what content should be taught in History classrooms and, though this chapter focuses on England, such debates have arisen across the globe (Phillips, 1998; Ismailova, 2004; Parkes, 2007; Hsiao-Lan, 2008; Clark, 2009; Guyver, 2011; Muñoz and Noboa, 2012; Martell, 2013; Burns, 2014). Many of these same studies show that in such debates – wherever they occur – contending political and press commentators tend to conceive of 'curriculum' far more narrowly than this chapter argues is appropriate. In the English context, many criticised the government's approach to reforms over the last decade precisely because of its narrow view of both the content and purpose of a History curriculum, where the government was seen to select the knowledge students should learn and the schools were to 'transmit' this knowledge (Young, 2011; Beck, 2012; Haydn, 2012). A wider definition of curriculum – as a process, rather than a body of knowledge to be transmitted – is crucial to understanding the equally contentious role of diversity in a curriculum.

When it comes to devising a curriculum for a diverse society, perhaps most particularly a History curriculum, commentators are divided as to whether schools should put more emphasis on the 'transmission of the achievements and cultural heritage of the nation' or 'reflect more fully the presence and achievements of those from ethnic minority backgrounds' (Grever, Haydn and Ribbens, 2008: 78–9). Although somewhat reflecting the narrow conception of curriculum held by many commentators, as noted above, either such approach should also take into consideration the preconceptions that students and teachers bring to the classroom. History teaching (and that of many other cognate disciplines) involves the individual interpretations and constructions not only of a single author and their text but also those of the teacher and the diversity of learners in a class. Not only are variations in student understanding predictable, but they are also often unrecognized. The Internet, television, film and music – not to mention families and friends – are but a few contributors to the cultural perceptions that students bring to the classroom. Young people's conceptions of 'race' and ethnicity owe a great deal to perceptions gathered from outside the classroom, and both students and teachers 'bring a variety of social identities into a classroom, ranging from identities forged through frequent encounters with racism to those living in bubbles of unexamined white privilege' (Elton-Chalcraft, 2009; Rozas and Miller, 2009: 25). While one can accept the need to take account of diversity within the curriculum, with so many variables in play, it is difficult to know how best to take account of it.

This chapter uses interviews with secondary History teachers in England to explore many of the issues mentioned above. Each interviewee teaches British imperial history to sixteen- to eighteen-year-old students and, for them, the place of British imperial history in the curriculum is essential to increasing student understanding of the diverse nation in which they live, and to gaining a greater appreciation of that diversity. Their views are a far cry from the one-dimensional perceptions still pushed in the British press. For example, a recent editorial for *The Times* (2018) argued that '[f]or many decades the Empire has been the subject of close to unanimous opprobrium. The average history teacher, musician, writer, film-maker or public figure routinely lambasts the imperial era', whereas another media commentator had earlier expressed fears that the potential prominence of imperial history in the curriculum would lead to a preponderance of 'bunting-and-bigotry' (Penny, 2010). The disparity between such media perceptions and the views of teachers themselves certainly has far wider implications for curriculum development in schools. However, the debate over a diverse curriculum and the place of British imperialism within it has raged well beyond the school sector. The 'Rhodes Must Fall' campaign, which began in 2015 in Cape Town, and other such movements to 'decolonize' both campuses and their curricula, have arisen at universities across the globe. Within academia, calls like that made in *The Times* editorial cited above, for a more nuanced, balanced – or more 'positive' – view of British imperialism are routinely met with a fervid response from those who see figures advocating such an approach as imperial apologists (see, for example, Lusher, 2017 or Adams, 2017). Never has the time been so ripe, across educational sectors, for a practitioner-led reflection on the place of empire and diversity in our twenty-first-century curricula.

The issue in context

At the start of the twentieth century, Britannia did indeed 'rule the waves', and the inevitability of British imperialism's place in the History classroom was beyond question.[1] Historian Peter Yeandle recently published a volume on this very subject, exploring schooling from the 1870s through to the 1920s, and the extent to which British imperialism influenced History educators. Yeandle draws clear links between his research and the education reforms of the UK Conservative-led coalition government (2010–15), and the former [English] education secretary Michael Gove's (2010–14) quest to return to a 'golden age' of History teaching with a 'content-led curriculum, devoid of educational theory, and intended to promote national identity' (Yeandle, 2015: 1). For many, this alleged attempt to promote national identity would also involve boosting the presence of British imperial history in the national curriculum for England.[2] Ultimately, Gove was forced to make a substantial U-turn when it came to his plans for curriculum change, and much of the new focus on British imperial history was removed following a significant backlash from leading historical figures and organizations (Burns, 2014: 110). Whether one agrees with Gove or his critics, what was clarified by this clash was that the issues of *which* history is taught and, more particularly, the inclusion of imperial history within the curriculum are issues that remain as contentious today as they ever have been.

Zajda (2015: 4) argues that a renewed sense of the importance of teaching national identity often results from periods of identity crisis. For him, the 2005 London '7/7' bombings (and the ongoing perceived threat of fundamentalist terror) were the start of such a crisis, and saw the then-prime minister, Gordon Brown, making clear the value of English/British national identity and its 'values of liberty and tolerance and the principle of fairness to all'. This renewed focus on so-called 'core British values' was reflected in the *Ajegbo Report* of 2007 on citizenship education, which also recommended paying greater attention to the legacy of British imperialism (as discussed in Osler, 2008). More than a decade on, recent UK government initiatives have echoed such projects, perhaps none so much as the integration (largely since 2014) into school curricula of so-called fundamental British values (FBV), which has since become a 'quasi-legal requirement' (Richardson, 2015: 37). Yet, as Richardson (2015: 37) rightly remarks, the idea of what constitutes a British identity (or an English one at that) has rarely been fixed or clear, but more of a 'muddle and mixture'.

In an overview of the complexity of what exactly, if anything, British identity is, historian Robert Colls points specifically to Britain's imperial past:

> British national identity was not born of a deplorable past. It is true that British dominion was not built according to the principles of the Equal Opportunities Commission and we have to accept, too, that it was interwoven with imperialism and what we now call racism. In this it was not alone among other imperialisms – including republican and socialist imperialisms. At the same time, we have to accept that British national identity survived because it was a broadly acceptable expression of the British people, to the British people, if not by the British people. (Colls, 2012)

For Colls (2012), writing during the period of coalition government (2010–15), the British had not stopped believing in themselves, but rather (since the 1950s) 'over a very short period the conditions of that belief had evaporated. Between the Festival of Britain and the Millennium Dome, say, British national identity was no more'. Perhaps, as Zajda (2015: 4) and Richardson (2015: 38) suggest, this was a reaction to internal existential threats from terrorism, or perhaps instead it was a partial reaction to stresses put on the very fabric of the United Kingdom, exacerbated by recent referendums on Scottish independence (2014) or membership of the European Union (2016). Whatever the primary stress, it appears that it is the pressures upon unity that have provoked a national (and governmental) response in trying to establish a stronger sense of national identity.

Coming at these issues from a somewhat different perspective, Cole and Stuart (2005), in their study of Asian and black trainee teachers working in south-east England, found that racism and xenophobia were widespread. Their conclusions suggested that the extent of racism was 'deeply worrying', but they also added that 'the teaching of imperialism, past and present, in schools [...] informs us most precisely about the historical and contemporary nature of

British society' (Cole and Stuart, 2005: 363). In an earlier piece, Cole argues that an honest evaluation of imperialism needs to be reintroduced to English schools in order to at least make students aware of the implications and ramifications of racism (Cole, 2004: 534). When one considers the place of British imperial history in the curriculum, and its role in identity forming, it seems to provide a valuable level of contextualization for the diverse student body of twenty-first-century Britain.

Whether studying imperial history helps widen one's understanding of modern Britain, forges broader understanding or exacerbates differences in identities is difficult to judge without further investigation. Research by Barton and McCully (2005) found that a balanced and standardized portrayal of history in Northern Ireland's curriculum led not to a lessening of tension between Unionists and Nationalists but rather had served to intensify students' partisanship. These authors' findings raise interesting questions for those who feel that, by selecting a certain type of subject matter, a certain way of thinking or type of identity might be inculcated in students. If indeed the government of the day wished to create an ideologically charged narrative of Britain's imperial history, there is little firm evidence that selecting facts and placing them on a 'syllabus-style' curriculum would have anything like the desired outcome.

Ladson-Billings (1998: 18) claimed in an early piece on critical race theory (CRT) in education that CRT [in the United States, at least] sees 'the official school curriculum as a culturally specific artifact designed to maintain a White supremacist master script'.[3] This is something Gillborn (2005: 499) feels applies just as directly to England, but in a far broader sense: 'education policy in England is actively involved in the defence, legitimation and extension of white supremacy'. When one brings together the ideas of Ladson-Billings and Gillborn, what they both suggest is that great power lies in the hands of those responsible for top-level curriculum design. However, though a government might well aim to achieve ideological goals through redrawing the curriculum (see Parmar 2010; Beck 2012), the way the curriculum is experienced in different schools might differ widely and, as such, the control the government might appear to wield could in reality prove largely illusory, or occur only on a broad scale due to dilution through mediation. Works by other CRT scholars, such as Gretchen McAllister and Jacqui Jordan Irvine (2000: 5; 2002: 441), highlight the importance of mediation, as might occur through the classroom teacher. Their studies consider the significance of the teacher's role in connecting with, and reflecting upon, difficult course content and relating it to students' experiences. In the best-case scenario, both students and teachers might effectively benefit from the varied 'cultural wealth' (Yosso, 2005: 82) within the classroom, shifting the lens from narrow, white middle-class privilege to a far broader range of vision. Such ideas, as shown below, are raised by the interviewees here, though without overt reference to this specific theoretical standpoint.

Methods

I adopted a purposive sampling approach when choosing the sites for this study in order to create a somewhat representative cross section of 'types' of English secondary institutions for sixteen to eighteen education, especially given the relatively small number of institutions involved. After this, the schools were somewhat self-selecting, as I also wanted to ensure teachers and their students had all covered a largely comparable section of British imperial history and were located in the same urban area. Given that the former was virtually impossible below A Level (sixteen to eighteen courses where core content is very specific), I chose teachers who taught specific modules on British imperialism to this age group (all three sites taught a module on British imperialism in India between 1900 and 1947 at AS Level, among others).[4] The interviews explored here are part of a wider study also involving data gathered from students, but this chapter's focus is solely on the teacher element of the project, due to constraints on space. The three different 'types' of institutions and the teacher aliases used in this chapter are listed below:

1. a state sixth-form college (James)
2. a state comprehensive school (Ruth)
3. an independent school (David)

In each school, I conducted a semi-structured interview, allowing for a clear agenda and a set of defined research questions that needed to be addressed. Each interview lasted for roughly half an hour and the questions were open-ended, allowing for modification of format and wording in relation to the interviewee's responses (Ary et al., 2010). I accept there are clear pitfalls to such an approach, notably interviewer bias and lack of direct comparability, but the clear benefits of the sort of answers gleaned from a more interactional interview hopefully make up for this (Mitchell and Jolley, 2010; Cousin, 2009).

When designing questions for the interview, I selected six questions closely linked to issues raised in my literature review for the wider study (Burns, 2017):

1. Do you feel that it is important for students in English schools to learn about British imperial history at school in the twenty-first century, and why?
2. By the time students study History at A Level, do you think students have already formed clear opinions of British imperialism?
3. Other than at school, how do you think students form views on the history of the British Empire?
4. Do History teachers have an obligation to provide a 'balanced' view of British imperialism, and how might this be achieved?
5. Is it possible during a student's school career – from Key Stage 1 through to post-16 (A Level) education – to gain a real understanding of the British Empire, given that it forms only a fraction of the curriculum?
6. Do you feel that a better knowledge and understanding of British imperialism has a generally positive or negative effect on how students view the United Kingdom today?

The questions were treated as part of an 'interview schedule' – flexible enough for questions not to need repeating if the matter had already been covered, and equally open to probing and follow-up questions (Thomas, 2009). A form of qualitative content analysis, as outlined by Schreier (2014: 170), allowed for the reduction of the resulting data, in a manner that was both systematic and flexible. Emergent categories were both concept and data driven, meaning key evolving themes did not need to be excluded. What follows in the next section is a thematic interpretation of the data from the interviews.

The evidence

It is argued above that teaching British imperial history as part of a History – and indeed a wider – curriculum speaks clearly to many ideas about diversity in schools today. In his interview, James led with this very theme:

> Well look at the make-up of the classroom you've seen today. We've got Pakistanis, Indians, Sikhs, Muslims [. . .] I think the way we've got the classroom, that diversity of the classroom, that diversity of the country now, is largely due to empire and if they're learning about the past and how people come to be here, maybe that can help bring in a bit more tolerance and less racial segregation within wider society [. . .] At least an appreciation, an understanding of why we've got the diverse society that we're living in Britain today.

Here, James focused quickly on the diverse ethnic make-up of his students, then expanded that to the United Kingdom as a whole, and how all students would benefit from a better understanding of how and why that society had arisen. David, whose class was predominantly white British, also felt it would help students to understand 'the make-up of what is British society today and many of the reasons why some of the initial waves of immigration – why they came [. . .] why they should and must be integrated'. So, for two of the three interviewees, the first idea raised immediately was that teaching imperial history today was important *because* Britain is a diverse, multicultural (and implicitly post-imperial) society, in line with the arguments of Cole (2004).

Another issue that comes to the fore in the discussion above is that curriculum is better understood as an interactive process, where a variety of different understandings enter the classroom, and that understanding does not simply come via a process of transmission and reception. The teachers interviewed all had something clear to say on this matter. James pointed to the media and its portrayals of the British Empire – in particular he noted the 2012 BBC documentary *Empire* presented by Jeremy Paxman. James felt that empire was 'mostly portrayed pejoratively, I don't think there's really much opportunity until you do a [school] course to see that there were perhaps beneficial aspects to the British Empire'. He felt that Paxman's programme was 'pretty negative, and helped reinforce a lot of negative views on empire'. David also noted the influence of the media, feeling that there was an

> increasingly set view from, you know, the channel I watch most, the BBC, the newspaper I read, *The Guardian*, but, you know, that sort of, that media establishment where it's just a word that has – it's a pejorative term and I don't think they know why, but they just know it's knocked about in a pejorative manner and they're not sort of wise, so they [students] kind of, they just have a vague seepage that it's a bad thing, but they can never justify it.

Both James' and David's comments would appear quite contrary to the picture of History teachers advanced by the *Times* editorial (2018) cited in the introduction here, suggesting that teachers routinely lambasted the British Empire when they taught the subject. Though David and James might be exceptions that prove the rule, their comments at least suggest that such a characterization of History teachers might be somewhat exaggerated.

Both David and James were united in seeing the media, in both cases the BBC, as generally portraying British imperialism as something broadly negative. In all of the interviews, the teachers felt that an in-depth exploration in History classes would – if not right this perceived wrong – at least allow students to form more nuanced opinions about British imperialism. However, though both David and James saw documentaries and news media as providing a form of mediation that slanted towards a negative view of imperialism, they differed over the influence of film entertainment. David suggested that, as well as less coverage in schools, there was less – what he termed – 'media seepage' regarding empire: 'when you're doing the Anglo-Zulu Wars and you put *Zulu* [the 1964 film about the defence of Rorke's Drift during the Anglo-Zulu War of 1879] on, you go "my God it's dated", you know, and they wouldn't sit in front of that as a family and watch it on a Sunday afternoon'. However, James felt quite differently, looking straight to films as a source of pre-existing ideas students might bring to class: 'if there are films like *Gandhi* [1982 film] around which deify him, of course'. Ruth suggested that the BBC television series *Horrible Histories*, which she felt had become far more influential than the original books, had 'actually done a good job in giving students [. . .] an alternative, less stereotyped view of the British Empire. So for some students, who've watched that, actually their view is probably a bit more rounded than students before them who hadn't seen those'. However, she felt that 'in general terms' television and film still gave a generally 'distorted view of empire'.

Moving away from the media, David, although suggesting that pre-sixteen schooling led to little development of students' views of empire, did note that one way in which school might have given students some opinion on the subject was what 'they've learnt from their Pakistani, Indian, whatever, classmates around the school, that actually, you know, there might have been a presentation at school, or something like that, or an understanding of that [. . .] but not *too* much'. This idea of peers bringing ideas of British imperialism into the classroom overtly in earlier years is an interesting one and certainly worthy of further investigation. James felt that the influence of family opinions on students' views of empire was important, but also varied: 'I do think even if white British students aren't getting it from their parents, but certainly the heritage is coming through to kids from Pakistani-British, or Indian-British, or Caribbean-British [backgrounds]'. As for white British students – as well as non-white students – James felt that there was potential for family influence through the wartime experiences of their parents and grandparents. Ruth felt similarly that family influence was 'diminishingly the case if you're talking about [. . .] an Anglo-centric view of it', but that the presence of perceptions that come from students whose families perhaps have emigrated from 'ex-colonies' could provide 'a different perspective on the empire, that again can be very useful in lessons'. Indeed, all three teachers seemed to indicate that pre-existing personal views of empire from beyond the classroom were more likely to come via non-white students.

Finally, on this topic, Ruth looked to the influence of politics and politicians in influencing student views, perhaps unsurprising as the interview was conducted in the run-up to the 2015 UK General Election. Ruth said,

> I think the current political climate is having an impact, whether directly or indirectly through their parents and the tabloid press. I think there's a lot of unfortunate, unhistorical nonsense peddled about the empire that doesn't necessarily determine how students think, but it is perhaps their way into understanding the empire, and that may be beneficial if you can use it as the springboard for a debate, but equally it can predetermine views that are hard to shift, and that may not be consistent with the evidence available. So, I'm thinking obviously of the UKIP phenomenon and the BNP phenomenon and a lot of even what came through in the latter stages of the last Labour government, this notion of British-ness shading over into almost fantasy versions of the empire – stripping out the bits of imperial history, the leftovers that suit a current political purpose, and I think that's something History teachers can use, but definitely need to engage with.[5]

Interestingly, although Ruth points to the potential influence of more right-wing, nationalistic parties such as the British National Party (BNP) and UK Independence Party (UKIP), she also includes the Blair-Brown Labour governments (1997–2010). This bears some resemblance to comments made by Politics professor Inderjeet Parmar (2010), who suggests that the 2010 coalition government sought to revive a project driven by the Blair-Brown governments whereby 'an imperial narrative in the school curriculum, contested though it would be, would keep alive the flame of the British empire'.

David felt that the way British people viewed empire today was quite different from how prior generations would have regarded it: 'we have moved away from the sort of [. . .] the British are best generation and actually now they are hypercritical. And actually to understand that we were one of the world's superpowers and we conducted an empire – often exploitative, um, never perfect, but probably, relatively, in a better, more moral, kinder, benevolent manner than the rest, and it's a sense of British identity'. David seemed keen to note that the teaching of imperial history should contain a balance between understanding past wrongs committed and the more benevolent side of British imperialism, but also that this understanding told us something about national identity – almost that the particular way Britain conducted its empire was inextricably linked to national identity.

In response to a prompt (given to all interviewees) on the study by Barton and McCully (2005) into the use of a 'balanced curriculum' in Northern Ireland, mentioned above, Ruth, from a Northern Irish Catholic background, related a personal tale:

> I was asked by family friends, shortly after I started teaching, because we were doing the Northern Ireland question for GCSE [. . .] 'But which version do you teach them?' There's an Irish one and there's an English one – he didn't say that but that's what he meant. And I was so outraged as a History teacher by that question, [. . .] I didn't know where to start to begin with to answer him, and that whole concept that there is *a* version that's not dangerous, that you've taken the dynamite out of (very difficult in Northern Ireland), or there are two opposing versions – as long as you pick the one in the middle it's ok. That's not History to me, it absolutely isn't. And, my reaction to that is it possibly, if that is the case, if they thought they were teaching neutral History, it was probably *bad* History. So no wonder. Because actually what – that word neutrality suggests to me an unwillingness to engage with what the controversial issues are, and really investigate the evidence and arrive at a considered judgement, and if you're not willing to do that then you just leave people with their original prejudices, I suspect.

Indeed, it was Ruth who responded most powerfully to the ideas of 'balance' and 'neutrality' throughout our interview. I include this long statement as it very much sums up a number of other points she made during discussion of the same idea. In a similar vein, James reasoned that 'if you feed to [students] everything that you as the expert can [. . .] inevitably people will hang their clothes on a peg somewhere. I think teaching History from a neutral standpoint, they're still going to take a side, because we're encouraged in History to look at interpretation and see what we agree with. People like a good debate, people like a good argument'. Both Ruth and James appeared to reach similar conclusions in the end, and these touched on the idea David broached in his comments on 'expertise', which are echoed here by James: that the History teacher's job is to provide students with sufficient knowledge to form their own opinion of British imperialism, however 'positive' or 'negative' that might be.

As to whether students came away from learning about empire with a particular positive or negative view on empire, the teachers had a number of observations. James suggested that students would reach their own decision based on the facts they had been provided with, but were likely to 'take a side'. David felt that, if taught well, it could only be 'a beneficial thing' and that 'a deep understanding of it will give people a better view of the UK today and the world they live in'. However, he warned that if people wanted to pick and choose certain elements, 'it could lead to flash points'. Finally, Ruth argued that it depended on the 'baggage' the students brought with them, and that 'it will affect the way they view the UK, but whether it leads to a positive or negative effect, I think that – I'd say that's really hard for me to judge'. She concluded that, ultimately, 'I'd like to think that by studying the British Empire they have a more nuanced understanding of the United Kingdom', and that it was not whether students gained a positive or a negative view of empire that really mattered, but that they had gained a 'deeper understanding'.

Discussion

Some critics of positioning empire centrally in the History curriculum, such as journalists Seumas Milne and Laurie Penny, have focused their criticisms on the potential desire to create pride in Britain's imperial past, and maintained that presenting even a balanced view of British imperialism was akin to presenting a balanced view of the Third Reich (Milne, 2010; Penny, 2010). The three interviewees here certainly felt that there was an intrinsic value to studying British imperial history, and that the fears of these media commentators would only be realized as a result of 'bad' teaching. Advocates of 'culturally relevant teaching' such as Martell (2013: 81) – though not engaging directly with the issue of British imperial history – suggest, like others cited above, that students 'of color' can be 'empowered by a curriculum that connects to their ethnic backgrounds'. British imperial history certainly achieves this for many. However, as Schmeichel (2012: 228) suggests, though culturally relevant teaching has its merits as an idea, it could potentially be a 'superficial transformation of thinking about culture that sticks children of colour within the same deficit mode of thought in which they were positioned in the 1960s and 1970s'. Further to this, there is the issue that a focus on ethnic/cultural difference might alienate or seem to vilify the 'owners' of the 'traditional' narrative. The idea of alienating such a group of students is raised by Nayak (1999: 197), who sees 'anti-racism' – a key part of much culturally relevant teaching – as having the potential to be viewed by white students and their parents as 'a bourgeois, *anti-white* practice' (italics in original). What the interviews explored above conclude is there is not an easy answer to the question of what the outcomes of teaching imperial history are likely to be. However, they also point to the idea that it is nonetheless important for students to address the key issues – many of which chime strongly with the theme of identity – which the study of British imperialism raises.

Like Grever, Haydn and Ribbens (2008: 78–9) and Rozas and Miller (2009: 25), the teachers remarked upon the influence of a multitude of potential forms of mediation within and beyond the classroom, from parents and peers to film and television. Clearly, all three interviewees acknowledged that classroom teaching of a prescribed curriculum was not the sole, or even necessarily the primary, route by which students came to form their ideas and judgements on British imperial history. This would add support to the idea that even if a government did seek to indoctrinate students through its authorship of a 'national' curriculum, perhaps this would at best have a much-diluted impact – after several tiers of mediation – by the time such prescribed content was received by the students.

Implications

This chapter certainly does not purport to give any definitive answers. However, even from this small sample of interviews, there arises a clear sense that teachers appreciate the value of studying the history of the British Empire. British imperial history touches upon so many controversial issues – especially 'race', ethnicity and identity – that are often evoked in education debates. Not unlike citizenship education, which touches upon often similar issues, such teaching presents challenges, especially in places with divided societies (McCully, 2006: 51). Nevertheless, what this study shows is that teaching British imperial history is deemed of importance not only by various historians, educationalists and media commentators but also by teachers themselves. These educators were united in seeing the variety of ways in which imperial history provides an invaluable context for young people regarding the nature of cosmopolitan, multicultural Britain today.

Far from being left to coverage by discrete lessons on 'citizenship', the evidence presented here underscores the importance of historical study in helping students become better equipped to understand modern Britain and play the role of critical and informed citizens. Following the May 2017 terrorist attack in Manchester, the *TES* ran a piece calling for the History curriculum to 'educate young people on the historical and present significance of diversity in British society', in order to help complement existing and contentious government strategies such as Prevent (Devon, 2017). Now, more than ever, additional curriculum time needs to be given to studying topics that could serve to better educate our young people on the diverse roots of British society. Though this chapter looks specifically at the role of imperial history in secondary education, the messages that come across in the data presented here have far wider implications for how we might approach curriculum and diversity across different sectors.

Conclusions

As the promotion of FBV continues to be part of the school landscape in England, it is worth concluding by showing how the findings here have clear links to such a curriculum-wide policy. Standard 5(1)(a)(v) notes that schools should 'assist pupils to acquire an appreciation of and respect for their own and other cultures in a way that promotes tolerance and harmony between different cultural traditions', which can be 'examined from a historical and a contemporary perspective' (DfE, 2013: 6; views echoed in DfE, 2014a: 5). Evidently, there is potential to see the wider applicability of the benefits of studying British imperial history to create a more enlightened citizenship beyond the History curriculum, and this can be accepted in line with the government's FBV agenda. British imperial history, as a topic, could be used to explore the long view of not only modern British history but also its politics and the nature of modern-day citizenship more broadly. Lord Nash, then-Parliamentary Under Secretary of State for Schools, outlined the aims of the FBV guidelines very much along such lines: 'A key part of our plan for education is to ensure children become valuable and fully rounded members of society who treat others with respect and tolerance, regardless of background' (DfE, 2014b). It does not seem too much of a stretch to link Lord Nash's words with those of Mike Cole (2004), in seeing that British imperial history has the potential to serve a far broader purpose than simply being a list of dry facts that would instead 'impart a tub-thumping English nationalism' (Evans, 2013).

There are a number of avenues that this chapter – largely due to restrictions of space – has not explored fully, and that therefore offer fertile ground for further research in this area. First, there are the perceptions of the students themselves, which have been approached in smaller studies such as Chapman and Facey (2004) and Burns (2016a, 2016b), but require far greater consideration and research. There is also the matter of the standpoint(s) of the teachers, which could hardly be generalized upon from such a small survey. It would, for example, be interesting to see how approaches to teaching imperial history differed (if at all) across a wider spectrum of teachers, especially when broken down into separate groups based on gender, ethnicity or socio-economic background, for example. Finally, it would be fascinating to conduct a similar study within a different nation that was formerly part of the British Empire, to see how different/similar perceptions of British imperial history and its place in the curriculum are among teachers elsewhere.

Notes

Much of what appears here is adapted from research presented in my doctoral thesis (Burns, 2017).

1   A reference to 'Rule, Britannia!', a still-popular nationalistic poem/song set to music by Thomas Arne and first performed in 1740.

2   For a number of reasons, the terms 'Britain' and 'British' are used throughout this chapter, despite being technically inaccurate on occasion. However, accepting that there is no useful adjectival form for citizens of the United Kingdom, this chapter uses the terms 'Britain' and 'British' to refer adjectivally to the United Kingdom, its citizens and its empire throughout. The frequent use of 'English' when discussing schools and education is not a misuse that presupposes England and Britain to be one and the same, but instead a positive affirmation of the devolved nature of the education systems within the constituent nations that comprise the modern United Kingdom.

3   Critical race theory addresses the interplay between race, racism and power. Originally starting life in the study of law, it has developed into an interdisciplinary movement in recent years. See 'Introduction', in Delgado and Stefancic (2001).

4   Prior to the effect of the 2015 A Level reforms, Edexcel, the examining body whose course was being followed in all three sites that took part in this study, provided an AS Level History course comprising three modules, and the 'India module' – referred to above – comprised one of these modules, worth 50 per cent of the total AS Level.

5   The UK Independence Party (UKIP) is widely characterized in the UK media as being to the right of the political spectrum, with their most prominent policies focusing on limiting immigration and leaving the European Union. The British National Party (BNP) is widely characterized in the UK media as being to the far right on the political spectrum.

References

Adams, R. (2017), 'Oxford University Accused of Backing Apologists of British Colonialism', *The Guardian* [UK], 22 December. Last accessed 24 February 2018: http://amp.theguardian.com/education/2017/dec/22/oxford-university-accused-of-backing-apologists-for-british-colonialism.

Ary, D., L. Jacobs, C. Sorensen and A. Razavieh (2010), *Introduction to Research in Education*, 8th edn, Belmont, CA: Wadsworth.

Barton, K. C. and A. W. McCully (2005), 'History, Identity, and the School Curriculum in Northern Ireland: An Empirical Study of Secondary Students' Ideas and Perspectives', *Journal of Curriculum Studies*, 37 (1): 85–116.

Beck, J. (2012), 'Reinstating Knowledge: Diagnoses and Prescriptions for England's Curriculum Ills', *International Studies in Sociology of Education*, 22 (1): 1–18.

Burns, A. (2014), 'The Jewel in the Curriculum: Teaching the History of the British Empire', *International Journal of Historical Learning, Teaching and Research*, 12 (2): 109–21.

Burns, A. (2016a), '"A Fit of Absence of Mind?" Learning about British Imperialism in the Twenty-First Century', *Frontier* 2: 16–19. Last accessed 6 January 2017: http://www2.le.ac.uk/departments/gradschool/current/frontier/issue-two.

Burns, A. (2016b), 'My Empire Is of the Imagination: History Student Perceptions of the British Empire in Secondary School', *International Journal of Historical Learning, Teaching and Research*, 14 (1): 93–112.

Burns, A. (2017), 'How Britannia Ruled the Waves: Teaching the History of the British Empire in the Twenty-First Century', EdD thesis, University of Leicester. Last accessed 31 May 2018: http://hdl.handle.net/2381/40656.

Chapman, A. and J. Facey (2004), 'Placing History: Territory, Story, Identity – and Historical Consciousness', *Teaching History*, 116: 36–41.

Clark, A. (2009), 'Teaching the Nation's Story: Comparing Public Debates and Classroom Perspectives on History Education in Australia and Canada', *Journal of Curriculum Studies*, 41 (6): 745–62.

Cole, M. (2004), ' "Rule Britannia" and the New American Empire: A Marxist Analysis of the Teaching of Imperialism, Actual and Potential, in the British School Curriculum', *Policy Futures in Education* 2 (3 and 4): 523–38.

Cole, M. and J. S. Stuart (2005), '"Do You Ride on Elephants" and "Never Tell Them You're German": The Experiences of British Asian and Black, and Overseas Student Teachers in South-east England', *British Educational Research Journal* 31 (3): 349–66.

Colls, R. (2012), 'British National Identity', *History Today*, 62 (8). Last accessed 9 May 2017: http://www.historytoday.com/robert-colls/british-national-identity.

Cousin, G. (2009), *Strategies for Researching Learning in Higher Education: An Introduction to Contemporary Methods and Approaches*, New York: Routledge.

Delgado, R. and J. Stefancic (2001), *Critical Race Theory: An Introduction*, New York: New York University Press.

DfE (Department for Education) (2013), *Improving the Spiritual, Moral, Social and Cultural (SMSC) Development of Pupils: Departmental Advice for Independent Schools, Academies and Free Schools,* November. Last accessed 8 October 2017: https://www.gov.uk/government/uploads/system/uploads/attachment_data/file/268826/dept_advice_template_smscadvicenov13.pdf.

DfE (Department for Education) (2014a), *Promoting Fundamental British Values As Part of SMSC in Schools: Departmental Advice for Maintained Schools,* November. Last accessed 8 October 2017: https://www.gov.uk/government/uploads/system/uploads/attachment_data/file/380595/SMSC_Guidance_Maintained_Schools.pdf.

DfE (Department for Education) (2014b), 'Press Release: Guidance on Promoting British Values In Schools Published', November. Last accessed 8 October 2017: https://www.gov.uk/government/news/guidance-on-promoting-british-values-in-schools-published.

Devon, N. (2017), 'Immigration Isn't a Threat to the UK. The Curriculum Should Reflect That', *TES,* 31 May. Last accessed 13 June 2017: https://www.tes.com/news/school-news/breaking-views/immigration-isnt-a-threat-uk-curriculum-should-reflect.

Editorial (2018), 'Empire State of Mind: Britain's Imperial History Requires Sophisticated Cultural Analysis', *The Times* [London], 24 February: 31.

Elton-Chalcraft, S. (2009), *'It's Not Just about Black and White, Miss': Children's Awareness of Race,* Stoke-on-Trent: Trentham Books.

Evans, R. J. (2013), 'Michael Gove's History Wars', *Guardian,* 13 July. Last accessed 8 April 2014: http://www.theguardian.com/books/2013/jul/13/michael-gove-teaching-history-wars.

Gillborn, D. (2005), 'Education Policy As an Act of White Supremacy: Whiteness, Critical Race Theory and Education Reform', *Journal of Education Policy,* 20 (4): 485–505.

Grever, M., T. Haydn and K. Ribbens (2008), 'Identity and School History: The Perspective of Young People from the Netherlands and England', *British Journal of Educational Studies,* 56 (1): 76–94.

Guyver, R. (2011), 'The Role of Government in Determining the School History Curriculum: Lessons from Australia', *History & Policy.* Last accessed 8 April 2014: http://www.historyandpolicy.org/papers/policy-paper-120.html.

Haydn, T. (2012), 'History in Schools and the Problem of "the Nation"', *Education Sciences,* 2 (4): 276–89.

Hsiao-Lan, S. C. (2008), 'A Critical Reflection on the Reform of the High School History Curriculum in Taiwan', in D. L. Grossman and J. Tin-Yau Lo (eds), *Social Education in Asia: Critical Issues and Multiple Perspectives,* 87–100, Charlotte, NC: Information Age Publishing.

Ismailova, B. (2004), 'Curriculum Reform in Post-Soviet Kyrgyzstan: Indigenization of the History Curriculum', *Curriculum Journal,* 15 (3): 247–64.

Ladson-Billings, G. (1998), 'Just What Is Critical Race Theory and What's It Doing in a Nice Field Like Education?' *International Journal of Qualitative Studies in Education,* 11 (1): 7–24.

Lusher, A. (2017), 'Professor's "Bring Back Colonialism" Call Sparks Fury and Academic Freedom Debate', *The Independent* [UK], 12 October. Last accessed 24 February 2018: http://www.independent.co.uk/news/world/americas/

colonialism-academic-article-bruce-gilley-threats-violence-published-withdrawn-third-world-quarterly-a7996371.html?amp.

Martell, C. C. (2013), 'Race and Histories: Examining Culturally Relevant Teaching in the U.S. History Classroom', *Theory & Research in Social Education*, 41 (1): 65–88.

McAllister, G. and J. J. Irvine (2000), 'Cross Cultural Competency and Multicultural Teacher Education', *Review of Educational Research*, 70 (1): 3–24.

McAllister, G. and J. J. Irvine (2002), 'The Role of Empathy in Teaching Culturally Diverse Students: A Qualitative Study of Teachers' Beliefs', *Journal of Teacher Education*, 53 (5): 433–43.

McCully, A. (2006), 'Practitioner Perceptions of Their Role in Facilitating the Handling of Controversial Issues in Contested Societies: A Northern Irish Experience', *Educational Review*, 58 (1): 51–65.

McKernan, J. (2008), *Curriculum and Imagination: Process Theory, Pedagogy and Action Research*, London: Routledge.

Milne, S. (2010), 'This Attempt to Rehabilitate Empire Is a Recipe for Conflict', *The Guardian,* June 10. Last accessed 29 February 2012: http://www.guardian.co.uk/commentisfree/2010/jun/10/british-empire-michael-gove-history-teaching.

Mitchell, M. and J. Jolley (2010), *Research Design Explained*. 7th edn, Belmont, CA: Wadsworth, Cengage Learning.

Muñoz, L. K. and J. Noboa (2012), 'Hijacks and Hijinks on the US History Review Committee', in K. A. Erekson (ed.), *Politics and the History Curriculum: The Struggle over Standards in Texas and the Nation*, 41–60, New York: Palgrave-Macmillan.

Nayak, A. (1999), '"White English Ethnicities": Racism, Anti-Racism and Student Perspectives', *Race Ethnicity and Education*, 2 (2): 177–202.

Osler, A. (2008), 'Citizenship Education and the Ajegbo Report: Re-Imagining a Cosmopolitan Nation', *London Review of Education*, 6 (1): 11–25.

Parkes, R. J. (2007), 'Reading History Curriculum as Postcolonial Text: Towards A Curricular Response to the History Wars in Australia and Beyond', *Curriculum Inquiry*, 37 (4): 383–400.

Parmar, I. (2010), 'Tony Blair, Gordon Brown, Michael Gove: Proud of the British Empire', Centre for Strategic Research and Analysis. Last accessed 12 February 2013: http://cesran.org/index.php? option=com_content&view=article&id=8 66%3Atony-blair-Gordon-brown-michael-gove-proud-of-the-british-empire-&catid=56%3Amakale-veraporlar&Itemid=314&lang=en.

Penny, L. (2010), 'Michael Gove and the Imperialists', *New Statesman*, June 1. Last accessed 29 February 2012: http://www.newstatesman.com/blogs/the-staggers/2010/06/history-british-ferguson.

Phillips, R. (1998), *History Teaching, Nationhood and the State: A Study in Educational Politics*, London: Cassell.

Richardson, R. (2015), 'British Values and British Identity: Muddles, Mixtures, and Ways Ahead', *London Review of Education*, 13 (2): 37–47.

Rozas, L. W. and J. Miller (2009), 'Discourses for Social Justice Education: The Web of Racism and the Web of Resistance', *Journal of Ethnic and Cultural Diversity in Social Work*, 18 (1–2): 24–39.

Schmeichel, M. (2012), 'Good Teaching? An Examination of Culturally Relevant Pedagogy As an Equity Practice', *Journal of Curriculum Studies*, 44 (2): 211–31.

Schreier, M. (2014), 'Qualitative Content Analysis', in U. Flick (ed.), *The SAGE Handbook of Qualitative Data Analysis*, 170–83, London: SAGE.

Smith, M. K. (2000), 'Curriculum Theory and Practice', *Encyclopaedia of Informal Education*. Last accessed 30 January 2013: http://www.infed.org/biblio/b-curric.htm

Thomas, G. (2009), *How to Do Your Research Project*, London: SAGE.

Yeandle, P. (2015), *Citizenship, Nation, Empire: The Politics of History Teaching, 1870–1930*, Manchester: Manchester University Press.

Yosso, Tara J. (2005), 'Whose Culture Has Capital? A Critical Race Theory Discussion of Community Cultural Wealth', *Race Ethnicity and Education*, 8 (1): 69–91.

Young, M. (2011), 'The Return to Subjects: A Sociological Perspective on the UK Coalition Government's Approach to the 14–19 Curriculum', *Curriculum Journal*, 22 (2): 265–78.

Zajda, J. (2015), 'Globalisation and the Politics of Education Reforms: History Education', in J. Zajda (ed.), *Nation-Building and History Education in a Global Culture*, 1–14, Heidelberg: Springer.

Part Two

Talent management and career progression

4

Talent, determination and resilience: Leadership accession and enactment for black, Asian and minority ethnic leaders

Tony Bush

Introduction

It is widely accepted that black, Asian and minority ethnic (BAME) leaders are under-represented in English schools. This is evident at the macro level, where the numbers of such leaders do not match their proportion in the national population. It is even more obvious in schools serving diverse communities, where BAME teachers and leaders fail to reflect the ethnic balance of pupils and parents.

There is some evidence that BAME teachers and leaders are likely to be better qualified than white leaders, often educated to the master's level, suggesting that their under-representation is not due to a qualifications 'gap'. This is partly because they are determined to succeed and partly because they feel that they may not be considered, let alone appointed, unless they are better than white applicants. They also require resilience to persevere despite the many, often subtle, barriers, which may discourage them. 'Gatekeepers' may limit their access to relevant training, while phrases such as 'you are not ready' may lead to self-doubt. BAME teachers who become heads despite such barriers often have special leadership qualities, honed by the many 'slights' experienced in their personal and professional lives.

This chapter explores the factors that inhibit accession for BAME leaders and the qualities that enable many to succeed despite the challenges. It also examines their experience as leaders, where their seniority does not protect them from discrimination, not least from parents. Ironically, there is some evidence that BAME parents want white teachers and leaders for their children, a form of 'reverse racism', suggesting that neocolonial attitudes persist through different generations. The chapter concludes that BAME leaders are often special people whose talent, determination and resilience enable them to succeed in a hostile or indifferent climate.

Under-representation of BAME leaders

The statistics show that BAME teachers are much less likely to be promoted to leadership positions than white teachers. Powney et al. (2003), drawing on a survey of 2,158 teachers, found that those from BAME backgrounds enter the profession later and have lower satisfaction levels. This seems to result in lower levels of participation in leadership roles (52% BAME remain as classroom teachers compared with 29% white women and 35% white males). Johnson (2017) shows that, while 14 per cent of the UK population identify as black or minority ethnic, only 3 per cent of heads are from BAME backgrounds. Miller (2019) also comments that BAME teachers are not proportionate to BAME pupil numbers. He adds that career progression of BAME teachers to leadership posts is also lower than for white teachers, suggesting that little has changed since the Powney et al.'s (2003) survey.

Bush, Glover and Sood's (2006) survey indicates that most BAME teachers are working in schools with a significant number of pupils from similar backgrounds. The proportion of BAME staff is much lower, and even schools with large numbers of BAME pupils are likely to have predominantly white staff. Their respondents expressed understandable frustration at such imbalances:

> I have been asked whether I am the cleaner or a teaching assistant – people don't expect to see coloured senior staff.
>
> It baffles me that the head and all senior teachers are white. It is not representative.

Family and community attitudes to teaching

Family and community attitudes to teaching influence whether BAME people embark on teaching careers and/or seek promotion. Papadopoulos (1999) identifies the ways in which BAME families form their own communities and then come to rely on tight local social contacts that may inhibit community and cultural integration until the second or third generations. Her conclusion is that this leads to a BAME view that is fatalistic with limited aspirations.

In referring to a wide range of professions, Davidson (1997) states that parental expectations that marriage is essential may conflict with career development and cause problems where this crosses racial groups. This leads to role conflict between home and career – not geographically mobile, not enough time for career, guilt feelings about career and motherhood, lack of emotional/ domestic support from husband, and need to take work home.

Parker-Jenkins et al. (1997), in a longitudinal examination of Muslim women and their career development, conclude that their progress is affected by the nature of family and professional support and the expectations of the teachers themselves. Those who did succeed reported that they had to work twice as hard as others in the face of discrimination and cultural problems within their communities. These arguments receive some empirical support from Bush et al.'s (2006) research, where eleven women referred to the importance of home support and family expectations of self-improvement.

Identity

Crow and Moller (2017) distinguish between professional and social or personal identities, while acknowledging that all three interact. They also discuss how professional identities differ from work roles. While the latter are 'scripted, deterministic and static', professional identities stress human agency and are dynamic. Armstrong and Mitchell (2017: 839) apply these ideas to black women principals in Canada, where 'educational administration continues to be dominated by strongly patriarchal and racialized practices that contain and circumscribe difference'. They add that 'women of colour are placed at the margins of administration' (ibid.).

The sense of 'identity' of BAME teachers strongly influences their attitudes to teaching and leadership. This has two aspects: the historical, in terms of the 'roots' of the individual, and the geographical, in terms of the concentration of people of similar BAME groups within an area.

Johnson's (2017) life history study of the lives and identities of UK black and south Asian heads included archival research, and interviews with family members of three deceased pioneer heads. She also interviewed twenty-five current and former BAME heads. She refers to 'situated portrayals' of her participants who offer diverse views about their identities. These ranged from emphatic endorsement of their black heritage (Carlton) to a 'colour-blind' perspective (Ken). She also notes distinct differences between British citizens of African, Caribbean or Asian descent, and first-generation migrants.

The concept of identity is complex when applied to multicultural schools in England. BAME leaders come from diverse backgrounds and may be working with pupils and colleagues from very different cultures. However, many of Bush et al.'s (2006) interviewees were able to point to advantages in being a BAME leader, including adopting a 'black to black perspective'. 'I remember what it was like to be a black child in a white school.' They also often understand the cultural background. 'I have lived in the community where the children come from for twenty-two years and I know the children and their families. I care about them and I am involved in community work.' They may also be a conduit for black parents. 'Angry parents want me to be their voice. Our voices are not heard.'

Bush and Moloi (2007) conducted research with cross-boundary leaders in South Africa. 'Cross-boundary' refers to leaders who are working in schools previously reserved, by the apartheid government, for a different racial group. These 'cross-boundary' leaders found their sense of identity challenged by the shift from a racially stratified education system to one that no longer prescribed where people could live or work, based on government-imposed racial identity. However, changing attitudes is much slower than changing people's legal status. As Johnson (2004) notes, black educators grew up with the ingrained belief that white people were 'superior' to those from other groups. One of the participants in Bush and Moloi's (2007: 47) research commented that black educators believe that white is 'good and clever'. These authors note that notions of identity in the post-apartheid era are 'complex' and 'fluid'.

Discrimination

There is widespread evidence of covert or indirect discrimination, coupled with a racial 'glass ceiling' and negative stereotyping. Harris et al. (2003), in a literature review of the career progress of deputy heads, note reliance on informal networks from which ethnic minorities are excluded. Miller (2019) also comments on the significance of 'in-groups', 'networks' or 'clubs', which may enhance or inhibit career development.

Bhatt et al. (1988: 150) argue that 'at all levels it is the white construction and interpretation of black reality that prevails', and this results in an alienating ethos where rules are not related to culture, and where the use of diagnostic tools favours the English cultural heritage. These factors contribute to an atmosphere that makes for problems in securing initial employment and career progression at all levels.

Bush et al.'s (2006) survey respondents were asked to assess the extent to which they had suffered from, or indeed, gained from discrimination. Fourteen reported 'no discrimination':

> I have never at any time or place felt that my ethnicity has helped me progress or held me back in my career progression. I firmly believe that it is my skills and experience (professional qualities) that have helped me progress, regardless of my ethnicity.

However, there was substantial evidence of discrimination, with thirty-six respondents detailing their negative experiences. The most frequently cited issues were 'racist attitudes'; the behaviour of managers, including being 'frozen out' of conversations; and discriminatory recruitment and selection practices. One of their survey respondents refers to overt racism within a predominantly white school. 'The chair of governors should not be allowed to get away with offensive remarks to black and ethnic people'. One of their interviewees notes that BAME people sometimes do not have confidence in black teachers and leaders, an example of 'reverse discrimination', echoing Bush and Moloi's (2007) South Africa evidence, reported earlier (and see below). 'Due to colonisation, many black people believe that "made in Britain is best", so are over respectful to white people and white heads.'

South Africa's legacy includes colonialism but also an extended period of statutory discrimination, through the policy of apartheid. Until 1996, the education system was stratified by race, and staff were prohibited from working outside their government-defined racial setting. The 1996 South African Schools Act produced a notionally integrated system, but many schools remain wholly or largely populated by one racial group, and working across racial boundaries is untypical. Bush and Moloi (2007) interviewed forty-six of these 'cross-boundary' leaders, to establish their perceptions of working in what were often unfamiliar school and community contexts. Their experiences differed markedly along racial lines. White, 'coloured' and Indian leaders were generally welcomed in the former black schools, but black leaders, in particular, experienced discrimination, and often racism, in the previously whites-only schools.

Facilitators for leadership accession

Despite the uncomfortable experience of many BAME educators, in the United Kingdom and elsewhere, there is also evidence of facilitators helping them access leadership roles. This may take the form of 'sponsorship', as white and BAME leaders seek to create opportunities for the career development of BAME colleagues. However, Miller (2019) cautions that BAME career progression may be 'fraught, complex and contentious', while also noting the significance of 'white sanction'.

Bush et al.'s (2006) survey respondents were able to identify certain factors which acted as facilitators for their career progression. Four referred to specific development opportunities, three mentioned respect for religious beliefs, while two noted positive discrimination policies designed to enhance ethnic diversity. Their interviews also provided evidence of 'enablers', notably in London. 'The head was very good at supporting my career. He believed in me.' Another participant in Bush et al.'s (2006) research noted that 'being black was an advantage in getting the head of year and assistant head posts; the latter being linked to ethnic minority achievement'. However, this latter point also has a negative dimension, in that BAME teachers may be considered suitable only for posts linked to ethnic issues rather than for wider leadership positions.

The overall view is that negative discrimination is widespread, while there are only limited examples of a positive approach. Negative discrimination may be most evident where the predominant ethnic group is white Caucasian, and may impact most strongly on those who have not been educated in Britain (Bush et al. 2006).

Recruitment and selection

Recruitment and selection strategies, and the composition of the 'selectors', may constitute a barrier to employment and promotion. Bariso (2001) says that progress is inhibited because of the lack of black role models, racism, negative personal experiences, poor prospects and a lack of career advice. As a result, underachievement, stereotyping, poor employment prospects, low pay and negative parental influence become embedded in institutional racism. Exclusion from teaching and promotion also operates through unrepresentative selection panels.

Manuel and Slate (2003: 25) list a range of inhibitors for BME women in the United States. These include lack of recruitment of women of all ethnic groups by school boards and failure at the hurdle of the mid-management career 'glass ceiling'. Their analysis links race and gender to suggest a 'double bind' for BME women leaders.

There is a growing body of American literature reporting on the problems of securing promotion once on the career ladder. Tallerico (2000), Ortiz (2000) and Manuel and Slate (2003) reach similar conclusions, that there are largely invisible criteria for selection. Powney et al. (2003) refer to evidence of hidden discrimination for teachers securing promotion in the United Kingdom. Singh (2002) refers to biased negative stereotyping by performance assessors, and misjudgement of potential and 'fit' by white leaders.

Seventeen of Bush et al.'s (2006) interviewees refer to racial or ethnic factors inhibiting their career progress. Their comments include 'being treated with suspicion', experiencing outright discrimination and working with 'difficult' superiors:

> I kept trying and finally got appointed as deputy head in a language school. The head teacher of this school challenged my appointment, saying it was based on favouritism. He repeatedly requested that I should be re-interviewed and I felt unjustly treated [. . .] my disgruntled head teacher made my working life unbearable by asking other staff not to cooperate with me.

Many different people and groups contribute to the perceived inhibition of BME career development. In Bush et al.'s (2006) survey, these included nine heads, seventeen senior leadership team (SLT) members, thirteen teachers and middle leaders, and one governor. The inhibitors include perceived racism by senior and middle managers, and by colleagues, and the negative attitudes of managers, parents and the community. There was also a lack of confidence, which may have been engendered by the negative attitudes. One African woman said that black people need to work harder to achieve career progress, while seven survey respondents mentioned the existence of a 'glass ceiling' affecting their promotion opportunities.

Experience of the appointments process

Bush et al.'s (2006) participants were asked to reflect upon the process of appointment to their present post to ascertain the extent to which this might be affected by hidden or overt racism. Nineteen interviewees commented that the appointment process was 'smooth', 'fair' or 'very positive'. However, fourteen spoke of negative experiences, including the following:

> When I told the head that I was from [country] [. . .] he was negative. Being a foreigner is an issue and that is sad. It is not openly said and blocks are created.

> Unlike Whites, I don't stand as many chances of being appointed to a senior management position.

Bush et al.'s (2009) study of English BAME National Professional Qualification for Headship (NPQH) participants produced mixed comments about the recruitment and selection processes. Those NPQH graduates who were successful in securing headships were mostly positive, although several had previous uncomfortable experiences. 'There is a lack of diversity in [local authority (LA)] and it was shocking to find how people [. . .] have negative attitudes towards diversity' (ibid.: 29). However, seven of the thirteen respondents who had been unsuccessful in their headship applications asserted that diversity issues might be responsible for their problems. For example, one Asian woman commented on the imbalance between pupil characteristics and those of staff and governors. 'One [. . .] school had about 70 per cent black intake but did not have a member of staff, volunteer or governor who was black' (ibid.: 27).

Overcoming the barriers

The literature provides significant evidence of a range of problems experienced by BAME teachers when seeking leadership positions. However, it is clear that many have been able to overcome the barriers, at least to some extent, because they have all become middle or senior school leaders.

Bush et al.'s (2006) research indicates a range of strategies, including self-confidence, resilience, perseverance and drawing on the support of family and friends. One participant noted that informal networking between friends and other BME colleagues is crucial. Seven of their participants refer to their determination to succeed. 'I am determined to do credible work. I do the best. Through determination I removed a barrier from my previous school.'

Leadership enactment

As noted above, despite experiencing racism, and negative attitudes during the selection process, some BAME applicants do succeed in being appointed to leadership positions, including headships. However, this does not bring an end to the problems experienced by some of these leaders. When BAME leaders are appointed, they may experience isolation or 'exclusion' within the school. Bariso (2001) distinguishes between external and internal exclusion and says that the latter may impact on the experience and internal promotion of BAME teachers and leaders after appointment.

Bush et al. (2009) report on racism experienced by three participants from London, in their research on diversity and NPQH. One was called a 'Paki' by a parent who was 'rampaging through the school'. Another had problems with a teacher union official in her borough, who was racist and sexist, and 'impugned my integrity'. She claimed that there was bullying, intimidation and a 'total lack of respect'. The third experienced difficulties, including racist remarks, from parents with low literacy levels and poor life skills: 'you're Chinky, aren't you?'

There is some evidence that British BAME people may have a different experience from those born or educated abroad. Singh (2002) notes that some BAME migrants experience difficulty arising from the use of English as a second language. Bush et al.'s (2006) research findings indicate that British BAME leaders are less likely to experience problems than those who were educated and/ or previously worked abroad. This seems to be attributable to factors such as accent, dress and cultural diversity.

Customized leadership development

There is an ongoing debate about whether there should be customized development opportunities for BAME teachers. Several of Bush et al.'s (2006) participants perceived a variety of gains from customized support, notably training with people from similar cultures, and with those who may have faced some of the same issues. 'BAMEs are overlooked and their contributions are overlooked. They make huge sacrifices, they give up a lot of time to inspire people but they are not recognised.'

However, far more participants (22) oppose such provision because it is perceived to be patronizing, inappropriate or because leadership is perceived to transcend ethnicity issues:

BAME teachers should have the same course and "the same treatment" as other teachers.

Leadership qualities and skills required to be a leader have nothing to do with ethnicity.

Ogunbawo (2012) argues that customized leadership helps address the under-representation of BAME leaders in England. She reports on research with participants of one such customized programme, the former National College for School Leadership's 'Equal Access to Promotion' (EAP) programme. These BAME teachers were overwhelmingly supportive of such programmes, with 91 per cent of Ogunbawa's respondents agreeing that participation in EAP encourages middle leaders to seek senior leadership positions. She cautions that such programmes should not become 'segregation camps' but concludes that they offer a viable way forward for BAME teachers seeking career progression. However, Moorosi (2014), offering an intersectional perspective, argues that single identity leadership development programmes privilege one aspect of identity over others, for example, race over gender and social class. She concludes that identity transformation cannot be achieved by all participants.

Bush et al. (2009) conducted research with BAME participants on undifferentiated NPQH programmes, including a full population sample (census) of such candidates. Their survey findings show many positive elements, but there were also some disturbing comments about diversity. Several respondents are concerned about the ethnic balance of tutors, the lack of attention to leading in multicultural contexts and the lack of differentiation for BME leaders. Nine of the ten interviewees in one London borough were strongly opposed to any customizing for BME candidates. Two described this notion as 'offensive', including one who said she wanted to take part in the research because she felt so strongly about this, and one who stressed that she would never have enrolled for a 'BAME focused' programme, even if that meant giving up the idea of being a head.

Providing specific training opportunities for BAME leaders signals determination to address the under-representation of such groups, and is likely to enhance discussion of multicultural issues, but it also risks 'ghettoizing' BAME applicants. This debate is likely to continue.

Discussion

The continuing under-representation of BAME leaders in English schools, and similar figures in other countries, demonstrates the intractability of this problem and the failure of previous initiatives to address the issue successfully. The views of some BAME parents, that white teachers are better for their children, may contribute to a perceived lack of commitment to tackle the problem successfully.

A further complication is that the term 'BAME' includes educators from many cultures, and that ethnicities and employment of a BAME leader may not align leadership with local community characteristics. However, a minimum requirement, in terms of social justice, is that BAME leaders should have equal access to leadership posts, but this remains an aspiration, not a reality.

Previous research and literature, including sources cited in this chapter, exemplify the issues facing BAME teachers and leaders at different levels in primary and secondary schools, and also in other sectors of education. Bush et al.'s (2006) study provides a detailed portrait of life as a BAME leader and of the many hurdles to be cleared in order to progress within the English education system. Similarly, Bush et al.'s (2009) study of BAME participation in NPQH training shows that racism and discrimination continue to blight the career development of such leaders, and inhibit the diversity of the teacher and leader workforce.

Personal experience

Much of the research on BAME leadership gives 'voice' to such leaders and aspirants, providing what are often deep insights into what it means to be a minority educator in a white-dominated profession. The views of BAME leaders are inevitably influenced by their experience as professionals and as members of their own communities. There are also important variations arising from their ethnic backgrounds and birthplaces. Teachers and leaders are shaped by their personal experience and that of their communities (Bishop, 2003; Bravette-Gordon, 2001; Johnson, 2017).

There is an important distinction between those BAME leaders and teachers who were born in Britain and those who were first-generation migrants. Nine of Johnson's (2017) eleven 'pioneer' BAME heads were in the latter group, while all of her seventeen experienced leaders were educated in the United Kingdom. Similarly, almost 70 per cent of Bush et al.'s (2006) interviewees were born in Britain and most of these choose to describe themselves as 'black British', 'British Asian' and so on. Others prefer to mention their family origins, for example, 'black African'. This connects to the concepts of 'identity' and 'roots', discussed in the literature, but also confirms that ethnic minorities are complex and cannot be treated as a homogeneous entity. For example, British-born BAME teachers are more likely to achieve senior positions than those born overseas. Some of Bush et al.'s (2006) participants believe that their foreign accents inhibited their career progression.

Beyond such differentiation, it remains clear that many BAME leaders have experienced racism and discrimination (Bush et al., 2006; Johnson, 2017; Miller 2019). This links to Powney et al.'s (2003) finding that most BAME teachers remain in the classroom. Several of Bush et al.'s (2006) participants refer to race, ethnicity, culture or religion as factors inhibiting their career progression. 'If you are black you have to be exceptionally good if you want to progress.'

Context

The importance of the context in which leadership is practiced is increasingly recognized (Hallinger, 2018). For BAME teachers and leaders, this has a particular meaning. Their professional experience is inevitably influenced by the nature of the community served by the school. Where leaders are working in their own ethnic communities, they are often able to derive the support needed to persevere in the midst of perceived racism and discrimination. Papadopoulos (1999) refers to BAME families forming their own communities, leading to concentrations of particular ethnic groups in certain areas and schools. In these circumstances, the community often regards the BAME teachers and leaders as their 'voice' because they understand their culture, speak their language and are perceived as more approachable than white teachers.

However, some BAME leaders work in predominantly white schools, where pupils, teachers, leaders and governors are overwhelmingly white. The challenges for BAME leaders may be even greater in such mono-ethnic schools and communities, with more evidence of hidden or overt racism (Bush et al., 2006).

Facilitating factors and support

Many BAME leaders are able to point to encouragement from different sources, notably families, colleagues, middle managers and heads. 'Sponsorship' from heads or community leaders is often the critical variable in enabling BAME teachers to progress into middle leadership and on to more senior positions. Many of Bush et al.'s (2006) participants also refer to personal characteristics, notably resilience, determination, courage and ambition, but some also mention support from family and friends. This confirms Davidson's (1997: 29) view that 'strong extended family support systems tended to act as an important stress buffer for many'.

Miller (2016) argues that support from white leaders may be helpful, or even essential, for BAME teachers to advance their careers. 'White sanction' occurs where the skills and capabilities of a BME individual are acknowledged, and promoted, by a white person, who acts as a broker or mediator, on behalf of the BME person. Brokerage here refers to leveraging opportunities for the BME individual. However, Miller (2016) concludes that BME people should not need to rely on white sanction to legitimize and enable them. Rather, changes are required to attitudes towards race equality and inequality.

Most participants in Ogunbawa's (2012) research express the view that BAME people need customized leadership development and support at various phases of their careers. Similarly, some NPQH graduates argue that such 'protected' opportunities may make BAME teachers more confident about accessing headship (Bush et al. 2009). One of Bush et al.'s (2006) participants mentions a racial 'glass ceiling', a problem also referred to by Manuel and Slate (2003: 25). However, some BAME leaders do not favour customized support, arguing that they are 'leaders' first and 'black leaders' second.

Barriers to career progression

The literature identifies several barriers that limit BAME teachers' progress to leadership positions. Powney et al. (2003) say that marginalization and indirect racism create barriers, while Harris et al. (2003) note the subtle influence of informal networks from which ethnic minorities are excluded. Bhatt et al. (1988: 150) add that this occurs in a context of white interpretation of black reality. Tallerico (2000) mentions invisible or 'behind the scenes' criteria for promotion, while Davidson (1997) notes that BME leaders may experience isolation as 'token blacks' and face a lack of acceptance by professional colleagues. Miller (2019) expresses concern that BAME career progression may be dependent on support and endorsement of white colleagues, a process which positions the latter as gatekeepers.

Bush et al. (2006) argue that the attitudes of heads, senior and middle managers, and colleagues, inhibit BAME career development for many respondents while some also allege direct or indirect racism from these groups. Some BAME leaders also point to racist attitudes from parents, mostly but not exclusively white, and from governors. These problems are exacerbated for women, who face a 'double bind' of racism and sexism in some schools and communities. 'There is the old-fashioned perception of men as better leaders. It would have been better for me to be an Asian man.'

BAME teachers and leaders adopt a range of coping strategies to deal with these problems. Most persevere in the face of such difficulties and several find comfort in the support of family, friends and professional colleagues. One of the participants in Bush et al.'s (2006) study says that she often cries, and two mention anger. 'I become angry and I sink into acceptance that the world is against me.' Those who experience racism and entrenched stereotypes often have to be assertive to deal with these attitudes – 'I want to show them that black people can do the job.'

Exceptional people: Talent and determination

BAME professionals who succeed in their careers despite the barriers may be regarded as 'pioneers'. McKenley and Gordon (2002) say that BAME teachers have a sense of vocation to their community, leading to a strong, pioneering feeling. Dhruev (1992: 45) adds that

> people of BME heritage can alternately transform their perspectives by seeing themselves as pioneering agents of change.

Johnson (2017) uses 'pioneer' to distinguish earlier BAME heads from more recent appointees, adopting a generational approach, with this group of eleven taking up their posts during the 1960s–1990s. Some of this pioneer generation self-identified as community leaders. Similarly, Bush et al.'s (2006) participants often referred to a pioneering role, notably in being role models for other BAME teachers, and in modelling for a wider audience, including pupils, staff and the community.

The weight of evidence about barriers to leadership progression for BAME teachers leads to a view that those who succeed despite the barriers are 'exceptional people', rather than being representative. Bush et al.'s (2006) sample of BAME leaders, for example, exemplified several 'exceptional' features, such as determination; hard work; commitment; courage and resilience; thorough preparation for leadership, including masters' degrees as well as NPQH; and professionalism, illustrated through meeting targets, dressing properly and demonstrating eloquence.

The literature shows conclusively that BAME teachers and leaders do experience barriers and either direct or hidden discrimination. Under-representation has some cultural dimensions but also arises from the 'invisible' criteria used by selection panels, a form of covert racism. Most of these leaders have progressed despite these barriers rather than as a result of positive discrimination or any other systematic support. Bush et al. (2006) argue that they have succeeded because their own talents and hard work justified it. One of their participants poses a question of fundamental importance:

The issue of ethnicity and leadership is one that is bound up with the whole history of race, colonisation and power, and the unconscious conflict that white people have in being led by black leaders especially in a majority white institution, whether it be a school, business or church. Also most black leaders would feel uncomfortable having to lead and exercise authority over a predominantly white institution [. . .] Our key question then is are we seeking to prepare ethnic leaders in order to lead predominantly ethnic groups, or to seek to develop leaders generally that will be able to lead any institution because of their leadership skills and talents.

Under-representation will continue unless there is a pool of teachers from BAME backgrounds who can and do progress to school leadership positions. The presence of these leaders at all levels is needed to provide the role models that will encourage others to enter the profession, progress to leadership positions and remain as leaders to become the role models of the future. The barriers and discrimination have not discouraged all BAME leaders. Johnson's (2017: 859) conclusion notes the 'commitment and optimism' of her sample of UK BAME heads:

Collectively, across the generations, they identified as outward facing leaders who support a multi-cultural vision of Britain, with high aspirations for their ethnically and religiously diverse students.

Conclusion: Implications for leaders

The research discussed in this chapter identifies a range of problems facing BAME teachers and leaders, in seeking to access and enact leadership roles. These can be seen as barriers to equity and social justice. These barriers are underpinned by cultural diversity and, in many cases, covert or overt racism. Senior school and system leaders, white and BAME, have a legal and moral responsibility to support career development for all current and prospective staff, but particularly for those groups which are under-represented in the workforce. This is important, also, to enable the staff body to be more representative of the community served by the school. There are several implications for leaders:

1. Encourage BAME teachers and leaders to apply for leadership positions. This should go beyond ritual 'we particularly welcome applications from groups under-represented in the current workforce'.

2. Provide training for school governors and others involved in staff recruitment and selection, to address covert racism.
3. Encourage parents from all community groups to engage with the school, as governors, and in other ways.
4. Stimulate succession planning, especially for BAME teachers and leaders, by providing leadership opportunities, both formal and informal. One example would be to enable BAME middle leaders to attend SLT meetings.
5. Make it clear, at public and staff events, that racist attitudes and discrimination are wholly unacceptable.

These steps, taken collectively, have the potential to change the climate for BAME professionals and to develop a wholly inclusive, non-racist, school ethos, which should also encourage and inspire pupils, parents and the local community.

References

Armstrong, C. and D. Mitchell (2017), 'Shifting Identities: Negotiating Intersections of Race and Gender in Canadian Administrative Contexts', *Educational Management, Administration and Leadership*, 45 (5): 825–41.

Bariso, E. U. (2001), 'Code of Professional Practice At Stake? Race, Representation and Professionalism in British Education', *Race, Ethnicity and Education*, 4 (2): 167–84.

Bhatt, A., R. Carr-Hill and S. Ohri (1988), *Britain's Black Population: A New Perspective*, Gower: Radical Statistics Race Group.

Bishop, R. (2003), 'Changing Power Relations In Education: Kaupapa Maori Messages For Mainstream Education in Aotearoa/ New Zealand', *Comparative Education*, 39 (2): 221–38.

Bravette-Gordon, G. (2001), *Towards Bicultural Competence: Transforming Our Lives, Handbook of Action Research*, London: SAGE.

Bush, T. and K. C. Moloi (2007), 'Race, Racism and Discrimination in School Leadership: Evidence from England and South Africa', *International Studies in Educational Administration*, 35 (1): 41–59.

Bush, T., D. Glover and K. Sood (2006), 'Black and Minority Ethnic Leaders in England: A Portrait', *School Leadership and Management*, 26 (4): 289–305.

Bush, T., T. Allen, D. Glover, D. Middlewood and K. Sood (2009), *Diversity and the National Professional Qualification for Headship*, Nottingham: NCSL.

Crow, G. and J. Moller (2017), 'Professional Identities of School Leaders across International Contexts: An Introduction and Rationale', *Educational Management, Administration and Leadership*, 45 (5): 749–58.

Davidson, M. J. (1997), *The Black and Ethnic Minority Woman Manager: Cracking the Concrete Ceiling*, London: Paul Chapman.

Dhruev, N. (1992), 'Conflict and Race in Social Work Relations', *Journal of Social Work Practice*, 6 (1): 77–86.

Hallinger, P. (2018), 'Bringing Context out of the Shadows of Leadership', *Educational Management, Administration and Leadership*, 46 (1): 5–24.

Harris, A., D. Muijs and M. Crawford (2003), *Deputy and Assistant Heads: Building Leadership Potential*, Nottingham: NCSL.

Johnson, L. (2017), 'The Lives and Identities of UK Black and South Asian Head Teachers: Metaphors of Leadership', *Educational Management, Administration and Leadership*, 45 (5): 842–62.

Manuel, M. E., and J. R. Slate (2003), 'Hispanic Female Superintendents in America: Profile', *Advancing Women in Leadership Journal*, Last accessed June 2018: http://www.advancing women.com/awl/fall 2003/MANUEL~1.html.

McKenley, J. and G. Gordon (2002), *Challenge Plus: The Experience of Black and Minority Ethnic School Leaders*, Nottingham: National College of School Leadership.

Miller, P. (2016), '"White Sanction": Institutional, Group and Individual Interaction in the Promotion and Progression of BME Academics and Teachers in England', *Power and Education*, 8 (3): 205–21.

Miller, P. (forthcoming), 'Race and Ethnicity in Educational Leadership', in T. Bush, L. Bell and D. Middlewood (eds), *The Principles of Educational Leadership and Management*, 3rd edn, London: SAGE.

Moorosi, P. (2014), 'Constructing a Leader's Identity through a Leadership Development Programme: An Intersectional Analysis', *Educational Management, Administration and Leadership*, 42 (6): 792–807.

Ogunbawa, D. (2012), 'Developing Black and Minority Ethnic Leaders: The Case for Customised Programmes', *Educational Management, Administration and Leadership*, 40 (2): 158–74.

Ortiz, F. I. (2000), 'Who Controls Succession in the Superintendency? A Minority Perspective', *Urban Education*, 35 (5): 557–65.

Papadopoulos, I. (1999), 'Health and Illness Beliefs of Greek Cypriots Living in London', *Journal of Advanced Nursing*, 29 (5): 1097–104.

Parker-Jenkins, M., K. F. Haw, B. Irving and S. Khan (1997), 'Trying Twice as Hard to Succeed: Perceptions of Muslim Women in Britain', Paper presented to British Educational Research Association, September, York.

Powney, J., V. Wilson and S. Hall (2003), *Teachers' Careers: the Impact of Age, Disability, Ethnicity, Gender and Sexual Orientation*, London: DfES.

Singh, V. (2002), *Managing Diversity for Strategic Advantage*, Report to the Council for Excellence in Management and Leadership, www.cranfield.ac.uk.

Tallerico, M. (2000), 'Gaining Access to the Superintendency: Headhunting, Gender and Colour', *Educational Administration Quarterly*, 36 (1): 18–43.

5

Race, origin, qualifications and the progression of overseas trained teachers (OTTs) in England

Paul Miller

Introduction

International migration has always played a key role in England's nation-building. England's economic and demographic interests are usually the push factors behind voluntary migration, skilled or otherwise, and migration on the whole has served as a means of social and ideological control. In deciding who are most desirable for 'admission', a state sets the parameters for the social, cultural and symbolic boundaries of the nation, which is sometimes manifested in racialized immigration policies (Miller, 2008). During the 1950s, migrant selection to England was racially motivated, with certain groups of individuals deemed more desirable than others (Grannum, 2002). Later, migrant selection was based on whether or not they could add to England's knowledge profile. Arguably, a hybrid of both these approaches is in in place today.

In the early 1970s, for the first time, the selection and admission of migrants to England was based more on their 'educational skills and resources' and not purely on racial background (Whitaker, 1991: 19), a move which, on the surface, appeared to suggest that England's policy towards migrants was both colour- and religion blind, which led to a new thrust of migration from the Caribbean, Africa and Asia, representing a counterbalance to pattern of migration from the United States, Canada, Australia and Europe. Whitaker (1991) described this period of migration based on skills over race a 'historic watershed' (19). By the mid-1970s, however, fewer migrants arrived in England from developed countries and more from developing countries, in particular from Asia, the Caribbean and Africa (Dustmann et al., 2003).

Since the mid-1990s, the selection of migrants based on their education and skills, favouring the highly skilled over family-class immigrants and refugees, has intensified. More than half the numbers of migrants admitted throughout the late 1990s were economic-class migrants (Dustmann et al., 2003), among them a considerable number of highly skilled professionals, particularly nurses and medical doctors, engineers and teachers. Despite England's preference for highly skilled migrants, however, and despite these professionals adding value to the labour force, an increasingly hostile policy environment was having, and continues to have, an adverse impact on their ability to thrive. In particular, the non-recognition of prior work experiences and qualifications have served as barriers to their integration and career progression (Haque et al., 2002; Miller, 2008).

The issue in context – The current position and status of OTTs in England

Although the opening up of England to migrants based on 'educational skills and resources' (Whitaker, 1991: 19), instead of their racial backgrounds, has been described as a watershed moment, and is arguably the foundation for the recruitment of overseas trained teachers (OTTs). Since the mid- to late 2000s, the openness and tolerance towards migrant professionals, from outside the European Union (EU), has come under increased social and political scrutiny and debate, which has led to the introduction of a myriad of government-led initiatives to curtail non-EU migration and to make it more difficult for those already in the country to obtain the right of abode (Miller, 2008; Achato et al., 2010). For example, in 2006 the Home Office changed the qualifying period for those in 'Employment Related Categories' (OTTs included) to be able to apply for Indefinite Leave to Remain (ILR) in the United Kingdom from four to five years with no recourse for those persons already in the United Kingdom at the time of the change. The Home Office also mandated that all migrants, including OTTs, were (and still are) required to complete English language and 'Life in the UK' tests as part of the requirements for obtaining ILR. A year later, the Department for Education and Skills (DfES) varied the conditions of employment for OTTs to allow for their deportation, if after four years of teaching in the United Kingdom, they had failed to achieve UK Qualified Teacher Status (QTS).

Overseas trained teachers in England

An OTT is any teacher who has undertaken teacher training outside of the European Economic Area (EEA) and Switzerland, and has been recognized by the competent authority in their home country (DfES, 2007). OTTs in England come from Organization of Economic Cooperation and Development countries, including the United States and Canada, and from other places such as Asia, Africa and the Caribbean. It is appropriate to make two important points at this juncture. First, as of 1 April 2012, the Department for Education removed the previous requirement for teachers trained in Canada, the United States, Australia and New Zealand to undergo any additional training leading to the award of UK QTS. As a result, once recruited, they can apply directly to the National College for Teaching and Leadership (NCTL) for QTS without undertaking further training or assessment in England (DfE, 2014: 2). Second, OTTs without UK QTS, or exemption from QTS, are considered 'unqualified teachers' and must undertake appropriate training and assessment leading to the award of QTS. OTTs considered 'unqualified teachers' are generally paid on the 'unqualified teacher scale', although the point on the scale at which they are paid is left to the discretion of their head teacher.

Data on OTTs has always been very patchy (Morgan et al., 2005; Miller, 2006), although in 2006, it was estimated there were approximately 43,000 OTTs in the United Kingdom. This was approximately 10 per cent of the total teaching workforce. The cultural backgrounds of OTTs differ considerably, and top supplying countries during the period 2001–08 were South Africa, Australia, the United States, New Zealand, Canada and Jamaica. Although the Home Office and the Department for Education now no longer collect nationality data on OTTs, there is evidence that several of the top supplying countries of migrant teachers to England remain the same. This is based on recruitment activities from 2014 to 2016, where the top sending countries were the Irish Republic, Australia, Canada, New Zealand, South Africa and Jamaica (Boffey, 2015). It is important to note here, however, that the official language spoken in the top six supplying countries is English, and that, with the exception of Jamaica and South Africa, the other four countries are primarily 'white', industrialized societies. It should also be noted, that of the top six supplying countries, the only two whose teachers must undertake further training for UK QTS are Jamaica and South Africa, non-white, non-industrialized developing countries. The *second wave* of teacher migration to England started in 2014 and is ongoing. This chapter, however, explores the promotion, progression of Caribbean OTTs who arrived in England during the period 2001–08, in the *first* wave of teacher migration.

Teacher progression in England

Teacher progression is highly subjective and, very often, teachers, school boards and policymakers have differing views regarding possible factors influencing an appointment or indeed a 'non-appointment'. Pioneering research by Morgan et al. (1983) found that the selection of head teachers was arbitrary and problematic, and that selection panels did not always have clear criteria for selection. Additionally, where criteria did exist, selection decisions were not always based upon these. In 2002, Earley et al. found that race/ethnicity was a problem in teacher progression, as evidenced by the few numbers of black and minority ethnic (BME) staff in senior leadership roles in schools. Ten years later, in 2012, Earley et al. reconfirmed that BME staff were disadvantaged in gaining senior leadership roles in schools due to race/ethnicity. Earley et al. also pointed to underlying essentialist stereotypes and the glass ceiling. Bush et al. (2006), and Lumby and Coleman (2007, 2016) also found that race/ethnicity is a factor in the career progression of some BME teachers. Coleman (2007) also indicated that 'in some cases women still meet prejudice from governors and others in the wider community' (389). Research conducted by Moreau et al. (2007) and by Bullock (2009) also showed women were disproportionately represented in senior leadership posts.

Research by Shah and Shaikh (2010) found that religious and ethnic affiliation plays a major role in the progression of Muslim teachers, in particular males. Other barriers that limit teachers' career progression to leadership positions include indirect racism (Powney et al., 2003); the subtle influence of informal networks that excludes some groups (Harris et al., 2003); discrimination at work (McNamara et al., 2009); government policy, social connections and school-level jockeying/interference (Miller, 2014); racial discrimination and the absence of/need for 'White sanction' (Miller, 2016); and race discrimination (Miller and Callender, 2018). Regarding OTTs specifically, Miller (2008) found the non-recognition and devaluing of their original qualification, and unfair policy treatment (Miller, 2018) contributes to their lack of progression. Furthermore, in a study for the Home Office, Haque et al. (2002) found that BME migrants, in particular those with high educational and occupational qualifications, experienced downward professional mobility after arriving in the

United Kingdom due to the non-recognition or devaluation of their overseas qualifications.

Conceptual framework

Critical theory is related to social theory, and is sometimes viewed as a philosophical approach to culture that considers the social, historical and ideological forces and structures which produce and constrain it. Critical education theory, on the other hand, is a sub-branch of critical theory which describes education as a product and a process, both of which are mediums of social control. Like critical theory, critical education theory also acknowledges the importance of culture and cultural identity in maintaining or transforming the status quo (Ward, 2006), and both sets of theories challenge the 'othering' of individuals and groups through key aspects such as racial and ethnic theory, hegemony, cultural dominance and cultural capital. These are discussed briefly below.

Critical Theory and Race: Discussions based on race, ethnicity and education usually imply that improvement in an individual's social status will result from their educational endeavours (McCarthy and Dimitriadis, 2004). However, sometimes insufficient regard is given to the fact that schooling and achievement (Bowles and Gintis, 1976), and indeed promotion, progression are closely associated with 'political' acts (Miller, 2013). Critical theorists challenge views that downplay or fail to acknowledge the marginality experienced by racial/ethnic groups (e.g. OTTs of Caribbean origin in England), who, through structural and institutional arrangements, are constrained and undermined (McCarthy and Dimitriadis, 2004). Put differently, education systems and institutions maintain existing social class structures for the benefit of a social and economic elite (Bowles and Gintis, 1976), thus galvanizing and reifying power relations and white authority (Giroux, 1993).

Hegemony: Hegemony is a process by which the disempowered are persuaded to participate in their own disempowerment. According to Ward (2006), it is a strategy of pacification where the oppressed must come to believe that their oppression is not really oppression, but that what they are going through is for the *common good.* As a result, the exercise of control by the dominant class or culture, over all facets of public life, is for the common good. For Gramsci (1971), hegemony is achieved and maintained in citizens by the creation and implementation of policies that keep the ruling class in their position, and which also require the mass of the population to acquiesce to their own domination. For example, by recruiting some OTTs to work as 'unqualified teachers' for up to four years without UK QTS, and by not providing them automatic exemption, the British government enlists the support of OTTs in its domination and their acquiesce. As Marx and Engels (1846) point out,

> The ideas of the ruling class are in every epoch the ruling ideas; i.e., the class, which is the ruling material force of society, is at the same time its ruling intellectual force. The class which has the means of material production at its disposal, has control at the same time over the means of mental production. (64)

Cultural dominance: Cultural theory asserts that in capitalist societies, the group with ownership of or power over the means of material and mental production will dominate (Sidanius and Pratto, 1999), thus leading to the creation of a *dominant* and a *subordinated* culture. Accordingly, it is in the interest of the dominant culture to exercise its power and control over resources, systems and other apparatuses, to sustain its position of dominance, and to do this, it gains the cooperation of the masses, through pacification or regulatory procedures that keep the subordinated culture or those representing the subordinated culture in check (Pratto et al., 1997). By requiring teachers from non-white, non-industrialized countries to undertake a programme of training and assessment for UK Qualified Teacher Status, which is not the case for teachers from white industrialized countries, the British government appears to be promoting and/or indeed attempting to maintain a form of cultural dominance built on whiteness.

Cultural Capital: According to Bourdieu (1986), status in society is determined by three kinds of capital, namely,

- economic – having large amounts of money and economic resources;
- social – having large numbers of influential friends; and
- cultural – having high-level skills and understanding of the codes used to describe objects of high aesthetic value. It is usually passed down within families as a set of understandings of the world – a *habitus*.

Cultural capital, however, Bourdieu points out, can be a major source of social inequality where certain forms of cultural capital are not as valued as others, and which, as a result, hinder one's social mobility (Nahapiet and Ghoshal, 1998). Put differently, some cultures have artefacts (e.g. an education system and/or the qualifications it provides) that are more highly valued than others. Thus, the standard of training received by OTTs from the Caribbean, India-Asia and Africa, for example, is believed to be of a lower status than that of those OTTs trained in EU member states and in other white, industrialized countries. Since capital, according to Bourdieu, is the foundation of social life, and since capital is believed to be responsible for one's position within the social order, the more capital one has, the more power one is able to exercise in society and vice versa. Thus, high-status cultural artefacts have high *cultural capital*, such as the qualifications issued in white industrialized countries, which provide automatic access to levels of social intercourse that augment their status in similar settings (i.e. white industrialized countries) or that confers on them a higher status in other settings (i.e. primarily non-white, non-industrialized developing countries).

The study

Data for this qualitative exploratory study was collected in two phases. Phase one was conducted between May and November 2015, and included six participants: four males and two females. Phase two was conducted between February and May 2016, and also included six participants: three males and three females. Across both phases, participants worked in secondary high schools in five London boroughs. Ten were employed as teachers and three had been promoted to the position of Head of Department. Convenience and snowball sampling were used to enlist participants. Among the questions asked of all participants were the following: What role, if any, do you think having overseas qualifications plays in your promotion/progression? What role, if any, do you think being an OTT plays in your promotion, progression? Do you think promotion, progression decisions are adverse for you because you are an OTT from the Caribbean? What, if anything, can you do to improve your chances of promotion, progression? What, if anything, can the system do to improve your chances of promotion/progression?

Participants

Together, the six teachers in phase one had 69 years of combined UK teaching experience, or an individual average of 11.5 years. Between them, they had taught in thirteen schools, with the one teacher having taught in five schools over a period of thirteen years. Together, they had submitted twenty applications for promotion both internally and externally, with one teacher having made ten applications. Of the six teachers and the twenty applications, four had been interviewed and two, one male and one female, had been promoted to Heads of Department (see Appendix 1).

Together, the six teachers in phase two had sixty years of combined UK teaching experience, or an individual average of ten years. Between them, they had taught in twelve schools, with the one teacher having taught in four schools over thirteen years. Together, they had submitted fourteen applications for promotion both internally and externally, with one teacher making four applications and two teachers making two applications. Of the six teachers and the fourteen applications, two had been interviewed and one female had been promoted to Head of Department (see Appendix 2).

Analysis

Descriptive and phenomenological approaches were used as a guiding framework for this study. Descriptive research provides a detailed picture of a particular situation (Neuman, 2006), in this case the experience of Caribbean OTTs regarding their promotion, progression in England, and their perceptions of the factors responsible for their promotion, progression or lack thereof. Phenomenology provides accounts from participants' viewpoints. Combining these approaches was consistent with the key aim of the study, which was to provide 'interpretive explanation and not prediction' (Doyle 2003: 326). Data were analysed using a thematic approach, which was well suited to be used with the descriptive and phenomenological approaches since thematic analysis integrates the identification and crossmatching of multiple concepts from different voices in order to make meanings.

The evidence

The role of overseas qualifications promotion/progression

Despite the United Kingdom's national qualification checking service, UK Naric, judging the original degree qualification of some OTTs to be as 'equivalent' to UK degree standards, the OTTs nonetheless considered their overseas qualifications a significant factor in promotion, progression decisions.

> At the start of my teaching career here, my qualifications were considered to be equivalent. However, I still had to go through the process of getting QTS. I think

although the QTS is a very good thing to have, the fact that I had to go through the process and others didn't have to, this slowed me down. (Male, phase 2)

My first degree from our well-respected national university was not considered an equivalent qualification. As a result, I had to do a two-years top up degree and an additional year doing QTS. I think having to go through this has held me back. (Female, phase 1)

OTTs also highlighted disparities created by the education policy environment in how they were treated.

I think the Department for Education does not value our overseas qualifications. It's a really interesting paradox. They will trust us to teach students – on the basis of our training overseas – but they will not promote us to leadership roles and they will not recognize our qualifications at face value. This is a bit hypocritical if you ask me. (Male, phase 1)

I think if I was trained here I would have been promoted a long time ago. You see, once people hear that you are an Overseas Trained Teacher, they suddenly think you don't know this or that and they have to bring you up to speed. So yes, I feel I have been overlooked for promotion based on the fact I am an OTT. (Female, phase 2)

OTTs also linked the non-recognition of their original qualifications to race, country of origin and to whether a country is regarded as 'developed' or 'developing'.

I have seen many White OTTs – mainly from Australia, Canada and New Zealand – get promoted to senior leadership role, and I think to myself: do our countries not all operate similar education systems? Do we not all speak English? Aren't we all former colonies of Britain? But then I resolve myself to the view that: one I am black and two I am from a developing country. So, the issue is really not about my competence, it is about the value that the UK places on my qualification, background, training – on me as a person, in comparison to the value it places on OTTs from White industrialized countries. (Female, phase 2)

Being an OTT counts against you in promotion, progression

All 12 participants suggested that being an OTT has a negative effect on their promotion, progression prospects.

I think that, despite being allowed to migrate here to teach, and, despite having the relevant qualifications and experience, my experience has taught me that school aims to subtly promote British teachers to positions of responsibility and leadership. (Female, phase 1)

More recently there has been a demand for recruiting teachers who attended top UK universities. These are the persons who will be fast-tracked to leadership – not us; not teachers from overseas. (Female, phase 1)

OTTs also proposed that their cultural identity, and cultural capital, instead of adding value to their prospects, appeared to have counted against them and not to be of equal value.

A lot of people do not understand us, our culture and they want us to fit into their system. If we try to retain our teaching personality from back home, this is going to lead to clashes and we are not going to get anywhere. OTTs tend to have more experience and a lot more paper qualifications than the average British trained teacher, but we do not get promoted in proportionate terms. (Female, phase 1)

Being an OTT from the Caribbean counts against you in promotion, progression

All twelve participants indicated that being an OTT disadvantages them in promotion, progression decisions, and that being OTTs of Caribbean origin places on them a double disadvantage.

I think that an OTT from the Caribbean serves three purposes in England: (a) filling a gap, (b) to manage poor behaviour and (c) to shut up and put up. Our ideas for improving teaching and learning are not appreciated, yet, when a counterpart from Canada, the United States, South Africa, New Zealand or Australia proposes similar ideas, they are thought of as being genius. These are the people who are promoted. (Female, Phase 1)

From my personal experience, I have seen many OTTs overlooked for promotion, especially those that were internally advertised. I often question why, and I can only narrow it down to either skin colour, accent or country of origin. (Female, phase 2)

How OTTs were perceived by senior school leaders was also believed to be problematic, and was a major obstacle to their promotion, progression.

There are some underlying factors that prevent OTTs from getting promotion to senior leadership roles – especially in certain key areas within school. This stems from the Senior Leader Team lacking confidence in the abilities of OTTs, and no matter how good you are, once they realize you are an OTT they assume you cannot understand the system – no matter how long you have been here. For a person from the Caribbean, this is much worse. From what I observe, it appears Caribbean teachers are good enough only for teaching, for keeping pupils on track, for marking, but not for strategic roles. (Male, phase1)

Improving the chances for promotion, progression

OTTs want to progress in their teaching career in England. Some offered very practical suggestions about what they feel they can do to enhance their own prospects of gaining a promotion. Some suggested undertaking professional training such as the National Professional Qualification for Middle Leadership (NPQML), whereas others suggested seeking opportunities to '*lead whole school activities*' as well as 'finding a mentor', although it was pointed out the mentor has to be '*someone liked by SLT*'.

Some OTTs, however, appeared resigned to things not changing and to not getting promoted. One suggested, '*I am not sure what else I can do. To be honest, I have done all I can do.*' Another reasoned, '*Although my native language is English, and since I cannot change my skin colour, I guess I should commit to speaking the Queen's English – and that may give me an edge*' (Female, phase 1).

Despite an apparent lack of clarity about what OTTs felt they could do to improve their chances of promotion, progression, they appeared very committed to their jobs and determined to prove to the 'system' they are capable of being school leaders in England.

System support in helping OTTs improve their chance of promotion/progression

OTTs were clear that much more needed to be done to support them, and they offered several suggestions about how schools and the education system could help them improve their chances of promotion, progression.

I think the government should recognize our original qualifications as equivalent, just like what is being done for some OTTs. I also think the government should create systems that support the progression of all OTTs and not just some. I think OTTs are just gap fillers although it is clear some gap fillers matters more [. . .] (Male, phase 1)

I have been in my school now for twelve years and I have seen a number of white teachers progressing and, in a sense, leaving me behind. I love my job and I love my school. However, despite applying for internal promotion four times, I have not gotten through. It's always, 'you are not ready yet'. If I am not ready after twelve years in one school working in several roles and amassing significant experience – when will I be ready? I guess when they tell me I am. (Female, phase 1)

Not all OTTs, however, were clear about what they felt schools or the education system should or could do to support them.

I have no idea to be honest. I have completed QTS; I have attended all CPD trainings on the offer; and I have built up eight years of teaching experience here. I think OTTs are like the forgotten teachers in the system. We are just 'there'. (Male, phase 1)

Discussion

The above findings point to epistemological and ontological issues of difference and recognition in England, where the government plays an active role in devaluing and discounting the original qualifications of some OTTs, and where school leaders also discount their prior work experiences, the combined effect of which contributes to their lack of promotion, progression. As a consequence, OTTs of Caribbean origin feel severely discriminated against. The denigration of overseas qualifications is problematic for the qualification holder, and is used as a political tool by governments (Basran and Zong, 1998; Haque et al., 2002; Miller, 2008) to justify hegemony and cultural supremacy. England's discriminatory policy context that undermines the promotion, progression of OTTs from the Caribbean, and institutional practices that combine to thwart their promotion, progression are discussed below.

'Levels of equivalency': Epistemological misunderstandings of difference

The non-recognition of overseas qualifications and prior work experience is attributable to a 'deficit model' of difference. One of the key expressions of a multicultural society is its commitment to cultural pluralism. However, some commentators argue that the claim of some countries to being a pluralist society amounts to 'pretend pluralism'. Fleras and Elliot (2002), for example, suggest that in those societies, society as a whole and individuals within them 'tolerate rather than embrace differences' (2). Such pretence is manifested in terms of recruiting and allowing OTTs from the Caribbean (and elsewhere) to teach in British schools, although not giving recognition to their overseas qualifications. Such pretence was correctly identified by one OTT who suggested that in order to improve her chances of promotion, *'I guess I should commit to speaking the Queen's English'*. This observation highlights an apparent paradox in England's education system, where a politics of knowledge exists and promotes two types of capital: a 'white' capital and a non-white capital, where 'white' capital has pre-eminence over non-white capital. As Guo (2005) asserts,

> Although minor differences may be gently affirmed in depoliticised and decontextualised forms such as food, dance and festivities, substantive differences that tend to challenge hegemony and resist being co-opted are usually perceived by many as deficient, deviant, pathological, or otherwise divisive. (4)

Put differently, making promotion, progression easier for all OTTs, and not just a few, can be a hugely problematic decision in a political context that does not value as equivalent, education systems in non-industrialized, non-white countries. It is not unreasonable, therefore, to acknowledge that one key barrier preventing Britain from fully recognizing migrants' overseas qualifications and professional experiences is its prevailing attitude towards difference. One OTT notes, *'the government should create systems that support the progression of all OTTs and not just some'*. Britain's negative attitude towards, and treatment of, OTTs, and other skilled migrants, coexists alongside its commitment to democracy, social justice, equality and fairness, and may be described as a form of 'democratic racism' (Henry et al., 2000: 10), or a situation which prevents the government from making changes to existing the social, economic and political order that might improve the low status of individuals and groups, in this case non-white OTTs, for fear that taking such steps would be in conflict with (and a threat to) the mainstream. Such fears, however, are borne out of, and reify notions of, hegemony and cultural dominance discussed above. Critical theorists (e.g. Bourdieu, 1986) have argued that knowledge is power, and that knowledge has power. And in England, I argue that the politics of knowledge is being used as a power tool to control the career progression of some individuals and/or groups. Indeed as Guo (2005) asserts, 'knowledge is socially constructed, culturally mediated and historically situated. It is never neutral; nor is it objective' (4). The nature of knowledge thus prompts a number of important questions: Whose knowledge counts as legitimate, and who sets the parameters for this? Whose knowledge is valued and whose knowledge is silenced, and on what basis? Is knowledge only to be found in white, industrialized societies?

As defined by the DfES (2007), an OTT is a teacher 'trained and recognized by the competent authority in his/her country'. And although their teaching experience and classroom skills are accepted in England as valid and essential, and thus they are recruited and allowed to teach, their overseas qualifications and/or their leadership experience are nonetheless devalued. This apparent paradox highlights two 'political' tensions. First, England accepts the skills of OTTs from the Caribbean gained from their training in a non-white, non-industrialized country, although not their overseas qualifications, which are arguably the basis for their skills. This tension highlights the differential regard England has for artefacts such as qualifications obtained in these countries. Second, there is an assumption that knowledge and experience gained in non-white, non-industrialized countries are substandard to those gained in England and in other 'white' industrialized societies, and that therefore, to progress in their careers, OTTs from the Caribbean need to be retrained (recultured). This tension highlights how the policy context in England is creating hegemonic and cultural domination whilst requiring OTTs from the Caribbean to participate in their own domination.

Li (2003) points out that the term 'migrant' has become a code word for people of colour, those from a different cultural background and those who do not speak fluent English. As a result, the knowledge and capacities possessed by these migrants are deemed inferior because their 'differences' are thought incompatible with the cultural and social order. This is precisely the point made by Ward (2006), who asserts that hegemony promotes the pacification and disempowerment of peoples and cultures, through regulatory frameworks, in the interest of the *common good*, and by Marx and Engels (1846), who argue that 'the class which has the means of material production at its disposal, has control at the same time over the means of mental production' (64). In the context of OTTs from the Caribbean in England, a hostile and discriminatory education and migration policy context, led by the government, is steadily undermining OTTs' belief in the ability of the system to be able to promote and deliver equality of access and outcomes to and for them.

The hierarchy of knowledge and power that elevates white OTTs and puts non-white OTTs at the 'bottom of the heap' is entrenched in Britain's ethnocentric past, where migrants from Europe, Switzerland, Canada, New Zealand, Australia and the United States were hitherto viewed as 'more desirable', and those from developing countries were viewed as 'undesirables'. Since skilled migration to England is no longer based on race and ethnic origin, the non-recognition of the original qualifications and experience of OTTs from the Caribbean and other developing countries, arguably, is the new 'head tax' used by the government for keeping out 'undesirables', and for keeping migrants already in the country, who are not from white industrialized countries, and therefore not of a certain ilk, 'in check'. The non-recognition of the original qualifications of OTTs from the Caribbean and developing countries is therefore a strategy for maintaining and reinforcing existing power relations in British society, and for appeasing those who are anxious about patterns and levels of migration.

'Levels of recognition': Ontological perspectives

The assessment and recognition of overseas qualifications in Britain appears to be grounded in two things: positivistic and racial/ethnic measuring. On the one hand, positivists believe an objective world exists 'out there' which is external to the individual (Boshier, 1994), and that if something exists, it can be measured. On the other hand, race and ethnic discrimination operates in the form of social categorization that exaggerates differences between individuals, groups and/or countries. In 2008, Miller proposed that 'this ontology has been the key determinant behind the current practice in overseas qualifications assessment and recognition' (18). A decade later, changes to education policy have not levelled the playing field, but instead have advantaged some OTTs over others. The result of this is the creation and normalization of a worldview that some teachers are more preferred than others, and that some teachers are more preferred for certain roles than others. Thus, OTTs stand a better chance of promotion, progression and of ultimately becoming British citizens where they, first, look like, and, second, share cultural habits and patterns of behaviour similar to British citizens, or third, are prepared to 'adopt', 'adapt' and 'adjust'. This process of 'adopting', 'adapting' and 'adjusting' is consistent with cultural domination and hegemonic principles. These concerns are compounded by the fact that positivistic and racial measuring adopts a set of value-free criteria which trivializes the social, political, historical and cultural contexts that have socialized OTTs from non-white, non-industrialized countries. Thus, claims of neutral qualifications assessment and measurement, professional standards, quality and excellence appear to be no more than thinly veiled disguises for keeping out some OTTs, and, among those who are admitted, to keep those from non-white, non-industrialized countries, in their place, and in check. For, although many OTTs were recruited to teach in England on the basis of skills, experience and qualifications received in their country of origin, it is clear that achieving UK QTS is a type of hidden criteria that delays, and in some cases denies, them access to the appropriate remuneration and to middle and senior leadership roles.

In using the criteria of a dominant culture to measure qualifications and experience gained by OTTs in a non-dominant culture, the resulting imbalance creates a politics of difference which has not considered a number of critical questions. Who establishes the criteria for measuring qualifications equivalence and for recognizing them? Whose interests are represented and served by said criteria? What should we do with/how should we treat knowledge that is valid but different? What forms of knowledge might become equivalent to 'ours'? Although the non-recognition or devaluing of the qualifications of some OTTs may be seen as an attempt by the government to ameliorate risk, these attempts stem from a fear of, and a misrecognition of, difference. By refusing to recognize as equivalent the overseas qualifications and experience of OTTs from the Caribbean and other developing countries, at the start of teaching contracts in England, like that of OTTs from white, industrialized countries, the government and the education system impose race, origin and country status barriers to progression that privileges a regime of truth which aids in perpetuating the oppression and disadvantage of the 'other'. These actions are consistent with those earlier described by Marx and Engels (1846).

Implications

OTTs provide an important function in the stability and continuity of teaching and learning in England's primary and secondary schools. Yet, OTTs trained in non-white, non-industrialized countries are disadvantaged in being promoted and progressing in their careers – the result of a hostile race and migration policy context. Previously, all OTTs entering Britain from outside the EEA and Switzerland had to undergo a period of training and assessment for UK QTS. In 2012, a change in educational policy added teachers trained in United States, Canada, Australia and New Zealand to the list. This, and other policy changes, have created two primary imbalances: one based on race and origin, and the other based on qualification and origin. OTTs from white, industrialized countries are given a head start to promotion, progression to leadership roles due to being exempt from additional training and assessment for UK QTS, whereas OTTs from non-white, non-industrialized countries must undergo additional training and assessment, since their qualifications, the educational systems that trained them and their experiences are not considered 'equivalent' to British standards. Qualifications, a form of cultural capital, should serve to narrow the gaps between individuals from different classes, races and origins. However, when the qualifications awarded by the 'competent authority' in a country of origin are not recognized or are devalued in England, this not only calls into question the qualifications of the bearer but also puts a limit on their progression and success, and calls into question the integrity of the education system (i.e. the competent authority) that awards these qualifications. Thus, and arguably a feature of competitive market environments, qualifications, as cultural capital, may increase or decrease in value, depending on the country of origin of said qualification, the destination country in which said qualification is presented and based on the market conditions existing in the country receiving such qualifications – at a particular point in time. Furthermore, although qualifications, as cultural capital, are believed to be one way of neutralizing imbalances in society, this is not always the case, for the ascribed and perceived difference in the value of qualifications held by different individuals (e.g. teachers in England) can lead to negative impacts for some individuals (e.g. OTTs from non-white, non-industrialized countries), although not others (e.g. OTTs from white industrialized countries). A key task for researchers and educationalists is therefore to critically examine and evaluate how political actions influence institutional and individual practices, in order to challenge systems of power imbalance that silence, exclude or otherwise disadvantage some individuals and groups.

Conclusions

OTTs are crucial to the delivery and sustainability of schooling in England. Although their precise numbers not known, they keep schools afloat and provide workforce stability for the compulsory sector and for the schools in which they work. Despite this, however, they are not first in line for leadership appointments, and responsibilities assigned to them are, in the main, usually limited to classroom teaching and behaviour management. A significant factor in the promotion, progression of OTTs from the Caribbean is an apparent misconstruction of their skills built on a view that they are 'fit to teach but not to lead'. This problematic nature of these misconstructions is sustained by the evidence from the present study, where the progression of OTTs from the Caribbean appears to have been flatlined. That is, of twelve OTTs interviewed, only three had been promoted to middle leadership roles (in this case, Heads of Department).

The non-recognition of the qualifications and experience of some OTTs in England privileges some OTTs over others, which creates a politics of knowledge built on a misrecognition and a fear of difference. Delivered through current education and migration policies, promotion, progression appears to be guaranteed for OTTs in England who were trained in white, developed countries. This raises crucial questions about the extent to which England's education and political systems value sameness or pluralism. In the current system, it appears that hegemony and cultural domination are preferred. Basran and Zong (1998) describe as 'double jeopardy' a situation where migrants must deal with the fact of their migrancy alongside adverse professional prospects due the non-recognition of their original qualifications and work experience. OTTs from the Caribbean and other non-white, non-industrialized countries appear to be caught in this 'double jeopardy' where race discrimination and stereotyping delivered through hostile migration and education policies in Britain, and not their qualifications, skills and work experiences, dictate how quickly, and how far, they are likely to progress.

Appendices

Appendix 1: Profile of Phase One participants

	Gender	Age	UK arrival	UK teaching years	UK Schools taught in	Promotion applications	Promoted	UK degree Equivalency	Qualified teacher at origin	UK teacher Qualified
P1	M	50–59	2005	11	3	2	No	No	Yes	Yes
P2	F	30–39	2007	8	1	1	No	Yes	Yes	Yes
P3	M	40–49	2008	7	1	3	No	Yes	Yes	Yes
P4	F	40–49	2003	13	5	3	Yes	No	Yes	Yes
P5	M	50–59	2001	15	1	1	No	Yes	Yes	Yes
P6	M	30–39	2001	15	3	10	Yes	No	Yes	Yes

Appendix 2: Profile of Phase Two participants

	Gender	Age	UK arrival	UK teaching years	UK schools taught in	Promotion applications	Promoted	UK degree equivalency	Qualified teacher at origin	UK teacher Qualified
P1	F	50–59	2003	13	4	2	Yes	Yes	Yes	Yes
P2	F	30–39	2003	13	2	3	No	No	Yes	Yes
P3	M	40–49	2006	9	1	3	No	No	Yes	Yes
P4	F	40–49	2005	11	2	4	No	Yes	Yes	Yes
P5	M	50–59	2007	7	1	1	No	Yes	Yes	Yes
P6	M	30–39	2007	7	2	1	No	No	Yes	Yes

References

Achato, L., M. Eaton and C. Jones (2010), *The Migrant Journey*. Home Office. Research Report 43. Last accessed 26 June 2016: www.homeoffice.gov.uk/publications/ science-research-statistics/research-statistics/immigration-asylum-research/horr43/.

Basran, G. and L. Zong (1998), 'Devaluation of Foreign Credentials as Perceived by Visible Minority Professional Immigrants', *Canadian Ethnic Studies*, 30 (3): 6–18.

Boffey, D. (2015), 'Dozens of Jamaican Teachers Hired to Work in British Schools', *The Guardian*, 11 October. Last accessed 26 June 2018: http://www.theguardian.com/ education/2015/oct/11/agency-hires-jamaican-teachers-for-english-schools.

Boshier, R. W. (1994), 'Initiating Research', in R. Garrison (ed.), *Research Perspectives in Adult Education*, 73–116, Malabar: Krieger.

Bourdieu, P. (1986), 'The Forms of Capital', in J. Richardson (ed.), *Handbook of Theory and Research for the Sociology of Education*, New York: Greenwood Press.

Bowles, S. and H. Gintis (1976), *Schooling in Capitalist America: Educational Reform and the Contradictions of Economic Life*, New York: Basic Book.

Bullock, K. (2009), *The Impact of School Leadership on Pupil Outcomes*. Research Report DCSF-RR108. London: Department for Children, Schools and Families (DCSF).

Bush, T., D. Glover and K. Sood (2006), 'Black and Minority Ethnic Leaders in England: A Portrait', *School Leadership & Management*, 26 (3): 289–305.

Coleman, M. (2007), 'Gender and Educational Leadership in England: A Comparison of Secondary Head Teachers' Views over Time', *School Leadership & Management*, 27 (4): 383–99.

Department for Children, Schools and Families (2007), 'Education (Specified Work and Registration) (England) (Amendment) Regulations'. Last accessed 10 June 2018: https://www.legislation.gov.uk/uksi/2007/2117/contents/made.

Department for Education and Skills (2014), 'Overseas Trained Teachers: Departmental Advice for Overseas Trained Teachers, Local Authorities, Maintained Schools and Governing Bodies'. Last accessed 10 June 2018: https://www.gov.uk/government/uploads/system/uploads/attachment_data/file/387894/OTTs_web_guidance_10_Dec_14.pdf.

Doyle, L. H. (2003), 'Synthesis through Meta-Ethnography: Paradoxes, Enhancements, and Possibilities', *Qualitative Research*, 3 (3): 321–44.

Dustmann, C., F. Fabbri and I. Preston (2003), *The Local Labour Market Effects of Immigration in the UK*, Home Office. http://www.homeoffice.gov.uk/rds/pdfs2/rdsolr0603.pdf.

Earley, P., J. Evans, P. Collarbone, A. Gold and D. Halpin (2002), *Establishing the Current State of School Leadership in England*. Department for Education and Skills research report RR336, London: HMSO.

Earley, P., R. Higham, R. Allen, T. Allen, J. Howson, R. Nelson and D. Sims (2012), *Review of the School Leadership Landscape*, Nottingham, UK: National College for School Leadership.

Fleras, A. and J. Elliot (2002), *Engaging Diversity: Multiculturalism in Canada*, Scarborough: Nelson Thomson Learning.

Giroux, H. (1993), 'Paulo Freire and the Politics of Postcolonialism', in P. McLaren and P. Leonard (eds), *Paulo Freire: A Critical Encounter*, 177–88, New York: Routledge.

Gramsci, A. (1971), *Selections from the Prison Notebooks of Antonio Gramsci*, New York: International Publishers.

Grannum, G. (2002), *Tracing Your West Indian Ancestors*, London: National Archives.

Guo, S. (2005), 'Difference, Deficiency, and Devaluation: Non-recognition of Foreign Credentials for Immigrant Professionals in Canada'. Presentation at the Canadian Association for the Study of Adult Education (CASAE) Conference, University of Western Ontario, 28–31 May.

Haque, R., C. Dustmann, F. Fabbri, I. Preston, J. Wadsworth, M. Shields, S. Wheatley Price and J. Kempton (2002), *Migrants in the UK: Their Characteristics and Labour Market Outcomes and Impacts*, London: Home Office.

Harris, A., D. Muijs and M. Crawford (2003), *Deputy and Assistant Heads: Building Leadership Potential*, Nottingham, UK: NCSL.

Home Office (2006). 'The Immigration (Leave to Remain) (Prescribed Forms and Procedures) Regulations'. Last accessed 12 June 2018: http://www.legislation.gov.uk/uksi/2006/1421/made.

Li, P. (2003), 'Deconstructing Canada's Discourse of Immigrant Integration', *Journal of International Migration and Integration*, 4 (3): 315–33.

Lumby, J. and M. Coleman (2007), *Leadership and Diversity: Challenging Theory and Practice in Education*, London: SAGE.

Lumby, J. and M. Coleman (2016), *Leading for Equality: Making Schools Fairer*, London: SAGE.

Marx, K. and F. Engels (1846), *The German Ideology*. Published 1932 by the Marx-Engels Institute.

McCarthy, C. and G. Dimitriadis (2004), 'Postcolonial Literature and the Curricular Imagination: Wilson Harris and the Pedagogical Implications of the Carnivalesque', *Educational Philosophy and Theory*, 36 (2): 201–13.

McNamara, O., J. Howson, H. Gunter and A. Fryers (2009), *The Leadership Aspirations and Careers of Black and Minority Ethnic Teachers*, London: NASUWT/NCSL.

Miller, P. W. (2006), 'Professional Lives in Transition: Overseas Trained Teachers in England', *Caribbean Journal of Education*, 28 (2): 187–215.

Miller, P. W. (2008), 'Downgrading and Discounting The Qualifications of Migrant Professionals in England: The Case of Overseas Trained Teachers', *Education, Knowledge and Economy*, 2 (1): 1–12.

Miller, P. (2014), 'Becoming a Principal: Exploring Perceived Discriminatory Practices in the Appointment and Selection of Principals in Jamaica and England', in K. Beycioglu and P. Pashiardis (eds), *Multidimensional Perspectives on Principal Leadership Effectiveness*, 132–48, Hershey, PA: IGI Global.

Miller, P. (2016), ' "White Sanction", Institutional, Group and Individual Interaction in the Promotion and Progression of Black and Minority Ethnic Academics and Teachers in England', *Power & Education*, 8 (3): 205–21.

Miller, P. (2018) 'Aspiration, Career Progression and Overseas Trained Teachers in England', *International Journal of Leadership in Education*, Doi: 10.1080/13603124.2018.1503838.

Miller, P. and C. Callender (2018), 'Black Leaders Matter: Agency, Progression and Sustainability of BME School Leadership in England in International Perspectives of Black Male Teachers, Teacher and School Leaders', *Journal for Multicultural Education*, 12 (2): 183–96.

Moreau, M. P., J. Osgood and A. Halsall (2007), 'Making Sense of the Glass Ceiling in Schools: An Exploration of Women Teachers' Discourses', *Gender and Education*, 19 (2): 237–53.

Morgan C., V. Hall and H. Mackay (1983), *The Selection of Secondary School Headteachers, Milton Keynes*, Buckingham: Open University Press.

Morgan, W. J., A. Sives and S. Appleton (2005), 'Managing the International Recruitment of Health Workers and Teachers: Do Commonwealth Agreements Provide an Answer?' *The Round Table*, 94 (379): 225–38.

Nahapiet, J. and S. Ghoshal (1998), 'Social Capital, Intellectual Capital, and the Organizational Advantage', *The Academy of Management Review*, 23 (2): 242–66.

Neuman, W. L. (2006), *Social Research Methods: Qualitative and Quantitative Approaches*, Toronto: Pearson.

Powney, J., V. Wilson and S. Hall (2003), *Teachers' Careers: The Impact of Age, Disability, Ethnicity, Gender and Sexual Orientation*, London: Department for Education and Skills.

Pratto, F., L. M. Stallworth, J. Sidanius and B. Siers (1997), 'The Sex Gap in Occupational Role Attainment: A Social Dominance Approach', *Journal of Personality and Social Psychology*, 72 (1): 37–53.

Shah, S. and J. Shaikh (2010), 'Leadership Progression of Muslim Male Teachers: Interplay of Ethnicity, Faith and Visibility', *School Leadership & Management*, 30 (1): 19–33.

Sidanius, J. and F. Pratto (1999), *Social Dominance: An Intergroup Theory of Social Hierarchy and Oppression*, Cambridge: Cambridge University Press.

Ward, T. (2006), 'Critical Education Theory: Education and State, Part 1'. Last accessed 17 July 2018: http://www.tonywardedu.com/images/critical_theory/critical%20 education%20part.1.pdf.

Whitaker, R. (1991), *Canadian Immigration Policy Since Confederation*, Ottawa: Canadian Historical Association.

6

The lived experiences of black women leaders: Barriers to progression

Claudette Bailey-Morrissey and Richard Race

Introduction

This chapter will explore the lived experiences of eight black women senior leaders so as to elucidate the ways in which their race, gender and social class have shaped their perceptions and experiences of senior leadership, particularly in the context of barriers to senior positions and promotion. Using a social constructionist, interpretivist paradigm, and an intersectionality lens, this chapter explores the complexities of black women senior leaders' multiple identities and the impact of these on their experiences. Due to the paucity of research into black women senior leaders' experiences in England, research from Europe, South Africa and the United States are also used to add international perspectives. Sixteen transcripts were generated from two semi-structured interviews with the participants to explore how their race, gender and social class intersect to shape their leadership perceptions, beliefs and practices. As education researchers, the concern has been to contribute both to gaining a better understanding of how black women senior leaders' gendered and racialized identities have shaped their senior leadership experiences, and what it means to them to be a black woman and hold a senior leadership position in a secondary school in England.

The context

This section provides a brief overview of the historical development of school leadership in England during the Thatcher and Major Conservative governments;

the New Labour government and the Coalition government, and how key educational reforms have socially constructed the role of the school leader and how the introduction of key policy has impacted the school leadership landscape. There is a large body of research about educational reforms that have taken place in England (Ball, 1993, 1997; Bush, 1999; Bottery, 2007; Gunter, 2008, 2012) and its impact on school leadership. Drawing on selected and relevant research, a social constructionist lens will be applied to present a brief historical overview to elucidate the relationship between intersectionality (Collins, 1993; Crenshaw, 1989; McCall, 2005) and school leadership. This, it is hoped, will illuminate the importance of these categories in shaping the lives, perceptions and experiences of black women senior leaders. There is cause for concern at the lack of black women and ethnic minorities securing senior leadership positions in schools (Coleman and Campbell-Stephens, 2010; Wyatt and Silvester, 2015), and it is in this context that this chapter will explore the meanings black women senior leaders attach to their senior leadership experiences. These are embedded in a notion of the social world, not as fixed or external to them but impacting on them in a deterministic way, as socially constructed by individuals through their social practices (Cohen et al., 2004).

Educational reform

Educational reform under the Thatcher and Major Conservative governments, and those implemented by New Labour and the Coalition governments, have impacted school leadership in two main ways: there was a shift in the perceptions of the role of the school leader and the introduction of a system that sought to encourage competition, accountability and standards but also with added state support and partnerships between schools and many state and private providers (Hargreaves and Shirley, 2009). Moreover, we draw on Burr (2003) and Gergen and Gergen's (2007) social constructionist theories so as to elucidate educational reform as a social construct.

Major changes took place under successive Conservative governments between 1979 and 1997, with neo-liberal ideas influencing education policy such as increased parental choice based on information made available, particularly from national test and examination results, leading to competition between schools. The central aims of these reforms were to create a marketized and more competitive school system (English, 2006), where the language of 'higher standards' was used to persuade parents that reform was necessary.

Moreover, during the Blair government (1997–2010), under New Labour, educational reform continued within the accountability framework of neo-liberal modernization (Lambert, 2007). In addition, the Education Reform Act (ERA) (1988) led to changes in the educational structure where 'low standards' were seen as an area of concern, identifying a societal problem, requiring an appropriate response, which had to be seen as more than the choices of authorized leaders in order to justify educational reform (Colebatch, 2006: 314). This, in turn, led to the modernization of school leadership, which was predicated on socially constructed neo-liberal ideas, associated with policy goals that include the commodification and privatization of public assets (Harvey, 2005).

The New Labour agenda added the social construction of 'leadership' because it was seen as providing a much stronger agentic thrust in instituting change and improving performance in the public sector, in general, and among schools, in particular, than the more conservative idea of 'management' (O'Reilly and Reed, 2010, 2011). This new leadership discourse led to the move away from 'management' of devolved responsibilities as it was no longer seen to be enough for new school leaders (Simkins, 2012: 625). Furthermore, following the General Election in 2010, educational reforms led to the English school system being hastily driven towards even greater levels of autonomy and choice for parents with a focus on improving standards. Coalition education policy set out the rapid conversion and expansion of 'academies' and 'free schools' (DfE, 2010). The rationale for these schools, similar to charter schools in the United States and free schools in Sweden, was to increase competition and drive up standards of educational attainment. From 2010 onwards, the Coalition government gave all state schools in the secondary sector the opportunity to convert to academy status as part of the government's vision of 'freeing' education from unnecessary controls, which were mainly seen as associated with local authorities (LAs) (Woods and Simkins, 2014: 327). The opportunity was initially given to those schools judged outstanding by the Office for Standards in Education. However, this policy was later developed so that 'low-performing schools' were made to convert, benefitting from what the Department for Education (2010: 56) identified as a move to ensure that schools deemed to be 'low performing' were connected to 'strong sponsors' and 'outstanding schools', seemingly, creating a comprehensive system of independent schools (Woods and Simkins, 2014). This illustrates Gergen and Gergen's (2007) social constructionist perspective about the use of discourse in creating meaning, and to some extent, an acceptance of change where language and all other forms of representation gain their meaning from the ways in which they are used within relationships.

Educational reforms have a number of implications for black women senior leaders, particularly in today's leadership landscape, for those working in inner city schools in deprived areas or those working in schools with challenging intakes. In these contexts, accountability measures fail to take into account considerable evidence that the effect of schools on student outcomes is dwarfed by other factors such as teacher quality (Hattie, 2003) and parental socio-economic status (Foreman-Peck and Murray, 2008). In addition, high levels of poverty can interfere with a school's ability to successfully improve student achievement (Rumberger and Palardy, 2005).

Methodology

One of the main purposes of conducting research into black women senior leaders' leadership experiences was to elicit and translate their stories of senior leadership so as to identify how they play a role in acting and performing on the senior leadership stage in the secondary school setting. As a result, the epistemological and methodological assumptions are that black women senior leaders' stories can be seen as a window into the discursive practices in which they locate themselves and how these, in turn, may reveal discrepancies in the official discourses of school leadership. Gathering data for the research involved two face-to-face, semi-structured interviews with eight black women, which occurred over a period of one year from July 2013 to June 2014. All the participants have taught in inner city secondary schools in London at some point in their careers. These schools could be described as operating in challenging circumstances, having diverse intakes. The average age of the participants was forty-six. Sixteen transcripts were generated from the interviews, which explored how black women senior leaders' race, gender and social class intersect to shape their leadership perceptions, beliefs and behaviours. Moreover, using a social constructionist, interpretivist paradigm and an intersectionality lens, the complexities of black women senior leaders' multiple identities were examined, exploring how each participant attributed different meanings to the reasons for their experiences. In this way, truth, as seen through one black woman senior leader's eyes, may be different to truth as seen through the eyes of another. However, each interview transcript provided invaluable insights into this research study into what it is like to be a black woman and a senior leader in a secondary school in England in the twenty-first century. Thematic analysis was used to analyse the data collected because it offers a fresh way to explore the meanings of transcripts in educational research, where key themes were identified from each interview transcript and categorized using coding.

Social constructionism

Social constructionism is being used in this chapter to understand how black women senior leaders socially construct their school leadership experiences. It is used to explore how barriers such as racism, institutional racism and discrimination can impact black women's experiences and the underlying assumptions about what is known about black women senior leaders' perceptions of themselves as school leaders, having multiple identities (Reynolds and Pope, 1991). Within the social constructionist paradigm, individuals are asked to be aware of the multiple realities that exist and the need to be ever suspicious about how the world appears to be (Burr, 2015: 5). Social constructionism might loosely be considered as any approach, which has at its foundation one or more of four key underlying assumptions (Gergen, 1985). First, social constructionism insists that we take a critical stance toward our taken-for-granted ways of understanding the world, including ourselves. In so doing, it challenges notions of reality as objective, fixed and, with the right instruments, knowable. Second, our understanding of the world must not be seen as static or inevitable but as historically and culturally situated, therefore, changing and developing over time. Third, 'knowledge is sustained' [. . .] 'through the daily interactions between people in the course of social life [. . .] our versions of knowledge become fabricated' (Burr, 2003:4). In other words, social interaction of all kinds, and particularly language, is of great importance to social constructionists. Fourth, knowledge is viewed as an interactive process. Therefore, social constructionism is helpful in seeking to understand the complex and multiple perspectives that individuals have of the world (Burr, 2003, 2015; Gergen, 1995, 1996).

Intersectionality and the social constructions of race, gender and social class

Intersectionality as a concept, derives from the activist critiques that black women in the United States and the United Kingdom made in the 1970s and 1980s about overly homogeneous political discourse, where black women's narratives have been distorted, maligned, appropriated, and rendered invisible in the interpretation and re/presentation processes (Hull et al., 1982; Brah and Phoenix, 2004). It has sought to expose how single-axis thinking undermines legal thinking, disciplinary knowledge production and struggles for social justice (Cho et al., 2013). Race, gender and class are social systems, patterns of social relationships among people, but they are also systems of oppression (Weber, 2013). According to Collins (2004), historically, race, gender and social class categories have been imposed on people as a means of justifying unequal social arrangements. However, people actively claim and manipulate race, gender and social class meanings through their everyday repetitive interactions (West and Fenstermaker, 1995). It is necessary to analyse and characterize the terms race, gender and social class because their meanings are contested. Intersectionality, therefore, is an important theoretical perspective that argues we should not study social categories (race, gender, social class) in isolation (Collins, 1993; hooks, 2000; Gillborn, 2008, 2015), but consider how the intersections of such categories can lead to multiple oppressions. An understanding of the ways in which black women senior leaders socially construct their race, gender and social class is useful and will help to elucidate their perceptions and experiences in relation to their multiple identities (Burr, 2003, 2015) and school contexts (Collins, 1998, 2000).

Gillborn (2008) suggests that 'race' is a system of socially constructed and enforced categories that are constantly recreated and modified through human interaction. Unfortunately, this does not stop people from talking about race in simplistic ways that ignore the realities of differentiated power and histories. Equally, notions and beliefs about gender led Bell and Nkomo (2001: 16) to conclude that gender is not only a social construct but also a 'set of assumptions and beliefs on both individual and societal levels that affect the thoughts, feelings, behaviours, references and the treatment of women and men'. In this structural conceptualization, gendering is the process and the gendered social order, the product of social construction. Moreover, social class can be identified as the fundamental means by which individuals are ranked on the social ladder of society (Kraus et al., 2013), where being at the top (or bottom) of the social class hierarchy shapes manners and tastes for art, music and culture (Kohn and Schooler, 1969); the social and economic opportunities people have across their life course (Stephens et al., 2012); and even the actual length of the life course itself (Adler et al., 1994).

Rollock et al.'s (2012) research into how black middle-class individuals in professional or managerial occupations position themselves in relation to the label 'middle class' provides useful insights into social class and black class identity. Rollock et al's (2012: 259) black middle-class identifiers tended to accept the label 'middle class' by making factual reference to income, the size of their home, occupation or pastimes. In contrast, middle-class ambivalent participants tended to regard themselves as middle class but did so with some degree of reservation or hesitation. Furthermore, whilst Rollock et al's (2012) research is a useful framework from which to examine black women senior leaders' perceptions and social constructions of their own social class identity, Phillips and Sarre's (1995) assertion that black, minority ethnic (BME) middle-class individuals constitutes a particularly interesting focus for analysis in that they occupy an ambivalent structural location that combines both (class) privilege and (racial) exclusion, providing further reasons for a study into the lived experiences of black women senior leaders. As we acknowledge in the data about to be analysed in this chapter, there were common features across the groups in terms of participants' reasons for hesitancy around inhabiting a particular location. This was attributed to the context of the relative newness of the black middle classes and respondents' broadly similar working-class trajectories alongside ongoing experiences of racism within a society that privileges and gives legitimacy to dominant White middle-class norms. Alternatively, working-class with qualifications participants ascribed to this label because it reflected their personal circumstances. For example, one participant described herself as working class but held middle-class values.

The complexities of Black multiple identities

'People live multiple, layered identities, derived from social relations, history and the operation of structured power' (Richardson and Loubier, 2008: 143). In other words, people are members of more than one category or social group, and can simultaneously experience advantages and disadvantages related to those different social groups. A discussion about multiple identities draws attention to the importance of multiple identities through multiple oppressions (Reynolds and Pope, 1991). There is a belief that black women leaders fare worse than either black men or white women because they possess a dual, as opposed to a single, subordinate identity (Rosette and Livingston, 2012), being insiders based on their gender and outsiders in terms of their intersection of race, ethnicity and gender (Fitzgerald, 2014). The term 'double jeopardy' has been used to describe the heightened disadvantage of black women due to the adverse consequences of black and female subordinate identities (Berdahl and Moore, 2006). Whilst identities are organized at the complex intersection of multiple categories of membership and meaning (Wilkins, 2012), for black women senior leaders the complex intersectionality of race, gender and social class raises important issues in enabling them to recognize stereotyping and, therefore, to work to socially construct a positive perception of Black women as senior leaders. Identities are socially constructed and emerge from negotiations between those imposed and chosen meanings. The imposed meanings, as derived from the intersections of race, gender and social class, stem from controlling images of Black women, which contain cultural contradictions that make it difficult, if not untenable, to perceive them in senior leadership positions (Collins, 1991, 2004). Ellemers et al. (2012) argue that when socially constructing their professional identities, BME academics felt these were shaped by the particular desires and stereotypes regarding them insisted upon by white colleagues. BME women in the data analysed below, for example, felt that in order to negotiate their professional roles as senior leaders, they had to exhibit a particular persona typified by high levels of professionalism, such as always meeting deadlines or publishing in high-quality journals. If they failed to exhibit such attributes, which they faced and in which they far exceeded the expectations placed upon white, female colleagues, then they were seen as failing to demonstrate their commitment and level of professionalism.

Black women senior leaders: Barriers

Gender is one of the ways in which individuals can be marginalized in accessing and exercising leadership (Coleman, 2007). In particular, women leaders may be seen as 'outsiders', as leadership is unconsciously identified with men (Schein, 2001). There is a stereotypical hegemonic masculinity that consciously and unconsciously influences our expectations of what a leader should be. As a result, women and others, who do not correspond to the leader stereotype of male, heterosexual, white and middle class, may feel and be perceived by others as outsiders in a leadership role (Coleman, 2007). For black women senior leaders, where their race and gender intersect, they can experience intersecting oppressions, or the convergence of being both black and female, and often they come from a lower socio-economic social class than whites (Collins, 2000).

Racism is a highly contested term and one that is almost always controversial. To be labelled a racist, for example, is generally considered derogatory. Moreover, traditionally racism has often been viewed as involving two key characteristics: a belief in the existence of discrete human races and the idea that those 'races' are hierarchically ordered (Gillborn, 2008). This is an extremely limited understanding of racism, and it has been argued that there are other forms that are both subtler and commoner. Indeed, racial discrimination is a pervasive phenomenon in the lives of many racial minorities (Sellers and Shelton, 2003), and it can take the form of blatant derogatory name-calling and can be subtle, for example, being stared at by security guards while shopping. These are behaviours that permeate the daily lives of individuals (Essed, 1991; Swim et al. 1998). In fact, racism is so widespread that Ryde (2009: 35) noted 'today's racism is hard-wired into our consciousness from the prejudices of the past'; it is embedded in the everyday practices of institutions and is therefore sustained by individuals, even though they may not be racist (Lander, in Knowles and Lander, 2011). When talking about racism, it is useful to distinguish between overt and institutional racism. Overt racism kills individuals, and institutional racism discriminates against individuals. Institutional racism exists where people decide to do nothing about the inequity, which they see or are aware of within their organizations, because it does not affect them, making them complicit in a similar way to violent acts of racism.

Moreover, a common theme emanating from research into black leaders' experiences reveals that racism is a fact of life for those whose race and gender intersect to create obstacles. For example, the respondents in Campbell-Stephens's (2010) research faced racism, arguing that they felt that staff were unwilling to take orders from a black leader and therefore undermined their authority. However, they were unable to prove it because the racism was not overt, supporting claims that black women are confronting a new version of workplace discrimination, a subtle bias, which 'unlike overt acts of bigotry that are punishable by law, subtle bias weeds through workplaces like an odourless vapour that, when left unchecked, stirs up feelings in black women that range from frustration to apathy to anger' (Taylor, 2007: 165).

Stereotyping is another form of discrimination and is the use of common-sense assumptions about groups of people to make predictions about characteristics of an individual (Crawley et al., 2013). Indeed, like physical objects, people are readily stereotyped based on visual cues of the physical body. Researchers note two related ways by which biases associated with role expectations affect leaders (Eagly and Karau, 2002; Heilman, 2001). First, because white males dominate leadership positions, women and ethnic minorities may appear less usual or natural and, thus, are perceived as a bad fit for these positions (Heilman and Okimoto, 2007). Second, women and ethnic minorities in leadership positions may seem 'inappropriate or presumptuous when they display the agentic behaviours often required in these roles (Koenig et al., 2011: 617).

Data analysis and discussion: Using Black women senior leaders' narratives to explore barriers

The method of data analysis we have used in this research is thematic analysis (Newby, 2014). A key theme emanating from research into black women senior leaders' experiences, as we have found, is how they perceive the ways in which their race and gender intersect with their social class to shape their experiences, and how they interpret and respond to stereotyping, discrimination and racism. The data analysis below examines the experiences of black women senior leaders where the participants talked about the challenges of being a black woman and holding a senior leadership position in a secondary school in England. Moreover, they also discussed challenges ranging from discrimination, racism and stereotyping, echoing what Rosette and Livingstone (2012) describe as others' perceptions of the incompatibility of being a black woman and a senior leader.

Black women senior leaders reported having a great awareness of their multiple identities and believed their ethnicity and cultural heritage were important parts of their identity (Richardson and Loubier, 2008). Some participants expressed a great sense of responsibility in guiding and supporting young people to succeed at school, describing themselves as role models, which they considered an important aspect of their senior leadership roles (Buckingham, 2008).

> My background originated in the Caribbean. There was [. . .] a British legacy in education so the head teacher was a very important figure in the school. For me, to become a teacher or a head mistress, it was an achievement; that was a definition of success when I was growing up. I bring diversity [. . .] I'm a visionary and that is something that I bring to senior leadership. I'm a woman, I'm from the Caribbean, I'm an immigrant, I'm black and I hear those are valuable things to bring to senior leadership. (Dee, IV: 1)

> First and foremost, I see myself as a Jamaican, and that comes out in many ways apart from the obvious, the way I sound, when I speak but I make no bones about the fact. [When] I go to sports day, I turned up in my Jamaican clothes. I remember someone came up to me and said: 'Oh, it's really nice to see you in the colours.' So, I don't hide my background. As an ethnic minority [. . .]

the school I've gone into [. . .] eighty percent of the year groups [. . .] are ethnic minorities. That whole role model thing really does apply to me [. . .] They know I'm Jamaican. I've got the same high expectations of them that everybody else [has] and the head teacher has. And it's just something that they can relate [to]. (Alisha, IV: 1)

There isn't a term on the ethnic minority form that necessarily fits but I suppose I recognize that I am British, I recognize that I am Caribbean and I recognize that I am African. I have spoken to some students recently who said that it was amazing that when you came to school, you dress stylishly, you wear colour and you're not afraid to express yourself. You're very down to earth. They had not come across a leader in a school like me. [For] other black students, in particular, it is important that they can see that it didn't matter what your background was, what race you are, if you wanted to aspire to a leader of a school in this educational system then you can do it. I really tried to reinforce the fact that you don't have to 'sell out' to become a leader. You can be yourself; you just have to know what is appropriate for what situation. (Jacqueline, IV: 1)

These narratives show a heightened awareness of the ways in which the participants' felt their racialized and gendered identities gave them an advantage in the context of their schools. These reflections reveal the added bonus of being an advocate for young people, going the extra mile and dispelling the myth that in order to achieve senior leadership status, the individual needs to change who they are, particularly if they dress or behave in a manner that reflects their cultural heritage.

Participants also reflected on ways in which colleagues perceived them due to their racialized and gendered identities as senior leaders and how these perceptions challenged their leadership:

And also being female I notice that there's very much different dynamics between male senior leaders and female senior leaders in terms of the way they do things. And how different staff react and gravitate naturally to different people. So, I feel I have a role, brought to the table, the fact that I am female, the fact that I am able to relate with people across different [. . .] cultures and nationalities. (Alisha, IV: 1)

In terms of colleagues, at times it was difficult because I think I was young and I was black and I was a woman. So, for some people that didn't sit well with them. It's like: 'Well, who's she?' Yes, staff that I line managed, I would say, who were older, often times [. . .] had been perhaps in that particular establishment for longer than I had been, and were white. (Jacqueline, IV: 1)

These narratives infer an awareness of the participants' racialized and gendered identities and highlight a common theme of their social constructions of what it means to be a male or a female senior leader (Heilman and Okimoto, 2007; Koenig et al. 2011). Whilst Alisha believes her multiple identities give her an advantage as a result of her ability to relate to a wide range of people from different backgrounds, Jacqueline's narrative is supported by Rosette and Livingston's (2012) view that black women fare worse than black men or white women, and they attribute this to the dual subordinate identity.

Participants reflected on the ways in which they believed their social class shaped their overall senior leadership experiences:

> Class isn't that important to me. I suppose [. . .] I'm working-class but my job is a middle-class job. It's hard to define class, because [. . .] like my dad, he owned his own business. His dad also had his own business. Does that make him middle class? And he wouldn't say he's middle class. (Deborah, IV: 1)

> Obviously, I've been through social mobility. I would definitely describe myself as working class; now I suppose I'm [. . .] sociologically, middle class. [I'm] very much a champion of the underdog and fairness [. . .] I'm not part of [. . .] that old boy's network. I know that I've had to fight for my place and so [. . .] I will help other people who I can see are in a similar situation. (Jacqueline, IV: 1)

> I don't even know. I kinda have a little tug of war with myself about it. Obviously, I'm middle class and I suppose [. . .] I was middle class before I came into the job that I am doing. The experiences that me and my brothers and sisters had with my mum and dad were pretty middle classed, I suppose, for the time that they were at. (Collette, IV: 1)

The participants' narratives reveal an ambivalence to social class, particularly in their use of the words 'I suppose' (Reay, 1996). They are supported by Mahony and Zmroczek's (1997: 4) claim that 'class is deeply rooted, retained and carried through life rather than left behind (or below) as some individuals find themselves in a different social class from that into which they were born'. Equally, there appears to be uneasiness in locating their social class, possibly because black professionals are uncertain of social class due to the shifting territory they occupy (Reay, 1996).

> I find the further up the ladder I get the more aware I am of not being properly middle-class because I don't classify myself as working-class [. . .]. I realize how much my identity's steeped in my culture. I feel inadequate a lot of the times because

I don't feel I've got the background or the experiences [. . .]. Going [on] holiday in France, or have been skiing. I've got my two-bedroom flat on the high road [. . .]. All of a sudden I feel very exposed and almost different. So that anxiousness that I just described to you I could have that every day with my peers. (Alisha, IV: 1)

Alisha, too, is uncomfortable with her social class position. Her narrative seems to suggest that there is a way of being that entitles individuals, to some extent, to claim membership of a particular social class (Mahony and Zmroczek, 1997; Skeggs, 2011). Interestingly, in Alisha's previous narrative she views the intersection of her race and gender as an advantage; however, when social class is added as a category, it creates a degree of uncertainty that leaves Alisha questioning her sense of belonging and uneasiness in her senior leadership position, echoing Lander, in Race and Lander's (2014) view that in contemporary society the norm equates to being white, male and middle-class.

The participants reflected on barriers and the challenges they faced as members of a senior leadership team:

The challenge came from trying to understand how my role fitted into the leadership team and what was expected of me. If you were new you had to work your way up to proving that you really earned your right to hold that position. There were so many unspoken ways of doing things, which made it very difficult if you were new because 'you did not know the rules'. There was a distinct lack of change; the phrase: 'we tried that' or 'we done that' were often used when any new ideas were suggested. (Claudette, IV: 1)

I think in comparison to white females I would say that, especially in secondary, [for] the black female leaders, it seems to take longer to achieve the same sort of position and it doesn't appear to be anything about merit. I have, especially in recent times, seen very young white females with no experience, haven't been a middle leader, and just fast tracked [. . .] to senior leadership, having not a clue what they're doing, in terms of how to treat people. They're very good at delegating and that's it. I can't really see anything else that they bring to bear except there seems to be a type. They kind of look a certain way, sound a certain way, got a similar sort of background and that I feel has really saddened me [. . .] I'm not going to go as far as, if I said blond, slim type that would just be too much of a stereotype. You do know it when you see it. (Jacqueline, IV: 1)

I can't think of a senior leadership team I have been on where I have felt a sense of belonging. I've always felt like an 'insider/outsider', if you know what I mean [. . .]

or 'outsider/insider'. A struggle to be valued [. . .] A struggle to be equal. Because I was accused of empowering the children so that they misbehave, so I was this crazy black woman that came in and encouraged the black children to misbehave [laughs]. And so, there was a sense in which I [was] being required to be somebody I wasn't in order to fit in it meant that I would have to, I suppose, compromise my own values and my own position by virtue of that fact, I was also 'othered'. I think that's a common feature of all my leadership positions. (Gloria, IV: 1)

I think people say that I'm quite headstrong and that she's very focused on getting the best. She doesn't settle for second best. I think people would say that she can be quite a force to be reckoned with. I don't know how to word this really, don't take any messing really, just kinda gets to the nuts and bolts of what the issue is. I think some people might say that I'm quite scary. I think that's what people have said before. I suppose because I mean what I say and I'll say what I mean. I put that expectation on myself and on others. (Collette, IV: 1)

I don't think I'm scary, but that's what I've been told. I think it's a historical thing. When you are quite confident or you know what you want people interpret that as being quite scary [. . .] You wouldn't say that about a white female or a white male Head. I think it's what they attach to ethnicity. (Collette, IV: 2)

The participants demonstrated different approaches to tackling stereotypical views others had of them and challenged misconceptions of what it meant to them to be a black woman and hold a senior leadership role:

I always felt that I had to have a bit of energy about me; [I would] then say he's not going to win this. I'm not going to allow you to get me to a point where I am a female; I am crying, because many did cry and leave the room, or calling in sick because you were that stressed or that you got so angry that you are no longer professional. There was kind of an understanding in the leadership team that you need to play that game to survive. And of course, I was not necessarily willing to do that. (Adwoa, IV: 2)

Everything about us is known and written. We are observed and researched; we are read about and so as far as our colleagues are concerned we are known. There's nothing to find out. And they bring that 'knowing' to the relationship that they have with you. Don't get bothered to find out who I am because it's been decided. I used to play opera, blaring out of my office at the end of the school day when I was marking books or relaxing. 'I had no idea you liked music like that'. Oh yeah, sometimes! (Laughs). (Gloria, IV: 2)

You shouldn't have ideas. You shouldn't have aspirations. My head teacher wrote on my NPQH [that I was] over-ambitious. You should not have any ambition. And you should be there [to do] the dirty work. When the head feels threatened by you, you know that you're a natural leader. I know you should play the game but [. . .] I draw the line [in] playing a game sometimes and then if you do that then you will get in because the other Assistant Head did all the stupidness but she got through. She's a Deputy now. (Deborah, IV: 1)

Your leadership is not validated because you're not what people expect a leader to be and so sometimes your colleagues make that role very difficult because they don't say: 'I am not going to be led by you', but they behave in ways, which undermine your capacity to lead. I know some people say: 'Oh you should play the game'. Well, I'm not playing any game that makes me feel bad about myself. I'm not offensive to people but I will tell them what my views are and why I hold those views. (Gloria, IV: 1)

One common theme emanating from the black women senior leaders' narratives above is who is entitled to be a senior leader (Rosette and Livingstone, 2012). The participants all spoke about being challenged in some way, either through racism and stereotyping, unspoken rules or by creating barriers such as promoting others who fit a certain profile. Their narratives demonstrate a refusal to comply and 'play the game' to get ahead at the expense of compromising their values (Brown, 2014). Gloria's narrative further illustrates the challenges black women senior leaders face as a result of their multiple identities, and her courage and determination to dispel the myths around how black women senior leaders are expected to behave through the use of music.

Conclusions

Securing a senior leadership position in a secondary school was an important fulfilment for black women senior leaders in this research. For a number of black women senior leaders, the education challenges and intersectional barriers of leadership far outweighed the triumphs, leaving three black women to conclude that senior leadership was not for them. One of the participants had left teaching and two were on the verge of leaving the profession. However, what research into black women senior leaders' experiences has demonstrated is that whilst incidents of stereotyping, discrimination and racism exist, those black women senior leaders who received guidance and support were able to gain the opportunities and experiences that enabled them to take risks, develop and grow

(Bailey-Morrissey, 2015; Race, 2015; Brown, 2014). Black women senior leaders' narratives reveal that despite the challenges, they were determined to work as dedicated members of their senior leadership teams, developing and maintaining professional relationships with colleagues through two-way communication and collegiality (Bailey-Morrissey, 2015).

However, it cannot be denied that barriers exist, preventing black women from successfully securing and maintaining senior leadership positions in secondary schools in England. In fact, this chapter has drawn attention to the intersectional barriers and challenges that have hindered black women senior leaders' career progression (Steinberg, in Race, 2018). Understanding black women senior leaders' experiences as something meaningful for black women themselves entails a continuing engagement with their narratives in an ethical way. While seeking to understand black women's professional identities is inconclusive, it is possible to understand the various ways in which they develop their own sense of school leadership identities, and this can be different from those imposed through stereotypical dominant models of what others consider it means to be a black woman senior leader (Hague and Okpala, 2017; Patton and Jordon, 2017; Guihen, 2018). Indeed, the journey into senior leadership is largely shaped by Black women's personal and professional experiences. This can be enhanced by challenging unconscious bias in the recruitment and selection process, and by tackling incidents of unethical leadership behaviour, such as racism, which continues to hinder career progression for black women senior leaders'.

References

Adler, N. E., T. Boyce, M. A. Chesney, S. Cohen, S. Folkman, R. L. Kahn and S. L. Syme (1994), 'Socioeconomic Status and Health: The Challenge of the Gradient', *American Psychologist*, 49 (1): 15–24.

Bailey-Morrissey, C. (2015), 'An Exploration of the Lived Experiences of Black Women Secondary School Leaders'. EdD thesis, University of Roehampton/Kingston University.

Ball, S. J. (1993), 'Education Markets, Choice and Social Class: The Market as a Class Strategy in the UK and the USA', *British Journal of Sociology of Education*, 14 (1): 3–19.

Ball, S. J. (1997), 'Policy Sociology and Critical Social Research: A Personal Review of Recent Education Policy and Policy Research', *British Educational Research Journal*, 23 (3): 257–74.

Bell, E. and S. Nkomo (2001), *Our Separate Ways*, Boston: Harvard Business School Press.

Berdahl, J. L. and C. Moore (2006), 'Workplace Harassment: Double Jeopardy for Minority Women', *Journal of Applied Psychology*, 91 (2): 426–36.

Bottery, M. (2007), 'New Labour Policy and School Leadership in England: Room for Manoeuvre?', *Cambridge Journal of Education*, 37 (2): 153–72.

Brah, A. and A. Phoenix (2004), 'Ain't I a Woman? Intersectionality Revisited', *Journal of International Women* Studies, 5 (3): 75–86.

Brown, A. R. (2014), 'The Recruitment and Retention of African American Women as Public School Superintendents', *Journal of Black Studies*, 45 (6): 1–21.

Buckingham, D. (2008), *Introducing Identity*, Boston: MIT Press.

Burr, V. (2003), *Social Constructionism*, 2nd edn, East Sussex: Routledge.

Burr, V. (2015), *Social Constructionism*, 3rd edn, East Sussex: Routledge.

Bush, T. (1999), 'Crisis or Crossroads? The Discipline of Educational Management in the 1990s', *Educational Management and Administration*, 27 (3): 239–52.

Bush, T. and D. Glover. (2014), 'School Leadership Models: What Do We Know?', *School Leadership and Management*, 34 (5): 553–71.

Campbell-Stephens, R. (2009), 'Investing in Diversity: Changing the Face (and Heart) of Educational Leadership', *School Leadership and Management*, 29 (3): 321–31.

Cho, S., K. W. Crenshaw and L. McCall (2013), 'Towards a Field of Intersectionality Studies: Theory, Applications, and Praxis', *Signs*, 38 (4): 785–810.

Cohen, L., J. Duberley and M. Mallon (2004), 'Social Constructionism in the Study of Career: Accessing the Parts That Other Approaches Cannot Reach', *Journal of Vocational Behavior*, 64 (3): 407–22.

Colebatch, H. K. (2006), *Beyond the Policy Cycle: The Policy Process in Australia*, Crows Nest, New South Wales: Allen and Unwin.

Coleman, M. (2007), 'Gender and Educational Leadership in England: A Comparison of Secondary Headteachers' Views Over Time', *School Leadership and Management*, 27 (4): 383–99.

Coleman, M. and R. Campbell-Stephens (2010), 'Perceptions of Career Progress: The Experience of Black and Minority Ethnic School Leaders', *School Leadership and Management*, 30 (1): 35–49.

Collins, P. H. (1990), *Black Feminist Thought: Knowledge, Consciousness, and the Politics of Empowerment*, Boston: Unwin Hyman.

Collins, P. H. (1991), *Black Feminist Thought: Knowledge, Consciousness, and the Politics of Empowerment*, New York: Routledge.

Collins, P. H. (1993), 'Toward a New Vision: Race, Class and Gender as Categories of Analysis and Connection', *Race, Sex and Class*, 1 (1): 25–45.

Collins, P. H. (1998), 'The Tie That Binds: Race, Gender and US Violence', *Ethnic and Racial Studies*, 21 (5): 917–38.

Collins, P. H. (2000), *Black Feminist Thought: Knowledge, Consciousness, and the Politics of Empowerment*, 2nd edn, New York: Routledge.

Collins, P. H. (2004), *Black Sexual Politics: African Americans, Gender, and the New Racism*, New York: Routledge.

Cox, R. H. (2001), 'The Social Construction of an Imperative: Why Welfare Reform Happened in Denmark and the Netherlands But Not in Germany', *World Politics*, 53 (3): 463–98.

Crawley, S. L., L. J. Foley and C. L. Shehan (2013), 'Creating A World of Dichotomy: Categorising Sex and Gendering Cultural Messages', in S. J. Ferguson (ed.), *Race, Gender, Sexuality, and Social Class: Dimensions of Inequality*, 33–47, Thousand Oaks, CA: SAGE.

Crenshaw, K. (1989), 'Demarginalizing the Intersection of Race and Sex: A Black Feminist Critique of Anti-Discrimination Doctrine, Feminist Theory and Antiracist Politics', *University of Chicago Legal Forum*, 139–67.

DFEE (Department for Education and Employment) (1997), *Excellence in School*, London: HMSO.

DfE (Department for Education) (2010), *The Importance of Teaching: The Schools White Paper*, CM 7980, London: DfE.

Eagly, A. H. and S. J. Karau. (2002), 'Role Congruity Theory of Prejudice toward Female Leaders', *Psychological Review*, 109 (3): 573–98.

Ellemers, N., F. Rink, B. Derks and M. Ryan (2012), 'Women in High Places: When and Why Promoting Women into Top Positions Can Harm Them Individually or as a Group (and How To Prevent This)', *Research in Organizational Behavior*, 32, 163–87.

English, F. W. (2006), 'The Unintended Consequences of a Standardized Knowledge Base in Advancing Educational Leadership Preparation', *Educational Administration Quarterly*, 42 (3): 461–72.

ERA (Education Reform Act) (1988), *Education Reform Act*, London: HMSO.

Essed, P. (1991), *Understanding Everyday Racism*, Newbury Park, CA: SAGE.

Fitzgerald, T. (2014), *Women Leaders in Higher Education: Shattering the Myths Research into Higher Education*, Abingdon: Routledge.

Foreman-Peck, L. and J. Murray. (2008), 'Action Research and Policy', *Journal of Philosophy of Education*, 42 (S1): 145–63.

Gergen, K. J. (1985), 'Social Constructionist Inquiry: Context and Implications', in K. J. Gergen and K. E. Davis (eds), *The Social Construction of the Person*, 3–18, New York: Springer-Verlag.

Gergen, K. J. (1995), 'Social Construction and the Transformation of Identity Politics', Paper Presented at the New School for Social Research Symposium, 7 April, New York City.

Gergen, K. J. (1996), 'Social Psychology as Social Construction: The Emerging Vision', in C. McGarty and A. Haslam (eds), *The Message of Social Psychology: Perspectives on Mind in Society*, 113–28, Oxford: Blackwell.

Gergen, K. J. and M. Gergen (2007), 'Social Construction and Research Methodology', in W. Outhwaite and S. Turner (eds), *The SAGE Handbook of Social Science Methodology*, 461–78, London: SAGE.

Gillborn, D. (2008), *Racism and Education: Coincidence or Conspiracy?* London: Routledge.

Gillborn, D. (2015), 'Intersectionality, Critical Race Theory, and the Primacy of Racism Race, Class, Gender, and Disability in Education', *Qualitative Inquiry*, 21 (3): 277–87.

Guihen, L. (2018), 'The Career Experiences and Aspirations of Women Deputy Head Teachers', *Educational Management Administration and Leadership*, 1–17, Last accessed 5 March 2018: http://journals.sagepub.com/doi/pdf/10.1177/1741143217751727.

Gunter, H. M. (2008), 'Policy and Workforce Reform in England', *Educational Management Administration and Leadership*, 36 (2): 253–70.

Gunter, H. M. (2012), 'The Field of Educational Administration in England', *British Journal of Educational Studies*, 60 (4): 337–56.

Gunter, H. and P. Thomson. (2009), 'The Makeover: A New Logic in Leadership Development in England', *Educational Review*, 61 (4): 469–83.

Hague, L. Y. and C. O. Okpala (2017), 'Voices of African American Women Leaders on Factors That Impact Their Career Advancement in North Carolina Community Colleges', *Journal of Research Initiatives*, 2 (3). Last accessed 5 March 2018: https://digitalcommons.uncfsu.edu/cgi/viewcontent.cgi?article=1122&context=jri.

Hargreaves, A. P. and D. L. Shirley. (2009), *The Fourth Way: The Inspiring Future for Educational Change*, Thousand Oaks, CA: Corwin Press.

Harvey, D. (2005), *A Brief History of Neoliberalism*, Oxford: Oxford University Press.

Hattie, J. (2003), *Teachers Make a Difference: What Is the Research Evidence?* Melbourne: Australian Council for Educational Research.

Heilman, M. E. (2001), 'Description and Prescription: How Gender Stereotypes Prevent Women Ascent up the Organisation Ladder', *Journal of Social Issues*, 57 (4): 657–74.

Heilman, M. E. and T. G. Okimoto. (2007), 'Why Are Women Penalized for Success at Male Tasks? The Implied Communality Deficit', *Journal of Applied Psychology*, 92 (1): 81–92.

hooks, B. (2000), *Where We Stand: Class Matters*, New York: Routledge.

Hull, G., P. B. Scott and B. Smith. (1982), *All the Women Are White, All the Blacks Are Men, But Some of Us Are Brave: Black Women's Studies*, New York: Feminist Press.

Koenig, A. M., A. H. Eagly, A. A. Mitchell and T. Ristikari. (2011), 'Are Leader Stereotypes Masculine? A Meta-Analysis of Three Research Paradigms', *Psychological Bulletin*, 137 (4): 616–42.

Kohn, M. L. and C. Schooler. (1969), 'Class, Occupation, and Orientation', *American Sociological Review*, 34 (5): 659–78.

Kraus, M. W., J. J. Tan and M. B. Tannenbaum. (2013), 'The Social Ladder: A Rank-Based Perspective on Social Class', *Psychological Inquiry*, 24 (2): 81–96.

Lambert, L. G. (2007), 'Lasting Leadership: Toward Sustainable School Improvement', *Journal of Educational Change*, 8 (4): 311–22.

Lander, V. (2011), 'Ethnicity, Whiteness and Identity', in G. Knowles and V. Lander (eds), *Diversity, Equality and Achievement in Education*, 49–64, London: SAGE.

Lander, V. (2014), 'Initial Teacher Education: The Practice of Whiteness', in R. Race and V. Lander (eds), *Advancing Race and Ethnicity in Education*, 93–110, Basingstoke, Hampshire: Palgrave Macmillan.

Mahony, P. and C. Zmroczek (eds) (1997), *Class Matters: 'Working-Class' Women's Perspective on Social Class*, London: Taylor and Francis.

McCall, L. (2005), 'The Complexity of Intersectionality', *Signs*, 30 (3): 1771–800.

Moore, K. (2008), 'Class Formations: Competing Forms of Black Middle-Class Identity', *Ethnicities*, 8: 492–517.

Newby, P. (2014), *Research Methods for Education*, 2nd edn, London: Routledge.

O'Reilly, D. and M. Reed (2010), ' "Leaderism": An Evolution of Managerialism in UK Public Service Reform', *Public Administration*, 88 (4): 960–78.

O'Reilly, D. and M. Reed (2011), 'The Grit in the Oyster: Professionalism, Managerialism and Leaderism as Discourses of UK Public Services Modernization', *Organization Studies*, 32 (8): 1079–101.

Patton, L. D. and J. L. Jordan (2017), 'It's Not About You, It's About Us: A Black Woman Administrator's Efforts to Disrupt White Fragility in an Urban School', *Journal of Cases in Educational Leadership*, 20 (1): 80–91. Last accessed 5 March 2018: http://journals.sagepub.com/doi/pdf/10.1177/1555458916689127.

Phillips, D. and P. Sarre (1995), 'Black Middle-Class Formation in Contemporary Britain, Social Change and the Middle Classes', in T. Butler and M. Savage (eds), *Social Change and the Middle Classes*, 76–91, London: UCL Press.

Race, R. (2015), *Multiculturalism and Education*, 2nd edn, London: Bloomsbury.

Reay, D. (1996), 'Dealing with Difficult Differences: Reflexivity and Social Class in Feminist Research', *Feminism and Psychology*, 6 (3): 443–56.

Reynolds, A. L. and R. L. Pope (1991), 'The Complexities of Diversity: Exploring Multiple Oppressions', *Journal of Counselling and Development*, 70 (1): 174–80.

Richardson A. and C. Loubier (2008), 'Intersectionality and Leadership', *International Journal of Leadership Studies*, 3 (2): 142–61.

Rollock, N., C. Vincent, D. Gillborn and S. Ball (2012), "Middle Class by Profession": Class Status and Identification amongst the Black Middle Classes', *Ethnicities*, 13 (3): 1–23.

Rosette, A. S. and R. W. Livingston (2012), 'Failure Is Not an Option for Black Women: Effects of Organizational Performance on Leaders with Single Versus Dual-Subordinate Identities', *Journal of Experimental Social Psychology*, 48 (5): 1162–67.

Rumberger, R. W. and G. J. Palardy (2005), 'Test Scores, Dropout Rates, and Transfer Rates as Alternative Indicators of High School Performance', *American Educational Research Journal*, 42 (1): 3–42.

Ryde, J. (2009), *Being White in the Helping Professions: Developing Effective Intercultural Awareness*, London: Jessica Kingsley Publishers.

Schein, L. (2001), 'A Global Look at Psychological Barriers to Women's Progression in Management', *Journal of Social Issues,* 57 (4): 675–88.

Sellers, R. M. and J. N. Shelton (2003), 'The Role of Racial Identity in Perceived Racial Discrimination', *Journal of Personality and Social Psychology*, 84 (5): 1079–92.

Simkins, T. (2012), 'Understanding School Leadership and Management Development in England Retrospect and Prospect', *Educational Management Administration and Leadership*, 40 (5): 621–40.

Skeggs, B. (2011), 'Imagining Personhood Differently: Person Value and Autonomist Working-Class Value Practices', *Sociological Review*, 59 (3): 496–513.

Steinberg, S. (2018), 'Advancing in Dialogue: Naming White Supremacy and Patriarchy as Power Blocs in Education', in R. Race (ed.) *Advancing Multicultural Dialogues in Education*, 279–94, Houndsmills: Palgrave Macmillan.

Stephens, N. M., S. S. Townsend, H. R. Markus and L. T. Phillips (2012), 'A Cultural Mismatch: Independent Cultural Norms Produce Greater Increases in Cortisol and More Negative Emotions among First-Generation College Students', *Journal of Experimental Social Psychology*, 48 (6): 1389–93.

Swim, J., L. Cohen and L. Hyers (1998), 'Experiencing Everyday Prejudice and Discrimination', in J. Swim and C. Stangor (eds), *Prejudice: The Target's Perspective*, 37–60, San Diego: Academic Press.

Taylor, T. S. (2007), 'Battling Bias: It's Still about Race but It's Not in Your Face', *Essence*, 4, 164–7.

Weber, L. (2013), 'Defining Contested Concepts', in S. J. Ferguson (ed.), *Race, Gender, Sexuality, and Social Class: Dimensions of Inequality*, 7–19, Thousand Oaks, CA: SAGE.

West, C. and S. Fenstermaker (1995), 'Doing Difference', *Gender and Society*, 9 (1): 8–37.

West, C. and D. Zimmerman (1987), 'Doing Gender', *Gender and Society*, 1 (2): 125–51.

Wilkins, A. C. (2012), 'Becoming Black Women Intimate Stories and Intersectional Identities', *Social Psychology Quarterly*, 75 (2): 173–96.

Woods, P. and T. Simkins (2014), 'Understanding the Local Themes and Issues in the Experience of Structural Reform in England', *Educational Management Administration and Leadership*, 42 (3): 324–40.

Wyatt, M. and J. Silvester (2015), 'Reflections on the Labyrinth: Investigating Black and Minority Ethnic Leaders' Career Experiences', *Human Relations*, 68 (8): 1–27.

7

Black, minority ethnic (BME) staff in further education: Progression and succession planning

Helen Deane

Introduction

As an independent trainer and consultant specializing in supporting the further education (FE) sector, I consider myself a practitioner researcher and in this role have a first hand in recognizing the strategic and political importance of addressing the under-representation of black, minority ethnic (BME) senior leaders. Amidst the backdrop of a major global recession and the UK government's austerity agenda in further education, which has over the last five years seen repeated cuts, redundancies and ongoing upheaval, it is even more important to consider the business, legal, educational and ethical imperatives for challenging this inequality. It is important that the FE sector maintain a dialogue and continually explore the reasons and implications for this inequality with the aim that this will encourage colleges and stakeholders in the sector to look at their internal and micropolitical organizational practices and review their approaches to succession planning strategies and continuing professional development approaches for all staff.

Ethically, a crucial part of this is the issue of being a black researcher working in the sector, and a heightened awareness of this sensitivity is always required and observed. As such, one of the ethical frameworks adopted is based on a 'model of responsibility' taken from a feminist research model put forward by Urban Walker (1997) and further developed and discussed in Edwards and Mauthner (2002). In addition to this, another model put forward by Ahern (1999) is used. Ahern uses reflexivity to identify areas of potential researcher bias in order to ensure that the process of collecting data and analysing and interpreting the findings is as impartial and objective as possible.

The issue in context

Succession planning

Succession planning for the FE sector senior leadership has, in the past, been overlooked, and in terms of supply issues, Greatbatch and Tate (2018) acknowledge that there are significant issues with recruiting leaders with the necessary skill set.

At the time of writing, 45 per cent of principals are over fifty-five, and traditionally a large majority retire at or around the age of sixty (McLoughlin, 2018). It is therefore critical that a pipeline of successors are identified and prepared. A 2017 research project undertaken on behalf of the University and College Union (UCU) demonstrates that the FE sector has made considerable strides in working with learners from diverse backgrounds and has a good track record of tackling inequality and transforming the lives of and communities for those learners (Duckworth and Smith, 2017).

Despite these significant steps, for those from some areas of the BME communities there are still some inequalities that need to be addressed. FE allows a second chance at education; however, there is consistent evidence of underachievement for some groups, for example, black Caribbean students (Avis et al., 2017). This inconsistency in terms of the experience for some learner groups is also seen amongst some staff groups. Research findings since 2002 consistently indicate that there has been little success in terms of increasing the number of BME staff in senior positions (Commission for Black Staff in Further Education, 2002; Deane, 2004; Network for Black Managers, 2005; Mackay and Etienne, 2006; Barnett, Deane and Gittens, 2008; Walker and Fletcher, 2013; Dixon, 2016).

Although there is a lack of data for most protected minority groups, analysis of (partial) FE workforce data for England from 2015 to 2016 suggests that the teaching population within the sector does not reflect the profile of learners, nor does it reflect the profile of local populations, particularly at leadership and governance level. The data provides evidence that 84.9 per cent of staff are of 'white British' ethnic background – which rises to 91 per cent for senior managers. Moreover, 4.5 per cent of staff are of Asian and 3.5 per cent of African/

Caribbean descent, but are only 2.4 per cent or 1.7 per cent respectively of senior managers. This contrasts with 8.2 per cent and 6.4 per cent of learners nationally. The Education and Training Foundation (ETF) workforce data contains national statistics, and we know therefore that there are even more pronounced differences at local levels.

Comparative issues

Similar issues and discussions have been raised in other public-sector organizations where there is clear evidence of the underrepresentation of BME staff in senior leadership positions. In the higher education (HE) sector, for example, Bhopal (2013) finds that BME academics continue to experience racism, confirming little change since findings reported by the Equality Challenge Unit in 2009, and Carter, Fenton and Modood in 1999.

In the local authority context, Andalo (2012) reported that 'just four out of 152 directors of adult services are BME and it is thought that the picture is similar in children's services.' Kline (2014) finds that the proportion of London NHS Trust Board members from a BME background is 8 per cent, an even lower number than was found in 2006 (9.6%), and that in the same period, the proportion of chief executives and chairs from a BME background has decreased from 5.3 per cent. It currently stands at 2.5 per cent.

Critical race theory

Critical race theory (CRT) emerged in the 1970s as a form of legal scholarship which considers judicial conclusions to be based on inherently racist social assumptions. The theory was developed out of the work of Derrick Bell (1987), who recognized that new theories and strategies were needed to address the more subtle forms of racism. CRT offers a framework that can illuminate areas of concern about the inequality of leadership and management progression in FE, and Deane (2012) used CRT to theorize, examine and challenge the ways race and racism implicitly and explicitly impact on BME leadership development practices and discourses in the sector. In this context, CRT asserts and takes the view that racism is ordinary, everyday, normal business and in some form or fashion is experienced by all BME people in the United Kingdom. There are a growing number of studies where CRT is being used in the FE sector, and in this context, rather than a theory, is being seen as a movement. CRT has been defined by Delgado and Stefancic (2001) as a movement that studies and attempts to transform the relationship between race and power by examining the role of race and racism within the foundations of modern culture [. . .] as a movement, it has moved beyond law and has now become common in the academic disciplines of ethnic studies, political science and education. (2–3)

Gillborn (2006) also posits that rather than a theory,

it is a set of interrelated beliefs about the significance of race/racism and how it operates in contemporary western society. (19)

CRT begins with five basic insights or main tenets: counter-storytelling; interest convergence; the permanence of racism; whiteness as property and critique of liberalism. In 2012 research, Deane utilizes all the tenets; however, for the purposes of this chapter, the first two tenets are focused on to be considered as a contribution of CRT to this debate.

Tenet One: counter-storytelling. This tenet demonstrates a commitment to the principle of experiential knowledge, in the form of narratives and storytelling, which is seen as appropriate and an integral part to analysing and understanding racial inequality. As indicated earlier, the use of this tenet is introduced as a key focus of analysis in this study and provides BME staff with the opportunity to tell their narratives with regards to marginalized experiences in colleges.

One example of this is where the experience of a BME member of staff highlights the impact of micropolitical behaviours on her opportunity for progression and is illustrated below (Deane, 2012: 106).

Mina's story

Mina has worked in her college for six years. She describes herself as ambitious and dedicated, and would love to get into a career in management. really because *'I'd like to have more of an influence on the way things are done around here.'* Mina's background is in commercial banking, where she had a successful career. She came into teaching when she started her family as she believed that the hours would fit in with her childcare and other domestic responsibilities. Things have not worked out quite like that, so she is now thinking about taking a step to move up the ladder.

One of the things she believes is stopping her is her unwillingness to get involved in office politics. She does not get involved in the *'it's who you know'* mantra and firmly believes that she will move up the ladder whether or not she *'plays the game'*.

She has, however, noticed that many times she has attended staff meetings where it appears that things have already been discussed, alliances have been made, and that these are not always activities that have taken place on the college premises. As a young mother and as a Muslim, she is not able and chooses not to engage in some of the social activities that she knows a lot of other staff get involved in. This means that she sometimes feels a bit excluded. She does not go to the pub on a Friday night, but knows that this is where a lot of discussion is had and, she believes, decision-making takes place.

Her dilemma is that, despite not wanting to get involved in this side of things, she has seen others who do, and who progress much more quickly up the ladder.

Mina's story gives a picture of how some informal organizational behaviour can impact on the progression of BME staff. The 2012 research found that micropolitically based racist behaviours and *'below the line'* activities are more insidious and damaging. It is these covert acts that currently operate as the main barriers to BME progression, and most BME respondents believed that these obstacles to their progression cannot necessarily be tackled by the further embedding of structural systems and positive action initiatives.

Tenet Two: Interest convergence – This important tenet purports that the interests of BME staff in gaining racial equality have been accommodated only when they have converged with the interests of white staff in power and decision-making positions. It is a view that considers moves to address racism as advancing certain groups materialistically and physically. In the context of BME staff progression, we can look to the positive action leadership development programmes that have taken place in the FE sector. The purpose of these programmes may not have only been to support the development of BME staff and thus address the succession planning issue, but also to address the self-interest of white leaders.

This is a controversial view, which echoes the sentiment of many who believe the emancipation movement would not have ended slavery at that time if it were not for the fact that financially and materially, the white elite were suffering due to the number of slave revolts and the commercial impact of the increasingly negative reputation of the slave industry.

Tenet Three: The permanence of racism. This tenet asserts that racism controls the political, social and economic realms of UK society and subsequently the FE sector. From the CRT perspective, racism is regarded as an inherent part of the FE system, privileging white staff over BME staff, and therefore there is the assumption that any succession planning or leadership development initiatives and plans are ineffective when racism and diversity is ignored in the planning process.

Tenet Four: Whiteness as property. This tenet originated from the embedded racism in American society, where the notion of whiteness operated on different levels, such as the right of possession, the right to use and enjoyment, the right to disposition and the right of exclusion. To better understand this tenet, and in the context of the 2012 study, we can consider the experience shared by one of the interviewees who related her story of a situation where her contribution and suggestions in head of department (HOD) meetings were always ignored. Yet when white colleagues made the same suggestions, these were then heard and acknowledged. Her view was that this was a form of everyday institutional racism experienced on a regular basis by her and her BME colleagues, a view not shared or acknowledged by her white-European counterparts.

To critically examine this situation from a CRT perspective, one would have to consider whether the response from the rest of those at the meeting would have been different if it were a white person who had attempted to make the first contribution. We might also think about what the reaction to her initial contributions would have been if the rest of those at the meeting were all black colleagues.

Tenet Five: Critique of liberalism. This tenet comes from the notion of colour-blindness, the neutrality of the law and equal opportunity for all. According to this tenet, colour-blindness is a mechanism allowing people to ignore racist policies that perpetuate social inequity. Colour-blindness is a perception that people from a BME background are no different from non-minority people. There are several factors that can cause some individuals to adopt this approach, including having deep-seated guilt about being racist, feeling uncomfortable about discussing 'race', having personal issues about 'race', trying to be protective of BME people and not wanting to hurt their feelings, simply misunderstanding issues of 'race' and discrimination and, for BME individuals, wanting to pretend that colour is 'not an issue'.

By using CRT as a framework to examine staff progression and succession planning in the FE sector, policymakers and senior leaders in our colleges and providers have to acknowledge that racism is endemic in our sector. The impact of such an acknowledgement can only be to take drastic measures to address the situation. In this regard, adopting a CRT framework for the discourse on BME staff progression and succession planning we know that

- CRT as a theory of 'race' and racism in the study of leadership and succession planning in the FE sector has not yet been considered as research framework;
- many CRT themes are based on 'race' issues in US terms; however, it cannot be ignored that the basic ideology of the concept of 'race' as discussed earlier, is common to both Europe and the United States; and
- CRT can seem threatening and alienating to the many people who believe that racism is a thing of the past and is no longer a major issue, particularly in the FE sector.

Positive action

The key form of positive action employed under UK law is the use of measures to support, enable and encourage people who share a protected characteristic (as covered in the Equality Act, 2010) to overcome disadvantage caused by that characteristic. In such circumstances employers are permitted to take proportionate action to enable or encourage persons who share the protected characteristic to overcome the disadvantage they face, to meet their particular needs, or to enable or encourage their participation in the relevant activity.

The recognition of continued under-representation of BME staff in senior leadership positions has led to the development of positive action initiatives in a wide range of public sector and some private-sector organizations. These include positive action recruitment practices in the civil service (Positive Action Pathway programme), graduate placement schemes, mentoring programmes and various BME leadership development programmes in a number of NHS trusts.

In terms of positive action in the FE sector, we know that positive action initiatives have taken place to support BME staff progression and have attracted mixed views in terms of the merits of this approach. We also know that there is considerable confusion and misunderstanding about the purpose and justification of positive action (CEL, 2008).

The main positive action scheme in the FE sector was the Black Leadership Initiative (BLI), which ran from 2002 to 2015. The overall brief of the BLI was to address under-representation by introducing practical measures to improve career development opportunities for BAME-sector staff, particularly those in leadership and management roles. The innovative programme developed and delivered a range of interventions, including secondments, work shadowing, mentoring and career development programmes. Initially funded by the Learning and Skills Council (LSC), then the Centre for Excellence in leadership (CEL) and finally the Learning and Skills Improvement Service (LSIS), the initiative initially exceeded its targets of reach (Zahno et al., 2004), and in a more recent evaluation of the project, Walker and Fletcher (2013) report that

> as well as engaging and being otherwise involved with approximately 4,580 BAME participants over the 10 year period, the activity of BLI has involved the voluntary participation and engagement of several hundred senior leaders, including college principals. (27)

The evaluation goes on to report that the project resulted in

> a powerful impact on the careers of participating BAME staff; an accelerated increase in sector leadership capacity; an effective professional network with good reach and participation across colleges, leadership levels, academic, business support and other roles, and teaching staff, especially in particular context; a substantially raised profile of BAME staff, issues and challenges; a shift in expectations with respect to the ethnic profile of senior and middle leadership teams evidence of progress in addressing issues of under-representation, particularly with respect to college principal positions and in particular contexts. (LSIS, 2012: 36)

A CRT lens may be applied to the positive action approach and, in particular, the tenet of interest convergence is particularly apt here, where the interests of the majority are also served by the interests of minorities. Many of those involved in the project included senior white staff and Office for Standards in Education, Children Services and Skills inspectors who were trained as mentors and who undertook a range of leadership and race training initiatives.

It can be argued that as the interests of BME staff were advanced, when they converged with the interests of white staff, the advances made became given up as the impact and effect of austerity and the cutbacks started to threaten the leadership status of white staff. 'Demand-led' and 'customer-driven' approaches to funding, austerity and political expediency have spurred decision makers to abandon positive action and, some would argue, revert to the old ways of doing things. For example, anecdotal evidence suggests that as funding cuts, mergers and restructures continue to dominate the FE landscape, the sector has returned to the most cost-effective ways of promoting from small pools of staff that are limited in diversity. However, it cannot be ignored that the issue of lack of racial diversity at the top was already present before austerity set in. Presently, it can be said that we are witnessing the reverse of this process: a period of pronounced *interest-divergence*, when senior sector leaders imagine that a direct advantage will accrue from the further exclusion of initiatives such as the BLI.

The study and evidence

The focus group

In order to locate the 2012 research within the current context, a focus group was conducted with five BME participants including a current principal, senior managers and the last chief executive of the key FE organization committed to supporting BME professionals (Deane, 2018). The group was held in order to augment the 2012 research and provide a review and update to the findings. A thematic approach was taken to analyse the findings from the focus group, and for small-scale studies of this nature, it is a flexible method that can be assigned to a range of research approaches. Braun and Clarke (2006) provide a six-phase guide which was a very useful framework for conducting this kind of analysis, and based on this framework four themes were identified. The themes were identified as (a) Succession planning, (b) BME staff attrition rates, (c) Attitudes and (d) Micropolitical behaviour.

The focus group interview began with an explanation of the purpose of the update to the research and included a discussion about why there had not been enough progress in the representation of BME staff in the sector and implications of this. A summary of the findings and evidence from the focus group are all consistent with the views found in Deane, 2012:

- FE institutions are still not taking a strategic approach to succession planning.
- Internal micropolitical structures and individual behaviours have a negative impact on BME professionals.
- The 'glass ceiling' effect is still in existence in FE within senior management and governing bodies.
- Austerity has been used as an excuse to allow the issue of race and leadership to drop off the agenda.

The findings from the focus group highlighted a range of factors that provided clear evidence that the inequality issue regarding senior leadership representation in FE is still due to racism, both institutional and individual.

Succession planning

The discussion highlighted the following key areas that were continuing to be of major concern when it came to succession planning strategies in the sector.

- FE institutions are not taking a strategic approach to succession planning, with internal unplanned activities involving the use of networks and other informal recruitment processes which can result in discriminatory practices.
- Individual, uncoordinated measures, including talent spotting and unofficial headhunting, increase the likelihood of discriminatory practice.
- There is high priority given to the idea of succession planning, and the ageing profile of the FE-sector workforce is recognized.
- The importance of better recruiting, retaining and progressing BME staff as part of effective succession planning is acknowledged; however, it is conceded that steps to support BME staff progression are mainly instigated as individuals and not as part of college-wide or corporate approaches, which are largely absent.

BME staff retention and attrition rates

When BME staff come up against the 'glass ceiling' syndrome, they choose to leave the sector for other professions, including becoming independent consultants and trainers. Colleges are placing a high emphasis on equality; however, in reality, the policies and strategies in place are not working. It is acknowledged that where senior managers actively support individual BME staff members, this succeeds in motivating and retaining BME staff.

Attitudes

- There is a lack of awareness and a lack of willingness to engage in discussions around the negative experiences of BME professionals.
- There is a lack of recognition of the relevance and appropriateness of multicultural leadership styles.

Micropolitical behaviours

Focus group participants concur with Deane (2012) and reported that the most significant barriers were the institutional and micropolitical behaviours that reflect a lack of understanding, awareness and value of the contributions that BME professionals bring to colleges. They believe the impact and outcomes of this level of institutional behaviour on BME FE professionals clearly parallels the behaviours associated with institutional racism. Comments included the following:

> Internal micropolitical structures and individual behaviours have a negative impact on the progression of BME professionals [. . .]

> Organizational cultures and micro-political practices in my college continue to determine who does and does not get promoted.

Discussion

The focus group discussion and current observations tell us what is already known and acknowledged in the FE sector. So the questions remain, what more can be done and what can be done now? The challenge and implications are to provide suggestions to a sector that already understands the need to address the lack of BME representation at the leadership level very well, and which has appeared to have tried a range of initiatives and strategies.

This chapter proposes key areas for further discussion if the sector seriously wishes to support the succession planning crisis and find a sustainable solution to the BME under-representation at senior levels in the sector.

It is clear that there are deeper issues to deal with that cannot be addressed by the further embedding of structural systems, leadership development programmes and positive action initiatives alone. The discussion and the suggestions offered are based on the fact that previous and current strategies to address the issue by breaking down the barriers to BME progression have not and are not working quickly enough.

The hypothesis for this discussion is that many people who claim to be supporting the agenda for BME progression are not really signed up because they have not honestly examined and/or had the opportunity to discuss their own understanding and position about 'race' and racism. Based on the experiences and thoughts of the participants from the focus group, this is not a surprising revelation, as many of the approaches, ideas and even the mindset that FE practitioners have around leadership, diversity and succession planning issues generally, have been driven by external policymakers. It is, therefore, not only the case that FE institutions need to internally address equality and diversity issues, but it is also important that the sector goes back to basics and encourages colleges and providers to address internal issues around race and racism.

Recommendations

The ETF in its first operational plan set out the aim to ensure that the senior leadership of the sector reflects the student population in its diversity by 2020. There are, however, no clear documented plans on how this is to be achieved. It is therefore recommended that in order to achieve this, the following should be discussed and considered by the sector.

Succession planning strategies

All FE colleges and institutions should develop succession management strategies that are published, and that include clear plans of how they intend to address the issue of BME staff representation. These plans could form part of their Equality and Diversity Impact Assessments and would therefore be subject to the monitoring processes that the impact assessments of all institutions in the public sector have to adhere to. To demonstrate true commitment to this agenda, the FE funding bodies should monitor the performance against the plan and, ideally, some allocation of funding should be attached to this performance indicator. The implication of taking this important step will have the effect of raising the strategic importance of the issue, and this will begin to address the culture and climate of our FE colleges as is always the case when funding is attached to a performance indicator.

The re-introduction of positive action initiatives

As early as 2009, the lack of BME representation at governor and board level for organizations in FE has been identified as an ongoing key factor in terms of the selection of BME senior staff in the sector (Equality Challenge Unit, 2009). For this reason, the sector must consider bringing in positive action policies and initiatives for a fixed period of time. Reintroducing the positive action initiatives that were in place under the sector leadership of CEL and LSIS, including increased opportunities for networking, mentoring and work shadowing for all BME staff, as well as access to positive action initiatives and training programmes in leadership development, is paramount. Evidence has shown that these steps have been successful in preparing BME staff for leadership positions (Walker and Fletcher, 2013). Although we know that not all BME professionals will necessarily attend positive action activities, further programmes of this nature should be made available so that the opportunity of 'levelling of the playing field' can be taken advantage of by all. Where providers only have a small number of BME staff, they should ensure that those staff are fully supported to attend externally run positive action courses.

Positive discrimination (affirmative action)

Given the importance and indeed the acknowledgement that we must address this issue urgently, a system of positive discrimination may also need to be considered and introduced for all senior management vacancies for a fixed period of time. It is recommended that the sector should consider allowing shortlists to contain a quota of 50 per cent of suitable candidates from a BME background. This policy should be widely communicated and publicized so that BME professionals can see the importance the sector is placing on addressing this issue and thus give them the confidence and motivation to apply for vacancies. This will have the added effect of not only addressing the numbers to better reflect the ethnic make-up of the student population and balance the representation of senior teams, but will also support the crucial process of tackling the internal culture in our institutions.

Content of leadership and continuing professional development (CPD) programmes

All sector leadership programmes run by government-funded organizations responsible for improving quality in the sector, should include an element or embedding of elements which allow for the raising of awareness and the understanding of the BME experience, cultural awareness and theories of 'race' including CRT. The implication of doing this will demonstrate that there is the motivation and governmental drive from the top and from the outset of succession planning initiatives.

As well as taking on board this structural approach, institutions need to strongly encourage individual members of staff to undertake continuing professional development (CPD) programmes that include an element of examining self, in terms of personal understanding and the practice of 'race' issues. This personal examination has to take place for all of those involved in FE, including stakeholder leaders, senior managers and all staff as well as those from a BME background, since it will be the fundamental basis for any structural and organizational cultural changes to be sustained and thus impact the succession planning crisis in the sector.

Over the past decade, CRT scholars in education have produced a significant body of work theorizing the impact of 'race' and racism in education. It is time that this is now adopted in the field of leadership. By linking theories of 'race' and CRT to everyday practices in our organizations, sector leaders and managers will understand how this development is relevant to a range of timely FE topics including the areas of succession planning and management, equality and diversity and positive action.

Detailed data collection

Running alongside this is the importance of accurate, detailed, transparent and good-quality data collection and analysis. Since the demise of the Lifelong Learning UK (LLUK), detailed information about the ethnic makeup of the staff in the sector according to roles and levels is no longer included in the Staff Individualised Record (SIR) data (ETF, 2018). The compilation of the information does place an administrative 'burden' on colleges, however, in terms of the importance of addressing the succession planning agenda. This will be justified by the value that the information will bring to discussion, debate and policy. It should also extend to qualitative data gathering, staff surveys and the monitoring of outcomes in different areas (e.g. promotions).

Develop and sustain dialogue about BME staff progression

The above steps cannot be taken in isolation, and in order that BME staff succession management strategies, positive action measures and the content of leadership development programmes can be clearly understood and remain relevant, open and honest discussions have to be encouraged and conducted into the nature of the ongoing prejudice faced by BME staff groups and why they continue to be under-represented in senior positions.

In order to ensure BME staff are both retained and attracted to working in the sector and thereby develop a diverse workforce of senior leaders, we need to have the confidence to develop a culture of openness and trust in which to develop a dialogue and to recognize the importance of maintaining a consistent focus on the agenda with a view not only to delivering policy and procedures but also to developing a culture of inclusion. As opposed to a debate, a dialogue should draw participants from as many parts of the FE community as possible to exchange information face-to-face, share personal stories and experiences, honestly express perspectives, clarify viewpoints, and develop solutions to concerns about BME staff progression and the impact on succession planning in the sector. Specific proposals of how this might be done include key stakeholders coming together to fund and organize

- a few small groups meeting once or twice;
- a large public meeting with panellists and questions from the audience;
- a series of small groups from across the FE community meeting for six weeks or more, concluding with a large meeting;
- a year-long commitment among a group of key FE leaders to study, reflect on and discuss BME staff progression issues; and
- college action research projects aimed at understanding the issues around BME staff progression concluding with a sector conference.

All of these approaches can be achieved; however, it will take commitment, courage and perseverance. It will mean that those who are in the position will have to take steps to create and change policies around human resourcing and staff training and development. This might include looking at staff induction processes, reviewing internal training policies and ensuring that they inform external leadership training and development content and other sector-run leadership programmes.

FE institutions should also review their organizational communication structures and ensure that there is an acknowledgement that micropolitical behaviour can and does have an effect on their decision-making processes in terms of BME staff progression. Micropolitics has to be recognized as belonging with any discussions about institutional discriminatory practices, and this message should be communicated and publicized so that all staff are aware that these practices will be observed and monitored, particularly in terms of their impact on the progression of BME staff.

And, most importantly, we must encourage the engagement of a more honest and open dialogue where those who are experiencing barriers to their progression are heard ands listened to.

Conclusion

Leadership is the key to the success of any organization, and senior leaders need to own leadership development activities within their organizations and build a systematic succession planning process that includes and provides BME talented individuals with the support they need to accelerate their own development. The readers of this chapter are strongly encouraged to consider the challenges which have emerged, reflect on the issues raised in the context of their own professional practice and academic interest and, where possible, support the opportunity to open up a dialogue and discussion. It is hoped that this work will contribute to the development of a view of leadership development within FE that will focus on the changing of internal organizational cultures, which are clearly the areas that need addressing in order to truly deal with BME staff progression and succession planning in the FE sector.

References

Avis, J., K. Orr and P. Warmington (2017), 'Race and Vocational Education and Training in England', *Journal of Vocational Education and Training*, 69 (3): 292–310, doe: 10.1080/13636820.2017.1289551.

Barnett, P., H. Deane and I. Gittens (2008), *Succession Planning and Racial Equality in the Further Education System*, London: Centre for Excellence in Leadership.

Bathmaker, A. M. and P. Harnett (2010), *Exploring Learning, Identity and Power through Life History and Narrative Research*, Abingdon: Routledge.

Belgutay, J. (Feb 2016), 'We're Losing the Fight for More Black Principals'. Last accessed 15 March 2018: https://www.tes.com/news/further-education/breaking-news/ were-losing-fight-more-black-principals.

Bell, D. (1980), 'Brown v. Board of Education and the Interest-Convergence Dilemma', *Harvard Law Review*, 93 (3): 518–34.

Bell, D. (1987), *And We Are Not Saved: The Elusive Quest for Racial Justice*, New York: Basic Books.

Blase, J. (1991), 'The Micropolitical Perspective', in J. Blase (ed.). *The Politics of Life in Schools: Power, Conflict and Cooperation*, 1–18, London, SAGE.

Braun, V. and V. Clarke (2006), 'Using Thematic Analysis in Psychology', *Qualitative Research in Psychology*, 3: 77–101.

Centre for Excellence Evaluation Unit (2006), *An Evaluation of the First Steps Programme*, Lancaster University: Lancaster University Management School.

Cole, M. (2009), 'Critical Race Theory Comes to the UK', *Ethnicities*, 9 (2): 246–69.

Commission for Black Staff in Further Education (2002), *Challenging Racism: Further Education Leading the Way*, London: Association of Colleges.

Deane, H. (2004), 'The Black Professional in Further Education', unpublished doctoral diss., Institute of Education, London.

Deane, H. (2012), 'Black and Minority Ethnic (BME) Staff Progression: A Leadership Succession Crisis in Further Education and Sixth Form Colleges', EdD thesis, Institute of Education, London.

Delgado, R. and J. Stefancic (2001), *Critical Race Theory*, New York: New York University Press.

Dixon, A. (2016), *Developing a Leadership Pipeline for BAME Staff in Further Education and Training: A Report on the Scoping Phase*, London: The Education and Training Foundation.

Dobson, M. and D. S. Dobson (2001), *Enlightening Souls – Office Politics, Understanding, Coping with and Winning the Game without Losing Your Soul*, New York: American Management Association.

Duckworth, V. and R. Smith (2017) *Transformational Further Education: Empowering People and Communities*. Available online at http://transforminglives.web.ucu.org.uk/.

Education and Training Foundation (2015), *Further Education Workforce Data for England: Analysis of the 2013–14 Staff Individualised Record (SIR) Data*. Last accessed 15 March 2018: http://www.et-foundation.co.uk/wp-content/uploads/2015/04/RPT-SIR22-230415.pdf.

Education and Training Foundation (2017), *Equality, Diversity and Inclusion Strategy 2017–2020*. Last accessed 15 March 2018: http://www.et-foundation.co.uk/wp-content/uploads/2015/05/EDI-Strategy-2017-20-PUBLISHED.pdf.

Education and Training Foundation (2018) *Further Education Workforce Data for England: Analysis of the 2016–17 Staff Individualised Record (SIR) Data*: Last accessed 15 April 2018: http://www.et-foundation.co.uk/wp-content/uploads/2018/03/Staff-Individualised-Records-Data-Report-SIR-25-2016-17.pdf.

Gillborn, D. (2006), 'Critical Race Theory and Education: Racism and Anti-Racism in Educational Theory and Praxis', *Discourse: Studies in the Cultural Politics of Education*, 27 (1): 11–32.

Greatbatch, D. and S. Tate (2018), *Teaching, Leasdership and Governance in Further Education*. Department of Education. Last accessed 15 April 2018: https://assets.publishing.service.gov.uk/government/uploads/system/uploads/attachment_data/file/680306/Teaching__leadership_and_governance_in_Further_Education.pdf.

Hirsch, W. (2000), *Succession Planning Demystified*, Brighton: Institute for Employment Studies.

Hoyle, E. (1982), 'Micropolitics of Educational Organisations', *Educational Management and Administration*, 10 (2): 87–98.

Hoyle, E. (1986), *The Politics of School Management*. London: Hodder and Stoughton

Kline, R. (2014), *The 'Snowy White Peaks' of the NHS: A Survey of Discrimination in Governance and Leadership and the Potential Impact on Patient Care in London and England*. Last accessed 15 March 2018: https://www.mdx.ac.uk/__data/assets/pdf_file/0015/50190/The-snowy-white-peaks-of-the-NHS.pdf.pdf.

Ladson-Billings, G. and W. Tate (1995), 'Towards a Critical Race Theory of Education', *Teachers College Record*, 97: 47–68.

Learning and Skills Improvement Service (2010), *The Voices of Women: Leadership and Gender in the Further Education*. Last accessed 15 March 2018: https://www.lancaster.ac.uk/media/lancaster-university/content-assets/documents/lums/lsis/0920r8.pdf.

LLUK (Lifelong Learning UK) (2009a), Further Education Workforce Data, SIR. London: LLUK.

LLUK (Lifelong Learning UK) (2009b), Impact of the professionalisation of the FE workforce. London: LLUK.

LLUK (Lifelong Learning UK) (2009c), *Workforce Strategy for the Further Education Sector in England, 2007–2012 (revised)*, London: LLUK.

Lumby, J., K. Bhopal, M. Dyke, F. Maringe and M. Morrison (2007), Integrating Diversity in Leadership in Further Education: Leadership for Learning and Skills Sector, CEL Research Programme 2006-07, Lancaster: Centre for Excellence in Leadership.

Mackay, F. and J. Etienne (2006), 'Black Managers in Further Education: Career Hopes and Hesitations', *Educational Management Administration and Leadership*, 34 (1): 9–28.

McLoughlin, F. (Jan. 2018), 'We Need to Prepare the Next Generation of College Principals'. Last accessed 15 March 2018: https://www.tes.com/news/further-education/breaking-news/we-need-prepare-next-generation-college-principals.

Murphy, N. (2009), 'Succession Planning in Practice', *IRS Employment Review*, 917 (9): 5.

Network for Black Managers (2005), *Survey of the Numbers of Black and Minority Ethnic Governors in the FE Colleges Sector of Englan*, London: Centre for Excellence in Leadership.

NBP (Network for Black Professionals) (2005), *Attrition Rate of BME Managers in the Further Education Colleges Sector of England*, Wolverhampton: NBP.

OEOD (Office of Equal Opportunity and Diversity) (2005), *A Brief History of Affirmative Action*. Last accessed 24 May 2009: http://www.oeod.uci.edu/aa.html.

Omi, M. and H. Winant (1994), 'On the Theoretical Status of the Concept of Race', in D. Gillborn and G. Gladson-Billings (eds) (2004), *The Routledge Falmer Reader in Multi-cultural Education*, 7–15, London: RoutledgeFalmer.

Skyers, S. and J. Poorman (2009), *An Evaluation of the Learning and Skills Improvement Service (LSIS) Positive Action Programmes*, London: LSIS.

Sturm, Susan P. (2001), 'Second Generation Employment Discrimination: A Structural Approach', *Columbia Law Review*, 101 (1). Last accessed 15 March 2018: https://ssrn.com/abstract=244407.

Taylor, E., D. Gillborn and G. Ladson-Billings (eds) (2009), *Foundations of Critical Race Theory in Education*, New York: Routledge.

The Guardian (Oct. 2017), 'Austerity Is Laying Waste to Progress on Diversity at the Top of Local Government'. Last accessed 15 March 2018: https://www.theguardian.com/public-leaders-network/2017/oct/12/austerity-waste-diversity-local-government.

Walker, E. and M. Fletcher (2013), *The Black Leadership Initiative – The First Ten Years; An Evaluation of the Impact Made by the Black Leadership Initiative over Ten Years 2002–2012*, London: Centre for Excellence in Leadership.

8

Understanding race and educational leadership in higher education: Exploring the black, minority ethnic (BME) experience

Jason Arday

Introduction

Within the UK higher education system diversification of academic staff has always been problematic, with the problem firmly embedded through inequitable structures (Mirza, 2017). As a sector, there are enduring and persistent institutional structures such as dominant Eurocentric curricula and poor representation of black, minority ethnic (BME) academic staff at junior and senior levels, which facilitate inequality. These enduring structures present a challenge for disrupting or dismantling racial inequality within higher education in the United Kingdom (Bhopal, 2014; Bhopal and Jackson, 2013). Fundamentally, such structures do not embrace the notion of valuing difference or diversification as a vehicle for inclusion (Chun and Evans, 2009). The notion that universities are a reflection of a postmodern, multicultural society is questionable given the lack of diversification throughout the academy (Andrews, 2016; Kezar and Eckel, 2008). This is evident in the low numbers of BME academic staff within the sector, particularly in senior leadership positions (Iverson, 2008; Shilliam, 2014).

The stimulus for this chapter derives from the ongoing debate within higher education, which situates racial inequality and discrimination as a barrier to greater diversification within the sector. Informing and mobilizing the ongoing debate regarding practical and penetrative actions on equality regarding the diversification of leadership within higher education is imperative in creating institutions that are reflective of ever-increasing diverse student populations. Importantly, this chapter will contribute to the ongoing discourse, which advocates that, although there have been significant advances in staff and student equality and diversity undertaken through widening participation interventions, there is still substantial work required to penetrate the deeply entrenched layers of inequality that permeate the sector. The under-representation of BME academic staff at senior leadership levels speaks to a need to evaluate existing policies, legislation and interventions, which aim to address inequity within higher education. In mobilizing the agenda for greater diversification within leadership positions, we are beginning to observe a disrupting of these normative and inequitable cultures as individuals within the academy begin to realize that such cultures are no longer tenable or reflective of an inclusive society (Singh and Kwhali, 2015). The Equality Challenge Unit (ECU) has been integral in attempting to challenge the sector to think more progressively about how they initiate inspiring and strategic approaches that aim to facilitate continuous cultural and systemic change, which embraces greater diversification within senior leadership levels. The Race Equality Charter initiated by ECU has worked with several universities to pilot and evaluate the effectiveness of the Charter Mark in determining how university institutions are attempting to disrupt patterns of hegemony and normativity that have ensured that ethnic minorities continue to remain on the periphery of the academy (Law, 2017; Singh and Kwhali, 2015).

After outlining the discrepancy in the proportions of BME staff in leadership positions in higher education, the chapter focuses on leadership issues in relation to the UK higher education landscape and explores why BME staff continue to be under-represented in these positions. Considerations illuminate the landscape of higher education regarding staffing, understanding the nuances of diversity and leadership and situating a personal, lived experience as a BME leader. Finally, the chapter concludes with some considerations for advancing greater diversification within senior leadership hierarchies within the academy.

Understanding the landscape: BME staffing in UK higher education

Understanding the landscape of higher education is complex particularly when illuminating patterns of inequity. Within the sector, inequality remains prevalent throughout all areas of higher education, including staffing, admissions and employment, with some of the most acute disparities occurring within academic professional and senior leadership roles (Alexander and Arday, 2015). Opportunities to access for BME academics have been problematic due to the structural inequalities and systems within organizations that enable others whilst disadvantaging minority ethnic groups. Many instances of racial inequity reside within conscious and unconscious biases, which lean towards showing preferential treatment based on a set of protected characteristics such as ethnicity, race, class, gender, religion and sexuality (Singh and Kwhali, 2015). An important distinction to note is that patterns and access to opportunity for BME academics differ in Russell Group and Post 1992 university institutions (Alexander and Arday, 2015). Within Post 1992 universities there has historically been a higher saturation of BME academic staff in comparison to Russell Group institutions (Bhopal, 2014; ECU, 2015).

Recent discourses and social commentaries have begun to explore and reveal the institutional racism which pervades higher education at the expense of BME individuals (Bhopal, 2014; Pilkington, 2011; Pilkington, 2013). Presently, higher education reflects an exclusive space which marginalizes ethnic minority groups with regards to gaining access and opportunity to certain types of prosperous capital and becoming socially mobile (Boliver, 2013; Pilkington, 2013). The packaging of higher education curricula has historically resembled a dominant Eurocentric curriculum, often leaving BME individuals on the periphery of academia (Arday, 2017; Mirza, 2017). Contention emerges when considering the types of embodied knowledge that are valued within normative white academic spaces (Leonardo, 2016). Attempts to decolonize the existing curriculum within higher education have often resulted in a reluctance to acknowledge the role that BME individuals play in explaining and relaying their own histories, in a way that is not distorted or conveniently processed for the 'consumer' (UCU, 2016; Smith, 2012). Such contexts are further exacerbated when aspects of representation and diversification are considered.

Recent research (Tate and Bagguley, 2017; Williams, 2013) indicates that while the numbers of ethnic minority students entering higher education continue to increase, this is not reflected in the recruitment of academic staff. This becomes even more pertinent when focusing on the lowly percentage of BME academics who constitute 7.8 per cent of the total UK population (Alexander and Arday, 2015; Bhopal et al., 2016; HESA, 2016; ECU, 2014). However, this could be interpreted as a 'fair' representative figure when compared with a BME UK population of 14 per cent (UK Demographics Profile, 2014). This figure, however, does not conceal the disparity concerning this discourse, as under-representation continues to reinforce the lack of equality and diversity within higher education.

Research examining (Alexander and Arday, 2015; Gillborn, 2015; UCU, 2016) racial discourse within education, aligned to inequality, has highlighted concern about marginalization and adequate career progression for BME individuals. The ECU suggests that BME individuals within higher education institutions (HEIs) are less likely to benefit from permanent or open-ended contracts of employment and opportunities to gain employment within the sector in comparison to their white counterparts (ECU, 2011; 2013). Despite legislation (Race Relations Act, 1976; Equality Act, 2010) to address inequality within society which often pertains to rhetoric, evidence suggests that BME staff and students continue to experience significant disadvantage in higher education in comparison to their white counterparts (Bhopal and Jackson, 2013; ECU, 2013; Pilkington, 2013). Within higher education matters of representation and diversification are often intertwined with race equality documents which are used as a barometer and indicator for equality and diversity practices and competence (Ahmed, 2007). Coincidently, Pilkington (2013) notes that such surface approaches often provide a masquerade for the underlying issues that allow racial inequality to be fluidly maintained through overt and covert discriminatory institutional mechanisms.

The concern to address issues of race inequality and systematic racism within higher education institutions lies in the hands of senior university stakeholders and administrators, best positioned to prioritize this agenda. Central to this argument is the matter of priority and where diversifying staff populations to reflect better representation ranks on the agenda of senior university stakeholders tasked with the responsibility of facilitating such endeavours (ECU, 2015). Current strategies for challenging inequality have led many to question the extent to which HEIs addressing issues concerning racial inequities, particularly regarding access to higher education for aspiring BME academics (Bhopal, Brown and Jackson, 2016; HESA, 2014; Pilkington, 2013). Further empirical research (Gillborn, 2010; Gillborn, 2014; Lymperopoulou and Parameshwaran, 2014; ECU, 2014) signifies the dearth of BME staff at the senior management level and the professorial level, when drawing comparisons with white counterparts. This inequity is compounded within the United Kingdom, with statistics revealing alarming disproportionate figures which indicate that overall, 92.4 per cent of university professors are white, while comparatively only 0.49 per cent are black (Bhopal, 2014; Khan, 2015). Further lowly figures reveal just 15 black academics in senior management positions such as directors, heads of department and deans within HEIs across the United Kingdom (Khan,

2015). In attempting to unpack such inequality, it is important to acknowledge recruitment processes which continuously facilitate unconscious and implicit biases that disadvantage BME individuals wishing to pursue a career in academia (ECU, 2013; 2014).

Understanding the barriers for BME leaders within the academy

Research undertaken by the ECU suggests that these types of biases occur automatically and are triggered by making judgements and assessments of people's capabilities, influenced by backgrounds, types of social capital and personal experiences (ECU, 2014). ECU state that individuals in positions of power and authority must recognize and acknowledge potential personal biases and mitigate their impact on distinct behaviours and decision-making. This anecdote becomes a powerful tool for the validation of existing racial inequality within higher education when we closely examine who maintains the power, and which types of individuals are in a position to exercise that power (Andrews and Palmer, 2016; Modood, 2012). Traditionally, Gillborn (2008) asserts that the beneficiaries of power and privilege within academia have been white middle-class individuals. The cycle of inequality has been maintained by prevailing, normative orthodoxies which are reinforced through various facets of inequity and disparity (Gillborn, 2008; Mirza, 2015). Consequently, the landscape of academia operates within a patriarchal, hegemonic normatively white backdrop, where white privilege is consciously and unconsciously advocated as habitual practice, which subsequently marginalizes and excludes ethnic minority groups (McIntosh, 1990; Warren, 2007). The context presented suggests that continually reinforced discriminatory practices often occur at the expense of BME individuals attempting to enter the academy or progress within academia (Leathwood, Maylor and Moreau, 2009).

The extreme paucity of black academic presence at the top, both in terms of professoriate and senior management, requires systemic transformational change, with the central focus for this transformation targeting better diversification and representation particularly at senior levels (Bhopal and Brown, 2016; Shilliam, 2014). Organizational cultures which continue to omit and marginalize the contribution of BME academics ultimately undermine their own diversity agendas towards challenging racial discrimination and creating inclusive spaces (Ahmed, 2012; Pilkington, 2011). Universities have a responsibility to implement cultural and organizational changes, which create inclusive spaces that embrace greater diversification and ethnic difference (UCU, 2016; Williams, 2013).

Understanding diversity and leadership

Diversity has become a ubiquitous term within education, often intertwined with inclusion. Frequently this term (inclusion) forms the basis for policy and practice discourses concerned with equity and equality (Law, 2017). Research undertaken by ECU (2015), HESA (2016) and Bhopal and Brown (2016), based on a combination of survey, focus group and interview data, confirmed the under-representation of BME staff at senior levels, and revealed a number of concerns amongst staff. The findings indicated the subtle silencing of BME staff in cases of discrimination, complacency on equality issues, a minimalist approach to statutory duties (e.g. simply complying with prohibited conduct on unlawful discrimination), and evidence of nepotism and personal discretion in promotion and employment (Bhopal and Brown, 2016; ECU, 2015). The disruption of these inequitable cultures for BME staff can leave residual effects which affect self-esteem, and leave BME staff open to claims of hypersensitivity or troublemaking when challenging racism (Alexander and Arday, 2015; Shephard, 2017). Further, notions of diversity continue to be undermined by a continuous lack of institutional awareness regarding the difficulties faced by BME staff (Singh and Kwhali, 2015).

Recent research (Bhopal and Brown, 2016; Singh and Kwhali, 2015; Mirza, 2017; Shephard, 2017) indicates that BME staff within higher education is less likely to be promoted to leadership positions than their white counterparts. While there have been some mechanisms to evaluate and identify patterns of BME leadership within the sector (HESA, 2016; ECU, 2015; Singh and Kwhali, 2015), institutions continue to remain unaccountable for not actively diversifying senior leadership teams within universities (Pilkington, 2013). A significant factor that has facilitated the spiral of racial discrimination is unconscious bias (Jarboe, 2016; Rollock, 2016). Recent literature has espoused that unconscious biases persistently affect aspects of racial inequality regarding the disparity in BME leadership appointments within higher education (Alexander and Arday, 2015; ECU, 2015; UCU, 2016). Jarboe (2016) states that while few individuals set out to consciously discriminate, we all obtain unconscious biases and preferences that influence our judgements and decision-making. This becomes a powerful indicator of how senior stakeholders within universities appoint and promote candidates or colleagues, which resemble tenets of their own cultural, gender, class or racial identity (Jarboe, 2016). The caveat to this particular narrative is that often many of these circumstances are situated within a dominant white male leadership hierarchy that has traditionally marginalized ethnic minority groups and women (Jarboe, 2016; Singh and Kwhali, 2015).

The landscape of inequality within the academy has ensured that BME academics continue to remain on the periphery of leadership opportunities. Often faculty of colour experience difficulties in trying to gain promotion to senior leadership roles, normally punctuated against a backdrop of racism discrimination, racist micro-aggressive cultures and inequitable levels of hypersurveillance, which often result in a questioning of professional capabilities (Bhopal, 2014; ECU, 2011; Leathwood et al., 2009; Singh and Kwahli, 2015). Recent narratives have attempted to proffer a changing landscape, particularly in reference to the installation of Valarie Amos in 2015 as the first black female vice chancellor at the School of African and Oriental Studies (SOAS). This can be misleading and detracts from the wholesale and penetrative change required within the sector to ensure more opportunities are provided to ethnic minority academics to pursue leadership trajectories (Andrews, 2016; Shilliam, 2014).

The impact of leadership thinking and practice on race

Leadership can play an integral part in either contributing to racial justice or reinforcing prevailing patterns of racial inequality and exclusion (Bogotch, 2015; Brown, 2006). Brown (2006) explains that within an ever-changing multicultural society, intertwined with racial complexities, the role that leadership plays requires continual re-examination, reflection and evaluation. Critically evaluating these processes provides a platform for considering greater equity and opportunity within societal structures. The dialogue concerning better representation diversification aligns with an urgency within the higher education sector to change leadership development thinking and approaches in order to dismantle racial inequalities (Furman and Shields, 2003). Leadership hierarchies within higher education have often failed to pay attention to the structural racism in leadership development pathways, consequently damaging the career trajectories and progressions of ethnic minority staff within the sector

(Bhopal and Brown, 2016). The structure of universities as traditionally being normatively and inherently white greatly impacts the connection between the leaders and the staff populations that they serve. Furman and Shields (2003) explain that challenging assumptions concerning leadership is particularly important, when considering the notion that people of colour can only improve their leadership as beneficiaries of highly prescriptive interventions. This assumption counters the idea of supportive and collective structures that should be nurturing and endorsing responsibility for self-determination within the institutional cultural context.

Mainstream ideas about leadership have often been situated in a rhetoric of meritocracy. The notion of meritocracy within a leadership context asserts that individuals have attained leadership tenures primarily based on their talent, natural ability or achievements (Ahmed, 2012; Singh and Kwahli, 2015). Miller (2016) asserts that this thinking overlooks the many ways in which structural racism has created economic structures that create advantage, opportunities and access (or lack of access) to leadership positions based on race. In considering the impact of leadership thinking, it is essential to note that leadership exists within a context. The focus on individuals in leadership thinking does not address differences within the social contexts. Bogotch (2015) explains that this is due to created systems of structural advantage and disadvantage and the effect they have on shaping societal and racial identities. For many BME academics, these collective identities create a shared experience from which collective grievances and aspirations emerge to motivate collective action (Alexander, 2017). This collective action coincides with a shifting paradigm that is now challenging university institutions to consider how their leadership hierarchies can be better diversified and representative of staff and student populations (Alexander and Arday, 2015; Rollock, 2016). By shifting the focus to collective action, the whole picture is considered in comparison to the focus traditionally being on the individual (Boske, 2014). Often this individual focus omits the influence of social identity as a context of collective leadership and penetrative action (Boske, 2014). Diversifying leadership can be problematic. Primarily, the authority of a leader is connected to the group that the leader oversees. Bhopal (2014) explains that difficulties can emerge in how leadership is perceived and to which extent it dismantles hegemonic and normative views of leadership. Miller (2016) provides that many ethnic minority leaders within higher education operate from a platform of limited power because of the structural racism that pervades the sector.

Unpacking social justice in leadership

Within the academy, the lack of a social justice perspective by some senior stakeholders can often compound this context. An important caveat to this recognizes that leadership is often characterized by the heroic, directive, high-profile individuals who exert influence over others by virtue of authority, position or persuasion (Shields, 2014). It is important to note that this only constitutes one form of leadership. Coleman (2011) explains that often we reward people whose leadership style is aligned with the dominant institutional culture, but not those who engage in more collective forms of leadership. Leadership through this particularly constrained lens fails to acknowledge the variances in leadership, particularly that of women and people of different races and ethnicities (Brown, 2006; Shields, 2014).

Given the cultural influence of individualism, many leadership development programmes are utilized as a tool for canvassing and selecting individuals perceived as able to demonstrate potential leadership ability (Shields, 2014). Essentially, these programmes provide potential leaders with additional knowledge and skills, with the objective of strengthening an organization's performance and ability to serve its wider professional community (Brown, 2006). Significantly, this approach does not take into account structural and systemic issues that inhibit and restrict individual power, or acknowledge the fact that dismantling structural racism requires collaborative and adaptive approaches (Boske, 2014; Brooks, 2008). Dismantling inequitable cultures that permeate leadership hierarchies is difficult. Changing the behaviour of individuals is not enough. Individual, behavioural changes do not necessarily support a system intervention that is penetrative and addresses the root causes of structural racism (Boske, 2014). The need for a systemic perspective and focus on leadership as a process and the importance of diversity to underpin this process requires individuals within the academy to embrace diversification as an essential component of equity and inclusion. Additionally, Bhopal and Brown (2016) suggest that support is required from senior leadership hierarchies to embed racial justice competencies in their ongoing practices, institutional cultures, networks and communities associated with the higher education sector.

In considering mechanisms for effectively supporting racial justice leadership, universities must be committed to prioritizing systemic change which recognizes diversification as an important tenet of leadership hierarchy. Boske (2014) explains that the commitment required must be explicit, with detailed targeted interventions which aim to provide greater equity and access to leadership opportunities for BME academic staff. In essence, conscious attention should be paid to racial justice in all aspects of organizing and mobilizing, in a variety of contexts ranging from organizations to networks and coalitions. Interventions immersed in equity and inclusion discourse are paramount to developing processes that support and nurture our BME leaders within the academy (Bhopal, 2014). Aligned to this, transparent conversations about power and privilege in decision-making and governance issues are integral to challenging inequitable leadership cultures within the sector (Adams, 2017; Rollock, 2016).

The Research Centre for Leadership in Action (2009) states that reflection on one's individual experience with institutional power and privilege, along with learning about barriers to access and opportunity through inequitable structures, is a continuous process that is integrated with positive and affirmative actions. Importantly, this speaks to custodians of the academy being collectively accountable for how we implement and measure our racial justice objectives. Anderson (2008) highlights that this competency within organizations and communities includes understanding how to use statistical and narrative data to diagnose issues and track progress.

Understanding leadership as a process makes more visible the natural connections between many organizations and individuals in different parts of a system, and encourages leadership that builds strategic alignment around problem analysis and vision with a diverse array of stakeholders (Research Centre for Leadership in Action, 2009). To achieve racial and social justice within a leadership context, Bhopal and Brown (2014) explain that universities need to move beyond the emphasis on the power of individuals towards a philosophy of interdependence and the building of connections with BME academic staff. In recognizing the limitations of leadership development programmes and strategies, Anderson (2008) asserts that these interventions cannot entirely dismantle structural racism. However, they can provide increased opportunities for individuals and groups who, because of racialized and structural systems, are less likely to have had equitable access to opportunities.

Situating the lived experience: Being a BME leader in higher education

Attracting BME people to prominent senior leadership positions within higher education is considerably difficult when mapped against a backdrop of minority ethnic academics concentrated at lower grades within university institutions. For many BME staff, the lived experience speaks to often being undermined, and to subtle forms of silencing and trivializing racist occurrences within the professional workplace (Singh and Kwhali, 2015; ECU, 2015). The lack of prominence given to race equality in higher education remains an issue. In part, Khan (2015) explains that this occurs because universities prioritize other endeavours which are normally aligned to significant funding streams, such as widening participation initiatives and gender equality interventions such as ATHENA Swan. Presently, there are no funding streams attached to advancing greater race equality within the sector. Having diversification within leadership hierarchies would provide opportunities to progress agendas concerning racial inequity (Leathwood et al., 2009; Rollock, 2016).

My own experience as a BME leader within higher education points towards not only negotiating aspects of leadership but also navigating deeply entrenched views about the capabilities of BME leaders within university spaces. I often found it very difficult to accept my own position as a BME leader due in part to feeling as though I were an impostor, continuously questioning my own capabilities (Ashe and Nazroo, 2016). There is a recognition that this continuous questioning of capabilities came as a result of enduring comments which were situated around whether I was capable of leading a group of colleagues competently. The default position often adopted advances a deficit approach which categorizes or renders ethnic minorities as not as capable as their white counterparts (Bhopal, 2015; ECU, 2015; Walumbwa et al., 2008).

In understanding my position as a BME leader within the academy, I became very aware of how I was perceived and treated by my colleagues. Collegiate environments often became the arena for voicing concerns, which undermined my leadership in quite a public and demoralizing way. There was an awareness that began to develop regarding my own position as a leader where I realized that I was being treated differently from my peers in similar positions of leadership. I became more aware of the inequitable structures, which invariably undermined my leadership as I became cognizant of the dearth of diversification regarding leadership, which made it difficult when encountering particular problems situated within a racialized context (Bhopal et al., 2015). Within that position you encounter a feeling of vulnerability and isolation as you become aware of how discriminatory cultures manifest and how dominant ideologies impact notions of leadership and, perhaps more pertinently, which types of people should be leaders (Aguirre and Martinez, 2006; Ashe and Nazroo, 2016). At this particular juncture, finding my voice as a BME leader within academia became important as I sought to conceptualize my experience and articulate the forms of discrimination that I had encountered. Often, as is the case, there was a resistance, which I was faced with when detailing and revealing my experiences of facing racism through a more insidious guise. Ultimately, the trivialization of my experience as a subjective opinion and hypersensitivity facilitated a culture of racism rarely being taken seriously by higher education institutions (Ahmed, 2012; Bhopal and Jackson, 2013). This then becomes another form of silencing for BME academics, who feel that there is not really a platform for them to voice their concerns about either witnessing or encountering racism.

In considering occurrences of racism within a leadership context, a pertinent consideration has always been situated around how I perceive myself and how sometimes my own mentality has rendered me not as capable as a white colleague, knowing that any comparison drawn will be made against this normative and white view of leadership (Adserias et al., 2017). For myself as a BME academic, I have often questioned whether I belong in the academy, and this has often been mapped against a feeling of exclusion within the academy. The trivialization of racism within universities is a barrier to successful leadership, particularly in the case of BME leaders who rely on strong university policy and direction regarding the disabling of discriminatory cultures. For BME leaders, such policies and penetrative interventions concerning discrimination are essential in ensuring that ethnic minorities are supported institutionally within their leadership positions (ECU, 2016; Iverson, 2008). Challenging racism in this way within the higher education sector is imperative if we are to develop a more inclusive academy that embraces and advocates greater diversification that is reflective of ever increasingly diverse student populations.

Developing communities of practice in leadership

Sharing best practice within a leadership context is integral to the development of other senior leaders. The language of collaboration is a powerful one, particularly within education. There is an emphasis for successful leadership hierarchies to share, disseminate and collaborate with other institutions collegially and communally to achieve particular sector benchmarks (Alexander and Arday, 2015; Arday, 2017; ECU, 2016). Situated within the context of race, this becomes pertinent when we consider perhaps how universities engage their ethnic minority staff and provide opportunities for them to progress to leadership trajectories. Increasingly, the landscape of leadership within the sector has been challenged because we are beginning to observe an emergent shift which has embraced the dissemination of racialized or inequitable experiences within the academy (Shilliam, 2014). This has provided BME academics with an opportunity to engage in communities of practice which facilitate professional development opportunities and provide access to greater networks that may facilitate potential opportunities to explore leadership trajectories within the sector (Ahmed, 2012; Lave and Wenger, 1991; Pilkington, 2013). Bhopal and Brown (2016) explain that for many BME academics access to these types of collegial environments that are nurturing, understanding and supportive are particularly difficult due to experiences that are continually situated in hypersurveillance, lack of access, marginalization and isolation. Typically, communities of practice are knowledge exchange and development hubs that bring together people from across the sector both nationally and globally (Lave and Wenger, 1991; Lieberman and Pointer-Mace, 2009; Tomlinson, 2004). In considering how normative patterns of leadership could be changed, this vehicle provides opportunities for ethnic minorities to illuminate their experiences of leadership or their experiences of being led in inequitable cultures (Tate and Bagguley, 2017). Importantly, for BME academics, communities of practice operate on a distributed leadership model which eliminates hierarchy in favour of greater equity and for faculty of colour (Ahmed, 2013; Miller, 2016). Significantly, where many ethnic minority academics will have been on the periphery of normative leadership models that operate within their own institutions, this type of community becomes powerful (Miller, 2016).

Wider access to opportunity is pivotal in mobilizing and diversifying leadership hierarchies. Activities within the community can facilitate networking and brokering across institutions nationally and internationally (Bhopal and Brown, 2016). This capital for BME academics is essential and provides them with access to sector opportunities that have been traditionally reserved or withheld from faculty or colour (ECU, 2016; Miller, 2016). The community also provides access to sector requirements for leadership. Due to the dearth and absence of visible senior BME leaders, this information becomes even more important in navigating leadership pathways (Adserias et al., 2017; Bogotch, 2015; Lieberman and Pointer-Mace, 2009). The autonomy of the communities provides a mechanism for sharing and gathering practice amongst members, which offers greater access to continuing professional development, in addition to highlighting the barriers and challenges that impact poor diversification within our leadership structures within the academy (Jarboe, 2016).

The use of technology would also be an effective tool in facilitating continuous support within the community. Adams (2017) suggests that the communities of practice could host 'live' discussions on themes of inequity or poor diversification, with activities such as webinars, blogs, network coordination, thought platforms and focus groups. Such interventions invariably are dependent on the participants within the community. Fundamentally, the communities for BME academics are agile, ideally supporting members to work together to consider current developments and the implications as they occur (Tate and Bagguley, 2017). The importance of this is central to ensuring that BME academics are provided with support mechanisms for their lived experiences of inequality or racism. Sharing such experiences can potentially be cathartic for faculty of colour and enthuse them in the quest to pursue leadership opportunities (Mirza, 2017). Other tenets which can be facilitated through a community of practice intervention could also involve collective problem-solving and engaging in opportunities to undertake research activity and projects with other BME academics and senior leaders (Law, 2017). For BME academics, this support structure would facilitate sector challenges through collaboration.

Engaging in reciprocity: Mentoring in leadership

Traditionally, mentoring is viewed as a process where an experienced individual provides information, expertise and in some cases emotional support to a novice over a period of time (Barrera, Braley and Slate, 2010; Le Cornu, 2005; Larson, 2009). Leadership at senior levels within universities often operates this conception of mentoring, which has also been historically hierarchical, frequently resulting in an imbalance of power between the mentor and the mentee (Angelique, Kyle and Taylor, 2002). The importance of mentoring as an instrument of support for BME academics attempting to navigate senior leadership progression is hugely significant. Mentoring provides opportunities for BME academics in particular to be guided towards the correct professional opportunities (Alvesson and Skoldberg, 2009). In this regard, BME academics can often be disadvantaged because they are operating on the margins of the academy.

The potential for penetrative and purposeful mentoring for BME academics to pursue senior leadership trajectories within higher education could potentially support them in fulfilling their professional aspirations (Bhopal and Brown, 2016; Miller, 2016). Due to the sensitive nuances of BME academics' experiences, which in many cases erode confidence, mentoring interventions should be targeted at enhancing and advancing career prospects through developing the confidence, motivation, experience and skills required to apply for (and ultimately gain) promotion to senior levels (Arday, 2017; Shilliam, 2014). Perhaps more importantly, targeted mentoring interventions should aim to make a positive difference to BME staff with sustainable outcomes that are measurable (Bogotch, 2015; Manathunga, 2007). One way for this type of intervention to be effective is to ensure that the knowledge transfer process is reciprocal, whereby senior leaders who are often considered to be the gatekeepers of knowledge are open to being mentored by more junior staff (Le Cornu, 2005; Scanlon, 2008). This could effectively be an innovative way to expose senior leaders within universities to the difficulties that ethnic minority group's face in attempting to navigate the academy.

In considering the potential for mentoring as an intervention to diversify leadership hierarchies, there must be a targeted focus which encourages BME staff to take on leadership and decision-making roles, whilst facilitating opportunities for BME staff to undertake formal and informal professional development (Adams, 2017; Bhopal, 2014; Miller, 2016). Mentoring relationships involving senior leaders within universities must also acknowledge and respond to the concerns regarding the dearth of diversification and representation at senior levels. This would be integral to reducing feelings of isolation amongst BME academics, who often obtain solitary positions within staff cohorts and faculties (Tate and Bagguley, 2017). The effectiveness of this process must also be determined by sufficient training for mentors, which should require compulsory unconscious bias training (ECU, 2015). Adams (2017) suggests that this should be accompanied by training which provides senior leaders with an understanding of the issues that place BME academics at a disadvantage, in particular those wishing to progress to senior leadership tenures. This form of mentoring could be penetrative and effective in engaging in a dialogue that eliminates hierarchy and embraces the notion of reserve mentoring (Le Cornu, 2005; Scanlon, 2008). This type of mentoring would facilitate greater equity and encourage all participants to have autonomy in the knowledge exchange relationship and becomes agents for change (Larson, 2009).

Utilizing reflection to dismantle racial inequity in leadership in higher education

The process of reflection is extremely effective and is utilized predominantly in education, nursing and mental health (Bradbury, Frost, Kilminster and Zukas, 2010). Making sense of lived experiences, particularly those that are negative or traumatic, is important in facilitating ways forward which allow those experiences to be positively converted. For BME academics in particular, their experiences of navigating the academy are often saturated within racialized occurrences which have often resulted in them being marginalized, victimized and isolated within faculties and departments (Bhopal and Brown, 2016).

Experiencing racism within the workplace is often a debilitating experience for many BME academics, and the process of reflection provides opportunities to make sense of these racist occurrences in attempting to understand the centrality and multifaceted nature of racism particular in its more insidious and covert forms (Rollock, 2016). Leadership encounters within higher education can be difficult to reflect on particular if this is a bad experience punctuated by episodes of covert racism. Ironically, Rollock (2016) explains that the opportunity to reflect on these experiences provides BME academics and BME senior leaders within the academy an opportunity to empower others encountering similar forms of oppression. Our experiences speak to the enduring legacy of institutional racism and how it permeates all of our major institutions within society. Personally, reflecting on my own leadership experiences as a black male within the academy has allowed me to make sense of particular occurrences that have left residual effects. The process of reflection allows practitioners to consider how they may utilize negative experiences to facilitate more positive future outcomes. Mirza (2017) explains that the process of reflection can help in attempting to deal with a racist encounter or experience within the academy. To this end, verbalizing these experience and highlighting the impact personally and professionally speaks to an emerging discourse which is encouraging BME academics to illuminate their experiences of racism.

The potential for targeted reflection as a tool for understanding and navigating the academy is potentially powerful (Mirza, 2017). Further, as an instrument for self-development, this has the potential to, if undertaken in a cyclical process, develop mechanisms to cope with insidious racism within the sector. Importantly, this also serves the dual process of challenging racism but additionally of allowing for these experiences to be documented and used for either personal reflection or research purposes. Adserias et al. (2017) explain that the conversion of these experiences into research is what fundamentally provides the higher education sector with evidence that the current leadership landscape requires closer scrutiny and better diversification which is more representative of ever-increasing multicultural, diverse student populations. The avocation of reflection as an instrument to dismantle racial inequity in senior leadership teams is important because our understanding of our lived experiences very much signpost our career directions and progressions (Loughran, 1996; Pollard, 2011; Schon, 1987). Experiences intertwined with inequity or inequality shape our view of leadership, particularly in higher education. Invariably, this will impact on the types of leadership we as BME academics respond to and, given the opportunity, would like to advocate (Adserias et al., 2017).

Conclusion

Racial discrimination within the academy remains problematic and continues to be a persistent barrier for BME individuals attempting to progress in academia. Paradoxically, universities continue to contradict egalitarian ideals associated with developing processes, which endorse access and inclusion for all (Gillborn, 2015; Leonardo, 2002). The persistent 'glass ceiling' faced by BME academics attempting to pursue leadership trajectories continues to undermine notions of equality and diversity often espoused in British universities. Anecdotes from BME individuals of exclusion, marginalization and overt and covert racism continue to remain the hallmarks of institutional and organizational racism and reaffirm the cycle of a lack of diversification in the United Kingdom's higher education institutions (Arday, 2017).

Importantly, we must recognize that the complexity of the BME academic experience means that in many cases they will have encountered or endured many occurrences of racism through multiple forms of oppression and silencing (Leonardo, 2016). Institutions must remember that many talented BME individuals are often reluctant to put themselves forward for leadership roles due to the lack of support that will invariably surround them whilst in that particular position (Bhopal, 2014; Law, 2017; Tate and Bagguley, 2017). Universities must engage with targeted leadership schemes for BME academics, which should be intertwined with unconscious bias training for all members of staff, particularly those who will have inherent views on the capabilities of BME leaders (ECU, 2015). It is important for some of these inherent views and mindsets to be challenged in a positive and enabling way to try and reduce the likelihood of resistance (Alexander, 2017).

A tectonic shift is required regarding the landscape of higher education, and this needs to be driven by university senior administrators who must be held accountable for not actively prioritizing and advancing the diversification of staff particularly at leadership levels (HESA, 2016; Mirza, 2017). Universities could measure their equality and diversity protocols by regularly engaging in audits which regularly monitor BME participation within their institutions, with regards to staffing and student attainment at the undergraduate and postgraduate levels (Law, 2017). Initiatives such as the ECU Race Equality Charter provide a framework for university institutions to examine, identify and self-reflect on institutional and cultural barriers, which disadvantage minority ethnic staff in pursuing leadership trajectories (Williams, 2013). This initiative attempts to remove the long-held complacency entrenched within university cultures which have previously disregarded issues of equity, diversity and equality (Singh and Kwhali, 2015). The importance of this issue has regularly received secondary status. Often, this is viewed as a compulsory procedure to satisfy university internal training (Ahmed, 2012; Pilkington, 2013). In many cases, such tasks designed to create and develop awareness of discrimination and equity are regarded as laborious and of no interest, resulting in the reinforcement of inequity and institutional racism (Mirza, 2017).

The importance attributed to valuing indifference is integral to advancing the equality and diversity agenda. In essence, judgements should be made on the capabilities of the individual based on their competency to perform. This competency should not be based on the colour of the individual. For universities to maintain their mantra as forward-thinking sites for egalitarian ideals, they must be prepared to reflect on some of the institutional cultures within the higher education sector which deepen racial inequality (Rollock, 2016; Shilliam, 2014). Targeted interventions must be focused on creating greater access for BME academics who wish to pursue opportunities to progress into leadership. Institutions must be held accountable for cultures that continue not to be diverse. The diversification of leadership hierarchies is also reflective of universities that wish to acknowledge inclusion as a platform for advancing greater access to opportunity (ECU, 2015; ECU, 2016). Disrupting patterns of inequality within the academy is difficult, particularly when we consider the dearth of BME leaders, but the terrain of academia as it presently exists, ensures that collectively much effort is still required if we are to continue to advance progressive change which ultimately dismantles racial inequality within higher education.

References

Adams, R. (2017), 'British Universities Employ No Black Academics in Top Roles, Figures Show', *The Guardian*, 19 January. Last accessed 10 February 2018: https://www.theguardian.com/education/2017/jan/19/british-universities-employ-no-black-academics-in-top-roles-figures-show.

Adserias, R. P., J. LaVar, L. J. Charleston, F. Jerlando and L. Jackson, L. (2017), 'What Style of Leadership Is Best Suited to Direct Organizational Change to Fuel Institutional Diversity in Higher Education?', *Race Ethnicity and Education*, 20 (3): 315–31.

Aguirre, A. and R. O. Martinez (2006), *Diversity Leadership in Higher Education*, ASHE-ERIC Higher Education Report 32 (3). San Francisco: Jossey-Bass.

Ahmed, S. (2012) *On Being Included: Racism and Diversity in Institutional Life*, Durham, NC, and London: Duke University Press.

Alexander, C. (2017), 'Breaking Black: The Death of Ethnic and Racial Studies in Britain', *Ethnic and Racial Studies*, doi: 10.1080/01419870.2018.1409902.

Alexander, C. and J. Arday (2015), *Aiming Higher Race, Inequality and Diversity in the Academy. London: AHRC: Runnymede Trust, (Runnymede Perspectives)*, London, Common Creative: Runnymede Trust (Runnymede Perspectives).

Anderson, J. A. (2008), *Driving Change through Diversity and Globalization: Transformative Leadership in the Academy*, Sterling: Stylus Publishing.

Andrews, K. (2016), *Black Studies University Course Long Overdue*, The Guardian, 20 May. Last accessed 27 February 2018: https://www.theguardian.com/commentisfree/2016/may/20/black-studies-university-course-long-overdue.

Angelique, H., K. Kyle and E. Taylor (2002), 'Mentors and Muses: New Strategies for Academic Success', *Innovative Higher Education*, 26: 195–209.

Arday, J. (2017), *University and College Union (UCU): Exploring Black and Minority Ethnic (BME) Doctoral Students' Perceptions of a Career in Academia: Experiences, Perceptions and Career Progression*, London: Creative Commons.

Ashe, S. and J. Nazroo (2016), *Equality, Diversity and Racism in the Workplace: A Qualitative Analysis of the 2015 Race at Work Survey*, Manchester: Centre on Dynamics of Ethnicity, University of Manchester.

Barrera A., R. T. Braley and J. R. Slate (2010), 'Beginning Teacher Success: An Investigation into Feedback from Mentors of Formal Mentoring Programs', *Mentoring and Tutoring: Partnership in Learning*, 18 (1): 61–74.

Bhopal, K. (2014), *The Experience of BME Academics in Higher Education: Aspirations in the Face of Inequality*. Stimulus paper, London: Leadership Foundation for Higher Education.

Bhopal, K. and J. Jackson (2013), *The Experiences of Black and Ethnic Minority Academics, Multiple Identities and Career Progression*, Southampton: University of Southampton EPSRC.

Bhopal, K. and H. Brown (2016), *Black and Minority Ethnic Leaders: Support Networks and Strategies for Success in Higher Education*, London: Leadership Foundation.

Bhopal, K., H. Brown and J. Jackson (2015), *Academic Flight: How to Encourage Black and Minority Ethnic Academics to Say in UK Higher Education*, London: ECU.

Bogotch, I. (2015), 'What is Social Justice Leadership? in D. Griffiths and J. P. Portelli (eds), *Key Questions for Educational Leaders*, 131–5, Burlington, Ontario Canada: Works and Dees Publishing and Edphil.

Boliver, V. (2013), 'How Fair Is Access to More Prestigious UK Universities?' *British Journal of Sociology*, 64 (2): 344–64.

Boske, C. (2014), 'Critical Reflective Practices: Connecting to Social Justice', in I. Bogotch and C. M. Shields (eds), *International Handbook of Educational Leadership and Social (In)Justice*, 289–308, Dordrecht: Springer.

Bradbury, H., N. Frost, S. Kilminster and M. Zukas (2010), *Beyond Reflective Practice New Approaches to Professional Lifelong Learning*, New York: Routledge.

Brown, K. (2006), 'Leadership for Social Justice and Equity: Evaluating a Transformative Framework and Andragogy', *Educational Administration Quarterly*, 42 (5): 700–45.

Chun, E. B. and A. Evans (2009), *Bridging the Diversity Divide: Globalization and Reciprocal Empowerment in Higher Education*. ASHE Higher Education Report 35 (1), San Francisco: Jossey-Bass.

ECU (Equality Challenge Unit) (2016), *Equality in Higher Education: Statistical Report Staff*, London: ECU.

Equality Challenge Unit (2015), *Equality in Higher Education: Statistical Report, Staff and Students*. Last accessed 21 March 2018: http://www.ecu.ac.uk/publications/ equality-higher-education-statistical-report-2015/.

Furman, G. C. and C. M. Shields (2003), 'How Can Educational Leaders Promote and Support Social Justice and Democratic Community in Schools'. Paper Presented at Annual Meeting of the American Educational Research Association, Chicago (21–25 April).

Gillborn, D. (2015), 'Racism as Policy: A Critical Race Analysis of Education Reforms in the United States and England', *The Educational Forum*, 78 (1): 26–41.

Gronn, P. and K. Lacey (2006), 'Cloning Their Own: Aspirant Principals and the School-Based Selection Game', *Australian Journal of Education*, 40 (2): 102–21.

HESA (2016), *Staff in Higher Education: Staff by Ethnicity 2015/2016*. Last accessed 17 December 2017: https://www.hesa.ac.uk/data-and-analysis/publications/ staff-2015–16.

Iverson, S. V. (2008), 'Capitalizing on Change: The Discursive Framing of Diversity in U.S. Land-Grant Universities', *Equity and Excellence in Education*, 41 (2): 182–99.

Jarboe, N. (2016), *WomenCount Leaders in Higher Education 2016*, London: WomenCount.

Kezar, A. J. and P. D. Eckel (2008), 'Advancing Diversity Agendas on Campus: Examining Transactional and Transformational Presidential Leadership Styles', *International Journal of Leadership in Education*, 11 (4): 379–405.

Khan, O. (2015), 'UK Study Finds Just 17 Black Female Professors, *The Independent*, 3 Febuary. Last accessed 21 February 2018: https://www.independent.co.uk/student/ news/uk-study-finds-just-17-black-female-professors-10019201.html.

Larson, L. (2009), 'A Descriptive Study of Mentoring and Technology Integration among Teacher Education Faculty, *International Journal of Evidence Based Coaching and Mentoring*, 7 (1): 119–35.

Lave, J. and E. Wenger (1991), *Situated Learning: Legitimate Peripheral Participation*, Cambridge: Cambridge University Press.

Law, I. (2017), 'Building the Anti-racist University, Action and New Agendas', *Race Ethnicity and Education*, 20 (3): 332–43.

Le Cornu, R. (2005), 'Peer-Mentoring: Engaging Pre-Service Teachers in Mentoring One Another', *Mentoring and Tutoring: Partnership in Learning*, 13 (3): 355–66.

Leadership Foundation (2015), *Why Does Ethnicity Matter in Higher Education Leadership? Leadership Insights*, London: Leadership Foundation in Higher Education.

Leathwood, C., U. Maylor and M. Moreau (2009), *The Experience of Black and Minority Ethnic Staff Working In Higher Education. Literature Review*, London: Equality Challenge Unit.

Leonardo, Z. (2002), 'The Souls of White Folk: Critical Pedagogy, Whiteness Studies, and Globalization Discourse', *Race Ethnicity and Education*, 5 (1): 29–50.

Leonardo, Z. (2016), 'The Color of Supremacy', in E. Taylor, D. Gillborn and G. Ladson-Billings (eds), *Foundations of Critical Race Theory in Education*, 2nd edn, 221–29, New York: Routledge.

Lieberman, A. and D. H. Pointer-Mace (2009), 'The Role of "Accomplished Teachers" in Professional Learning Communities: Uncovering Practice and Enabling Leadership', *Teachers and Teaching: Theory and Practice*, 15 (4): 459–70.

Manathunga, C. (2007), 'Supervision as Mentoring: The Role of Power and Boundary Crossing', *Studies in Continuing Education*, 29 (2): 207–21.

McIntosh, P. (1990), 'White Privilege: Unpacking the Invisible Knapsack', *Independent School*, 49 (2): 31–6.

Miller, P. (2016), ' "White Sanction", Institutional, Group and Individual Interaction in the Promotion and Progression of Black and Minority Ethnic Academics and Teachers in England', *Power and Education*, 8 (3): 205–21.

Mirza, H. S. (2017), 'One in a Million: A Journey of a Post-Colonial Woman of Colour in the White Academy', in Deborah Gabriel and Shirley Anne Tate (eds), *Inside the Ivory Tower: Narratives of Women of Colour Surviving and Thriving in Academia*, 39–54, London: Trentham UCL Press.

Pilkington, A. (2013), 'The Interacting Dynamics of Institutional Racism in Higher Education', *Race, Ethnicity and Education*, 16 (2): 225–45.

Pilkington, A. (2011), *Institutional Racism in the Academy: A UK Case Study*, Stoke-on-Trent: Trentham Books.

Pollard, A. (2011), 'Ethnography and Social Policy for Classroom Practice', *Social Crisis and Educational Research (RLE Edu L)*, 164–71.

Research Center for Leadership in Action (2009), *Taking Back the Work: A Cooperative Inquiry into the Work of Leaders of Color in Movement-Building*, Robert F. Wagner Graduate School of Public Service, New York University. Last accessed 14 April 18: http://wagner.nyu.edu/leadership/reports/files/TakingBacktheWork.pdf.

Rollock, N. (2012), 'Unspoken Rules of Engagement: Navigating Racial Micro-Aggressions in the Academic Terrain', *International Journal of Qualitative Studies in Education*, 25 (5): 517–32.

Rollock, N. (2016), *How Much Does Your University Do for Racial Equality? The Guardian*, 19 January. Last accessed 9 September 2017: https://www.theguardian.com/higher-education-network/2016/jan/19/how-much-does-your-university-do-for-racial-equality/.

Scanlon, L. (2008), 'The Impact of Experience on Mentors' Conceptions of Mentoring', *International Journal of Evidence Based Coaching and Mentoring*, 6 (2): 57–66.

Schon, D. A. (1987), *Educating the Reflective Practitioner*, San Francisco: Jossey-Bass.

Shephard, S. (2017), 'Why Are There so Few Female Leaders in Higher Education: A Case of Structure or Agency?' *Management in Education*, 31 (2): 82–7.

Shields, C. M. (2014), 'Leadership for Social Justice Education: A Critical Transformative Approach', in I. Bogotch and C. M. Shields (eds), *International Handbook of Educational Leadership and Social (In)Justice*, 323–39, Dordrecht: Springer.

Shilliam, R. (2014), 'Black Academia in Britain', The Disorder of Things, 28 July. Last accessed 15 September 2018: https://thedisorderofthings.com/2014/07/28/black-academia-in-britain/.

Singh, G. and J. Kwhali (2015), *How Can We Make Not Break Black and Minority Ethnic Leaders in Higher Education?* Stimulus Paper, London: Leadership Foundation for Higher Education.

Smith, E. (2012), *Key Issues in Social Justice and Education*, London: SAGE.

Tate, S. A. and P. Bagguley (2017), 'Building The Anti-Racist University: Next Steps', *Race Ethnicity and Education*, 20 (3): 289–99.

Tomlinson, H. (2004), *Educational Leadership (Professional Growth for Professional Development)*, London: SAGE.

UCU (University College Union) (2016), *The Experiences of Black and Minority Ethnic Staff in Further and Higher Education*, London: UCU.

UK Demographics Profile (2014), United Kingdom Demographics Profile, IndexMundi.com. Last accessed 2 May 2016: http://www.indexmundi.com/united_kingdom/demographics_profile.html.

Walumbwa, F., B. Avolio, W. Gardner, T. Wernsing and S. Peterson (2008), 'Authentic Leadership: Development and Validation of a Theory-Based Measure', *Journal of Management*, 34 (1): 89–126.

Williams, D. A. (2013), *Strategic Diversity Leadership: Activating Change and Transformation in Higher Education*, Sterling: Stylus Publishing.

9

Systemic changes to Crack the Concrete Ceiling: Initiatives from the leadership foundation for higher education

Alice Johns, Jan Fook and Vijaya Nath

Introduction

Despite the fact that there have been increasing calls to address the under-representation of black, minority ethnic (BME)[1] people in leadership positions in higher education (HE) in the United Kingdom, inequality persists (Equality Challenge Unit, 2017: 130). The 'concrete ceiling' (Davidson, 1997) is a term which has been used to refer to the blocks to advancement experienced by BME people in HE, similar to the 'glass ceiling' experienced by women in many different occupations. This is an issue which the Leadership Foundation for Higher Education (LFHE)[2] (recently amalgamated with the Equality Challenge Unit and the Higher Education Academy to become Advance Higher Education (Advance HE)) has sought to explore and stimulate thinking on. Whilst many different initiatives exist, including those which help develop leadership potential in individual BME HE staff, there is also now an increasing need to focus on the more systematic or organizationally targeted strategies. In this chapter we aim to detail these specific initiatives developed by the LFHE, outlining the underlying philosophy and approach, the initiatives themselves and outcomes of these. We hope that these details will produce an overall picture of the current state of thinking and contribute to the sector's further thinking on strategies to address the problem of inequality of BME staff at senior levels in HE. For this reason, the chapter primarily seeks to describe the initiatives in detail rather than include critical evaluation, as most of the initiatives are still in progress. There is no intention to compare or evaluate these activities against those of similar types elsewhere, but where appropriate, evaluative comments have been made in terms of what is known from the literature elsewhere, or from our reflections on learning to date from initiatives in progress.

We begin with a brief background on the LFHE and its interest in BME equality in HE. We include a brief overview of approaches and strategies to address these issues in a more systemic or organizational way. The bulk of the chapter then describes the different LFHE initiatives which have recently, or are currently, being undertaken. It concludes with discussion of what further developments are needed.

Background of the LFHE and interest in BME equality

The Leadership Foundation was established in 2004 as the HE-sector agency dedicated to leadership, governance and management (LGM) development. A membership organization that delivered leadership development and consultancy advice to higher education institutions in the UK and around the world, its remit was to unite research and practice, identify 'what works' and pathways to impact and provide practical resources to support LGM development.

A commitment to equality, diversity and inclusion has always been enshrined within its values and strategy. Aurora, the Leadership Foundation's flagship women's development programme, has its genesis in the findings of Morley's (2013) 'Women and Higher Education Leadership: Absences and Aspirations'. This programme attracted some criticism for not taking adequate account of BME women. In recent years, the organization has embarked upon an ambitious programme of work to make the leadership of higher education institutions (HEIs) more equitable with regard to different aspects of diversity. These initiatives have taken a multidimensional approach, aiming to stimulate systems change at all leadership levels, driven by the belief that a diverse leadership will best serve the interests of the sector and society (Morrow, 2015). The report by Bebbington et al. (2009) provides a broader context to the LFHE's interest in diversity and leadership and summarizes this multidimensional approach as including organizational development, leadership development and strategic level recommendations.

Overview of systemic approaches and initiatives to address BME equality

As mentioned in the introduction, strategies to address the under-representation of BME people in leadership roles in HE fall into at least two categories – those focused primarily on the development of BME staff themselves, and those focused more on the systemic, workplace cultural or organizational changes which need to take place in order to support BME people to attain positions of leadership (Bhopal and Brown, 2016). We are aware that the distinction may be be somewhat blurred (e.g. development of individual BME staff might nonetheless include a focus on strategies for dealing with systemic bias). However, we believe it is important to draw the distinction, as it can be all too easy for strategies which are individually focused to neglect the broader environment that plays a crucial role in the potential progression of BME staff, and to implicitly 'blame the BME victim' for lack of success in attaining positions of leadership. This latter type of approach is often characterized as the 'deficit' model, which focuses on 'fixing' the individual (Morrow, 2015).

Strategies which are more focused on systemic support and changes include the following:

- Mentoring and sponsoring schemes. Given that BME staff often feel excluded from the personal development needed to succeed in seniority, mentoring and sponsoring schemes have been suggested as a way to overcome this. There is often confusion regarding the difference between such schemes, and this lack of clarity around the purpose of sponsorship has worked against minority groups (Ibarra et al., 2010). Whilst mentorship focuses on the personal development of high potential employees, sponsorship is predicated on power and focused on the active advancement of the individual by someone within the organization with sufficient influence (Ibarra et al., 2010). Mentorship has been criticized as being based on a deficit model, while sponsorship implies more of a two-way relationship (Alexander and Arday, 2015). Other literature confirms that informal processes like sponsorship can be very powerful and influential (Tharenou, 2001).
- Strategies focused on changing institutional bureaucratic policy and practices, for example, ensuring BME representation on selection/promotion panels; ensuring that recruitment practices provide equal access for BME people (e.g. Singh and Kwhali, 2015); and recognizing the role of

executive search firms in supporting the recruitment and selection of BME people to senior positions is also important, and therefore it is important to involve such firms in raising awareness of equality issues in decision-making about the composition of selection panels, and the processes of selection (Manfredi et al., 2017). Transparency regarding statistics on BME equality is also commonly recommended (e.g. Aouad et al., 2012) as is the ongoing need to ensure that staff are aware of equality-related policies.

- Strategic outcome targets. These focus on aims for institution-wide measures or outcomes regarding BME staff equality, for example, working towards equal representation of BME staff at senior leadership levels (Bhopal and Brown, 2016) and inclusion of diversity targets as performance indicators in senior management positions such as the NHS Workforce Race Equality Standard (NHS, 2017). The use of metrics to measure and support the case for diversity (Balter et al., 2014) is an important aspect of outcome-focused targets.

- Training/continuing professional development. Training initiatives cover a wide range of different types from those which focus on development of individual BME staff for leadership (e.g. Stellar HE, Diversifying Leadership) to programmes which focus on general training for staff across the Higher Education Institution (HEI). For example, diversity awareness and unconscious bias training which build cultural capacity in HEIs (Morrow, 2017). Training programmes may also include shadowing schemes (for BME staff to experience working at more senior levels) or reverse mentoring schemes, whereby senior white leaders are mentored by BME staff or students (Morris, 2017).

- Network formation for BME groups within or across HEIs. This is often recommended because networking is seen as critical in obtaining senior positions and for effective leadership (Fenton, 2000). Unfortunately, as noted above, since BME people are often excluded from the cultural practices within some existing networks, just joining any network may not provide relevant opportunities. In addition, BME people may not belong to networks which can assist them. For example, black women students on predominantly white campuses are rarely integrated into the life and culture of institutions (Moses, 1989). However, of course, the support which being part of a network of BME people with similar experiences and identities can provide is often novel and welcome. A major issue, though, revolves around what opportunities there are to create and also to participate in networks.

- Assessment of organizational performance. These strategies include tools and criteria for assessing an institution's performance in terms of BME equality. The best known of these is perhaps the Race Equality Charter, established by the Equality Challenge Unit in 2016. Another useful example is the self-assessment tool (Aouad et al., 2012) for leading culturally diverse communities in higher education. This tool suggests foundational indicators as a basis for organizing strategies (includes vision/mission, leadership, management, strategic planning, community engagement and budgetary support).
- Curriculum content and development. Whilst curriculum development may not directly affect the numbers of BME staff employed at more senior levels, what is does do is contribute to the culturally diverse climate in the university and send a message that BME input is valued (Morrow, 2016). Examples of actual content and/or specific courses or strategies which should be developed are race/racism content; black studies courses; involvement/participation of BME staff/students in curriculum development; and internationalization of the curriculum, so that students are aware of comparative differences and can apply different cultural or ethnic perspectives in their analysis of policies or situations.
- Public/civic engagement. Given the need for HEIs to reach out and contribute to their immediate and broader communities, relevant BME communities should be included, as both communities should be engaged with, but also communities which can and should participate in the life of the university (Morrow, 2014). This can happen in many different ways and at many different levels. For example, it can happen in more generic ways by the staging of festivals or awareness events, or more specific ways through ensuring BME representation on governing bodies.
- Research-focused initiatives. Universities can also ensure that appropriate administrative and academic research on BME issues is conducted and supported (e.g. Singh and Kwhali, 2015). This can take the form of special schemes or research centres being established.

Whilst there is clearly a large range of possible strategies to encourage more equal representation of BME people at more senior levels in HEIs', what we know less about is how extensively which of these initiatives have been taken up, and what are the overall outcomes. In the remainder of the chapter we detail the rationale behind several programmes undertaken by the LFHE to address these concerns; the programmes themselves; and also what is known about outcomes.

LFHE initiatives

Although not explicitly stated as overarching policy or intention by the LFHE, an underpinning framework for understanding the rationale behind the broad range of initiatives is provided with reference to critical race theory (CRT) (Ladson-Billings and Gillborn, 2004; Delgado and Stefancic, 2017). CRT is commonly used in research and writing on diversity in leadership (e.g. Ogunbawo, 2012; Gooden, 2012; Liu and Baker, 2014) and functions as a wide-ranging but also focused analysis of how different social and cultural conditions interplay in creating conditions of racism. The particular tenets that are relevant include a recognition that racism is a 'normal' rather than aberrant occurrence; the social constructionist nature of knowledge about difference; the recognition of white privilege and its role in constructing the flipside of race and racism; and the importance of the 'voices' and knowledge of the experiences of people of colour in framing our understanding of race. Each of these principles can be said to provide impetus for these particular LFHE programmes with their emphasis on approaching the need for diversity in leadership from a systemic angle (e.g. the sponsorship toolkit), including the voices and experiences of individual BME academics and leaders (e.g. the 'Cracking the Concrete Ceiling' study and the senior BME leaders project), and including a focus on organizational policies and practices (e.g. the Equality Diversity and Inclusion (EDI) senior leadership retreat), rather than a sole focus on individual BME leader development. These themes are assumed in the design and implementation of the following initiatives.

The following section outlines some of the initiatives that the Leadership Foundation has undertaken or begun between 2015 and 2018 as part of its core priority to support the sector in addressing the under-representation of BME leaders in UK HEIs. All such initiatives were funded by the Higher Education Funding Council for England (HEFCE), the Scottish Funding Council (SFC), the Higher Education Funding Council for Wales (HEFCW) and the Department for Education, Northern Ireland (DfENI).

1. Diversifying Leadership Programme

Introduction

During 2014–2015, the Leadership Foundation published a number of studies and stimulus papers exploring the barriers to progress for prospective BME leaders (Bhopal and Brown, 2014; Morrow, 2015; Singh and Kwhali, 2015). In order to make the leadership of the academy more equitable, such studies pointed to the need for targeted leadership development and networking opportunities for BME academics.

A key recommendation of the inaugural BME Leadership in Higher Education Summit was that the sector was in need of further support to develop the BME talent pipeline. It was proposed that there should be a programme developed in parity with the Leadership Foundation's women's development programme, Aurora.

With funding for three pilot cohorts, the Diversifying Academic Leadership (DAL) programme was launched in January 2016. The first was run free of charge, the second part subsidized and the third at full market rate. Such an approach was taken to assess the appetite and take-up for such a programme, as well as to reflect the co-creational aspects of the programme. Participants were asked to directly feed into programme content, thereby creating a dynamic learning environment that would produce a programme suited to the developmental needs of BME colleagues, as identified by them.

Combing leadership theory, networking opportunities, facilitated action learning and exposure to senior leaders through the sponsor role and guest speakers, the programme was based on good practice in leadership development for excluded or minority groups.

In 2017, as a result of an independent evaluation conducted by Bhopal and Brown (2016), it was decided that professional service staff should be included in the programme, and thus, the title changed to Diversifying Leadership (DL). The length was also extended to four days, with a full day for action learning and an orientation webinar. This was based on participant feedback because they felt they needed more reflexive space to discuss their experiences with career progression as BME people within the academy, as well as to plan strategies to advance their careers.

Aims

Aimed at BME early career academics and professional service staff, up to and below senior lecturer level or equivalent, the DL programme includes an orientation webinar, three development days, a facilitated action learning set, a networking forum and virtual discussion using Jiscmail. There is also a requirement for participants to identify and secure a sponsor to act as promoter of their talents and strengths, and who for the duration of the programme and beyond uses their position as sponsor to influence the thinking and mindsets of other colleagues inside and outside of their specific HEI.

Specific support for sponsors has been developed and is detailed further within this chapter.

Challenging the belief that developing the individual reflects a deficit model approach, the programme uses an asset model approach to combine four key elements: preparation through a series of development activities; collaboration through action learning with peer reflection; the providing of space between modules to think and act strategically, and opportunity through access to a sponsor.

The programme introduces participants to key leadership theories, explores 'authentic leadership' and what this might look like for each individual, and helps participants develop their own leadership style. A key benefit is that the programme provides a 'safe space' to explore experiences of being BME and working within HE with colleagues across the sector. Themes around increasing visibility, cultural identity and capital, power and influence are explored throughout. Each development day also includes a leadership insight from a senior HE leader or other sector leader from a BAME community, which gives direct access to role models. The final day includes a storytelling workshop which develops presentation skills and instils confidence and pride through celebrating difference.

Participant profile

Across the seven cohorts, post-92 institutions have engaged with the programme more than Russell Group institutions, and as of yet, there has been no engagement from alternative providers. Geographically, the majority of participants come from universities based in London and the South East, followed by the Midlands. There have been fewer participants from institutions based in the North East and South West. This is perhaps expected as HEIs in London and the South-East tend to have higher proportions of BME staff (Universities and Colleges Union, 2012). The following chart shows the ethnic background of participants, with the highest proportion being black/black British Caribbean. The data does not distinguish between UK domiciled and non-domiciled. The Cracking the Concrete Ceiling research, which focuses on the impact of the DL programme, has uncovered significant differences in the experiences of these two communities. Although not as yet completed, the broad aims and some preliminary findings of this research project will be outlined later in this chapter.

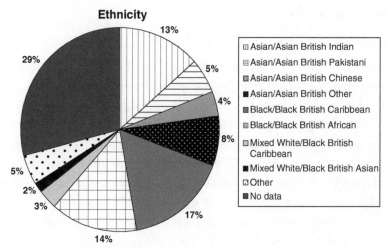

Figure 1 Data provided by participants of the Diversifying Leadership programme to the Leadership Foundation for Higher Education.

Conclusions

The DL programme has had a difficult journey in terms of establishing equivalence with Aurora within institutions, providing evidence to the often held belief that BME activities are not invested in or taken as seriously as gender-based development activities. Morrow (2015) discusses the difficulties that BME staff have in gaining support for career development. Evidence from the programme reflects this also. When the programme was advertised at full market cost, it did not receive as many applications as when it had been offered at a subsidized cost. Feedback from participants provided evidence to the fact that they had struggled to gain support, in terms of time out of the office and in funding to attend the programme. Only in recent times have some HEIs begun to develop similar resources for DL as with Aurora.

The DAL evaluation showed that as a result of completing the programme, participants felt an increase in: the perception of their visibility and personal value; motivation within their role and confidence in carrying out their duties. It was also found that respondents felt more equipped to move forward and apply for leadership roles. Furthermore, participants valued the 'safe space' in which they could discuss their career journeys with others who had experienced similar barriers in terms of exclusion and marginalization. Fuller findings on the impact of DAL will be published in the Cracking the Concrete Ceiling research, due in 2019.

2. Sponsor toolkit

Introduction

Much research focuses on the use of sponsors as an enabler to career progression for under-represented groups in leadership positions (Ibarra et al., 2010). While mentorship arguably takes a deficit model approach where the individual is 'fixed', sponsorship looks beyond the individual to the environment within which they operate, working to remove institutional barriers to drive positive change. The benefits of sponsorship have been briefly outlined within the introduction of this chapter. Other research supports the idea that sponsorship, especially that by white leaders, can be a major factor in facilitating BME leadership. The concept of 'white sanction', discussed by Miller (2016), captures this belief on the part of BME staff, that being sanctioned by a white person can aid their progression.

For the BME sponsor relationship, research has shown that there may be cultural differences that need to be overcome before effective relationships can be built between a white sponsor and a BME participant (Ragins, 1997). Feedback from DL participants in cohorts 1–4 indicated that it was challenging to establish productive intercultural relationships with their sponsors. Similarly, feedback from sponsors showed that in many cases they were not confident in addressing issues of race and under-representation with participants and often were not aware of the specific barriers faced by BME staff in advancing their careers.

The DAL evaluation found that participants valued the inclusion of a sponsor within the programme, but there was a mixed response to how useful they felt their sponsor had been. This was shown to be the case for a number of reasons:

- There were inconsistencies across institutions in terms of how sponsors were selected.
- There were varying levels of information provided to sponsors in terms of their involvement with the programme.
- There were differing understandings of the sponsor role and their expectations in terms of time commitment.
- Often, sponsors did not know the differences between sponsorship/mentorship and indeed, the difference between sponsoring in the sense of lending support in an application and a formal sponsoring relationship.

It was found that sponsors were appointed in a variety of ways: through centralized process managed by HR/EDI departments; automatically chosen as line manager or approached by the participant themselves. Therefore, outcomes and levels of engagement were mixed with some participants reporting that they had only met once with their sponsor, whereas others had been given constructive advice on current and future roles, improving their curriculum vitae and routes to promotion.

An emergent theme was that HEIs could be more proactive in monitoring the activity of sponsors and their engagement with the programme. While the Leadership Foundation was unable to compel universities to monitor sponsor engagement, it was decided that the support provided to sponsors could be enhanced. It was also determined that it would be beneficial to provide clarity on the difference between sponsorship and mentorship to offer clearer guidance for line managers in how they might support participants alongside a senior sponsor.

Aims

The Sponsor Toolkit (authored by Jannett Morgan, programme director, Diversifying Leadership, and Tinu Cornish, senior training and learning adviser, Advance HE) comprises five modules, designed to be used by participants and sponsors at key stages during the programme.

- Module One: 'The role of the sponsor' provides specification of what the role of the sponsor is, what their expected contribution will be and what qualities they will bring to the role.
- Module Two: 'Race matters' tackles issues related to race and how a willingness to 'talk about race' can strengthen the relationship and increase the chances for protégé career success.
- Module Three: 'The long and winding road – leadership in academia' encourages the sponsor to share their own leadership journey, identifying career enablers, barriers and critical junctions.
- Module Four: 'The tallest poppy: visibility and the double bind' introduces sponsors to the complex ways that bias can play out in institutions and what they can do to counter this in their advocacy of their protégé.
- Module Five: 'Mapping the journey-career planning' introduces sponsors to a process of working with their protégé to create a five-year career plan, identifying future career opportunities and barriers.

As the issue of being ill-equipped to have conversations about race was raised frequently, it was decided that there was a need to have a forum where sponsors could be 'primed' in having conversations about race and the importance of openly discussing barriers faced by participants. A webinar based on the 'Race Matters' module was decided to be the most time effective way to engage sponsors. A workshop at the BME Leadership in Higher Education Summit 2017 was also held on sponsorship and a 'Champions Network' established in November 2017.

Conclusions

Evaluations of the webinar show that sponsors are now better equipped regarding how to have conversations about race and are clearer about the differences between sponsorship and mentorship. Greater understanding of unconscious bias and cultural humility was also found. However, as of the date of publication, three sponsor webinars have been run, with less than a quarter of participant sponsors attending. This shows that despite the development of this support, there is still a significant challenge in convincing senior leaders of the value of giving their time to such initiatives. An evaluation on the use and effectiveness of the toolkit was planned for academic year 2018–19.

3. BME Leadership in Higher Education Summit

2015

The inaugural BME Leadership in Higher Education Summit was co-convened with the Equality Challenge Unit (ECU) in June 2015. The summit aimed to assemble key stakeholders and interested parties to develop practical steps that the sector, the Leadership Foundation and ECU could take towards supporting BME staff to realize their potential and ensure that HEIs benefit from the diversity of talent in the academic and professional workforce. It was hoped a road map for apt, active and relevant leadership development interventions that work for BME staff and their institutions, would be developed as a result.

Parallel round-table discussions were held to consider the following thematic areas: development of cultural understanding in leadership and management; the politics of race, class and gender in developing BME leadership; changes needed at the institutional level; barriers to BME representation in senior academic and professional service staff; action priorities for systems-level change; strategies to increase ethnic diversity at the top and ways to achieve culture change, in order to overcome the perpetuation of stereotypes of BME staff as 'non-leaders'.

A series of recommendations came from the event: to create a networking space and a leadership development programme specifically for BME staff, to provide a space for good practice in developing BME talent pipeline, to run unconscious bias workshops and to establish strategies to engage the executive in this agenda. Subsequently, with further funding, the Leadership Foundation developed the Diversifying Leadership programme, the BME Champions Network, unconscious bias workshops for governing bodies and the senior leadership equality, diversity and immersion retreat for the executive and governing body.

2017

With renewed funding, a second summit was held in May 2017. In the two years since, there has been little progress in diversifying the leadership of our institutions, and the numbers of staff in senior leadership positions has fallen. For example, in 2015 among UK academic staff 8.3 per cent were BME but just 3.9 per cent were classified as senior managers (Equality Challenge Unit, 2015). By 2017, the overall levels of BME UK academic staff had increased to 9.1 per cent but those classified as senior managers had decreased to 2.9 per cent (Equality Challenge Unit, 2017). It must be noted that one theory (Equality Challenge Unit) provided for the decrease is that there has been a skills drain, with many senior academic leaders seeking employment in the United States where it is perceived that there are more opportunities for BME.

The 2017 summit, therefore, aimed to be actions led and to create a practical environment to empower leaders to equip themselves with tools for change. Rather than focus on the deficit, it aimed to focus on enabling system-level change, looking beyond individual development and drawing on evidence-based practice and what works. The summit took the format of a panel discussion, comprised of senior leaders and chaired by Baroness Valerie Amos, director, School of Oriental and African Studies. The question posed to panel members and the audience was 'How can all HE leaders create a step change to advance race equality for BME leaders in universities?' Key areas of consideration were how to challenge organizational culture and how to get strategic buy-in to further advance the race-equality agenda. Workshops were also held in the following thematic areas: sponsorship; white privilege; institutional case studies in good practice; and what works in workforce race equality.

A series of recommendations for action were made by delegates to engage student unions more in terms of developing the talent pipeline; hold HEIs to account through the future role of the Office for Students (OfS); create spaces to have conversations about race at the Executive and the Board level; and provide funding for BME staff development. Feedback from delegates was that the summit created a sense of possibility in terms of what could be done and was energizing.

2018

In 2018, the summit followed a similar format, but the panel and workshops were constructed for a senior audience to respond to the recommendations set out by the 2017 summit. It aimed to provide a balance between areas of policy, practice, advocacy, leadership and influence as well as differing stakeholder perspectives around race equality in HE. With the change from the HEFCE to the OfS and the sector priority in providing value to students, it was felt there was a need to bring in the student perspective through the inclusion of the National Union of Students (NUS). To note, there is little research on whether a diverse workforce improves student attainment and outcomes for BME, and this is an area that requires future and further research.

Nicola Dandridge, chief executive officer, Office for Students, chaired the panel discussion, which included senior leaders who provided the institutional, student, EDI practitioner and policy perspective. The workshops focused on policy and practice at a national level, looking across institutions at the sector as a whole. The themes covered in the workshops were equality and diversity in REF; priorities for OfS in widening participation at all levels in HE; and diversity in governance and conditions for success in senior BME leadership. It was hoped attendees would leave having contributed to the shaping of national initiatives and next steps, and that the summit would provide powerful networking opportunities.

Conclusions

Whilst it is hard to measure the impact of these summits, with an increase in senior leaders attending from 2015–2018, the number of strategic allies interested in the agenda is increasing. However, getting strategic buy-in from the very top remains difficult. The 2018 summit was covered in BBC News and the *Guardian*, with Baroness Amos commenting on the issue of institutional racism within universities. At the time of writing, the *Equality Statistics in Higher Education Report 2018* is yet to be published, so it remains difficult to ascertain the contribution of these summits in bringing about change in the overall landscape.

4. 'Cracking the Concrete Ceiling' study

This study was commissioned by the LFHE in 2016 to follow up on the longer-term impact of the DL programme on participants' experiences, but also to map some of the institutional contexts in which they worked. The overall aim was to learn more about in-depth individual experiences of BME academics seeking to develop their leadership, and the influences of and interplay with contextual factors; and about changes over time. It was hoped that this focus would give a better idea of how to support BME progression in HEIs in a multiplicity of ways. More specifically the project aimed to investigate how leadership development (through the DAL/DL programme) can address contextual and institutional issues surrounding the BME staff pipeline in higher education; and how leadership development for BME staff impacts, and can impact, on facilitating the path to BME leadership in higher education. The study team comprised researchers from across several universities and organizations (Dr Terri Kim (University of East London), co-principal investigator; Professor Jan Fook (visiting professor, Royal Holloway, University of London), co-principal investigator; Amanda Aldercotte (Equality Challenge Unit); Kevin Guyan, Equality Challenge Unit; and Professor Udy Archibong, University of Bradford)).

Design and methods of the project

In broad theoretical terms, the study takes an intersectional approach (Meers, 2014) in the analysis of participant experiences. An intersectional approach recognizes that a number of social factors can intersect to construct the experiences of marginal people.

The study therefore takes into account how multiple factors such as class, age, gender and ability can interplay with racial and cultural/ethnic identity to influence career trajectories of academics to complicate the picture. In this way an intersectional approach should allow a more complex, but nevertheless more accurate, understanding of the influences affecting potential BME leaders.

The study is mixed method in design (Denscombe, 2008) in order to provide both an overview and an in-depth understanding of contextual (structural and institutional) perspectives, as well as individual experiences at a more micro level (Archibong et al., 2009). The qualitative aspect of the project uses a narrative-constructivist methodology (Andrews et al., 2013; Squire et al., 2014) and an intersectional approach. The narrative constructivist methodology is useful for gaining an in-depth understanding of individuals' experiences and interpretations. The narratives are analysed thematically.

Analysis of HESA staff records will be undertaken to provide a picture of BME leadership and identify potential pinch points within the academic trajectory, both at the national and the institutional level for those institutions included in the current study. Second, a longitudinal survey of BME academics will be undertaken, with a first wave at the onset of the project to establish a baseline, and a second one year later. Data collection will be undertaken across a sample of participants involved in the DL programme stratified by institutional type, together with a sample of BME academics not involved in the programme, which will act as a comparison sample.

Mixed methods in collecting data will also allow comparative case studies at the HEIs in which DL participants are based (five consented to be involved). These include both a longitudinal survey of a comparison sample of staff (two waves) and semi-structured interviews with key institutional players (mentors, professional service managers and sponsors). These interviews will focus on perceived changes, especially with regard to cultural changes around being BME.

The study to date and preliminary findings

The study officially began in late 2016, and data collection will finish in late 2018. Interviews are conducted with volunteer participants from cohorts 1–5 (nineteen participants) of the DAL/DL programme (sessions held between January 2016 and the first part of 2017). All of these participants were interviewed at least two to three times over an eighteen-month period.

Given that data collection is not yet complete, only very preliminary findings can be reported at this stage. These tend to echo much of what is already known about the experiences of BME academics in HE. Further analysis is yet to be done to explore the interplay with contextual factors. Below is a summary of themes which have emerged to date.

From DL participant interviews:

- Empowerment and support of BME staff results from being able to network and undertake the DL programme together. Individuals are able to find a group with whom to identify (one participants spoke of 'finding a tribe'.
- However, there is also a need to recognize cultural differences within the group. For example, British-born and non-British-born BME people may have quite different identities, depending on whether they experienced racial or cultural discrimination in their country of birth or where they were raised.

- There is also a clear need to address some of the complex identity and political issues which might arise from raising awareness of BME issues. Not everyone is aware of racial discrimination, or is able to make constructive use of a political analysis of such issues.
  - ° The fact that there is an ongoing role of discrimination in workplace progression was reinforced, in particular the role of hidden cultures which support exclusion of BME staff.
  - ° There is a need to address BME staff support and progression on a range of different fronts.

From the quantitative aspects of the study:

- The sample of institutions selected for the case studies and comparison samples within them are well suited for comparison with the DL participants, both in the similarity of their survey responses and the overlap in themes discussed by DL participants, the comparison sample, DL sponsors and institutional key players.
- The individuals who joined the DL training programme were more likely to be in role model positions and felt less confident in their leadership abilities.
- BME and white respondents experience bias in their departments/ institutions very differently, with BME respondents reporting a strong bias towards the promotion of white individuals and white respondents remaining more neutral on average.

Emerging recommendations reinforce the need for networking, increased transparency with regard to processes for progression and more systematic sponsorship of BME staff.

5. Senior BME leaders study

Whilst many studies of BME staff in higher education highlight the impediments to attaining progression or leadership positions, it is important also to profile factors which might support or facilitate BME staff to achieve leadership, especially very senior leadership positions. With this in mind, the LFHE commissioned another project which focused on stories from BME leaders who had attained positions of seniority. The project was conducted by Jan Fook (Royal Holloway, University of London) and Vijaya Nath (at the time director of leadership development, the LFHE). As both researchers are from BME backgrounds, it was hoped that this might encourage more open discussion of some of the experiences that BME people might normally be more reluctant to share with white colleagues.

There is current interest in narratives of experiences from BME staff, partly because this potentially provides a more holistic view of how different aspects of a person's life or career interacts to result in the attainment of success in leadership. This potentially gives a more complex and perhaps comprehensive focus than simply focusing on either barriers or supports in a career trajectory. Such a focus necessarily implies a polarized view of a career trajectory, whereas in fact different incidents or situations might interact, and be interpreted or constructed differently, and acted upon differently, by different people. For example, what is initially experienced as a barrier, may in fact be reworked and provide an impetus to learning in a way which underpins future progression. Initial hindrances may in fact become opportunities. Experience may consist of a range of different incidents or situations which, working together, help produce an orientation to one's career that works for a particular individual.

In this project, it was hoped that learning in some depth from the actual experiences of BME people who had attained positions of leadership would add some insight into how these different factors worked together. This in turn would help identify how systemic or organizational conditions might support or enhance personal aspirations or abilities, or vice versa, in order to enable leadership progression for BME staff.

For this project, twelve individual BME people who had attained positions of relative seniority were interviewed (either in a focus group or individual interview). Positions ranged from Readership level to very senior management. Most people held professorial positions, and about 70 per cent held positions of academic management. One person held a senior professional services position. Below is a summary of themes which arose from interviews and discussion with this group.

It was common for people to speak of the importance of mentoring, being encouraged to apply for positions which they might not normally have considered, and in general of the role of trusted colleagues. These were not necessarily of BME background. The support of others, such as family members, was mentioned for quite a few participants.

The importance of networking was emphasized, in particular networking with senior colleagues so that they felt some familiarity with BME colleagues. This might involve seeking or taking up opportunities (e.g. sitting on university-wide committees; arranging secondments) which would expose the BME colleague to situations in which they could mix socially with senior colleagues.

The skills and knowledge which participants spoke about as being important varied somewhat. For instance, some participants emphasized the importance of personal qualities such as resilience, persistence and courage. Related to these qualities was the idea of developing self-belief. In relation to this, what might be seen as a relatively contentious point was the place of ethnicity in identity, and how there is a need not to let ethnicity overwhelm identity which might ensure that a negative interpretation becomes a 'self-fulfilling prophecy'.

Others spoke of the need to know and understand university culture, how the organization works, and the ability to appreciate different perspectives on it. In relation to this, having good interpersonal skills and the ability to engage with people helps establish good and trusting relationships with colleagues.

Several people emphasized the need to do a good job and to work hard '*being good (the best) at your present job*' brings recognition. This introduces the idea of what values are important many people spoke of having a clear work ethic, being selfless in your university (i.e. wanting to make a contribution and having this perceived by others).

Lastly, a clear theme was that of identity, and how this may be different for British-born, and non-British-born BME people. The latter may not have been raised in a culture or society where they were a minority, and therefore may not necessarily take on the stigma felt by some British-born BME people. This might make it easier for such people to construct their own identity. Many participants spoke of the need to '*identify a path for yourself*' which '*enables you to be yourself*'. This might involve having a clarity of vision and purpose.

Possible recommendations arising from both studies ('Cracking the Concrete Ceiling and the Senior BME leaders study)

It is important to re-emphasize that there needs to be a suite of initiatives at all levels and of many types. These could include the following:

- Ensuring visibility of BME staff in as many different aspects of the university environment as possible. Obviously this applies particularly at senior levels where the paucity of BME leaders is apparent.
- Working with (and sometimes questioning) more subtle workplace cultures such as 'fitting in' – exposing them, making people aware of

them, so that pathways to seniority and leadership are more transparent. Asking whether a particular idea of practice includes or excludes, and who? Also awareness of commonplace micro-aggressions, for example, assuming a BME person is not a staff member, and certainly not a senior staff member; mistaking a person of colour for someone else of the same colour

- Seeking greater depth than unconscious bias in order to introduce transformational change. Promoting reflection on decision-making regarding recruitment and promotion or when scrutiny is required
- More complex training which acknowledges cultural differences within the BAME group.
- Increased attention to creating and sustaining different types of networks which might work for BAME people in different ways. For example, networking can be done across universities, and may not be exclusively for BME people but perhaps for common interest groups.
- Thinking proactively about exposing BME people to new and different opportunities, for example, committee membership; shadowing.

6. Equality, Diversity and Inclusion (EDI) Senior Leadership Retreat

The EDI retreat aimed at supporting institutions to explore and understand the issues around EDI, with a specific lens on race inequality in HEI culture. The broad intention was to provide an experiential and resourced space to enable participants to identify and explore change strategies, and to develop further strategic thinking for overcoming barriers to change. Based on a pilot for governors that was run in May 2017, the retreat was expanded to include the executive, recognizing the need for both parts of leadership functions to work in tandem.

In order to support organizations and their leaders in their commitment to diversity, the twenty-four-hour retreat included immersive conversation, group work, featured speaker session with a representative of the Office for Students (OFS) and provided a peer-to-peer networking opportunity. The event was facilitated by Vijaya Nath, former director of leadership development, Leadership Foundation, Roger Kline, research fellow, Middlesex University Business School and Simon Fanshawe, partner, Diversity by Design.

Members of university executives and governing bodies were invited to take part. A mixture of Russell Group and post-92 universities attended, with 44 per cent of attendees being governors (including a serving chair) and 56 per cent being executive members.

Structure of event and themes arising

Themes are presented in general terms and not attributed to any one individual or institution, in order to preserve confidentiality.

Participants subscribed to the need for the sector and their individual institutions to do more to bring EDI to the fore in enhancing teaching and learning, research, the student experience and the reputation of the institution. Participants were particularly open about the presence or absence of visible minority ethnic role models in senior leadership roles as well as at the executive board/council level. All individuals attending had plans to set targets to redress the real and perceived imbalance. Over half acknowledged a desire to make EDI core to their business and values. The same number expressed a concern that an austerity culture could encourage HEIs to approach this as a 'tick box exercise'.

After an introduction in which it was emphasized that the retreat intended to provide a safe and non-judgemental forum in which participants could share and explore 'what works' and what changes were needed to take the EDI agenda forward in their HEI, five specific sessions were held.

These were the following:

Session One: Introductions – participants were given an opportunity to speak about their reasons for attending, which indicated a serious appetite for wanting to change their HEI's approach to EDI. They were clear that accountability was central to this. They also made the point that strategies could not just focus on compliance (otherwise, there was risk of a 'tick box' mentality), but also that improvements in racial equality should also bring improvements for people with other protected characteristics.

Session Two: Learning from others – what works? – this session explored the research and practice around some specific successful strategies. These examples were presented as vignettes from the NHS, the United Nations SWOP tool and Diversity by Design's work at Nottingham University – School of Engineering.

Session Three: Exploring Diverse approaches – this was run as two separate groups (Executives and Governors) each exploring two strands as follows:

- What is the Exec's responsibility regarding diversity and inclusion?
- What would be the priorities for action and why?
- How would they articulate the case for effective action on diversity and also communicate it to the staff?
- What is the Council/Board's responsibility regarding diversity of staff and diversity of the Council/Board?
- Why would a more diverse Council/Board be a better one?
- What does governance of diversity mean?
- What governance questions should you be asking of the Executives?

Ideas arising were prepared for presentation to the whole group in session four.

Session Four: Sharing Next Steps and Reflections – below are the key points which emerged from this session.

- Participants wanted to find questions to ask that 'really understood the problem'.
- The tactics of influencing the Board was one consideration – how to take what they had learned/discovered/discussed during the retreat back to their institution and have impact was also important.
- For one group the scale of the task (working towards EDI) facing their current organizational culture was overwhelming. They sought advice on how to begin to communicate the learning from the retreat.
- Both groups sought to understand where their institution was currently – they shared a desire to obtain the data (not just quantitative but also qualitative).
- One group were keen that exec and board really should hear the voices of their staff – especially women and staff with BAME backgrounds.
- They wanted to know what good looked like. What would be realistic and yet ambitious goals for their HEI?
- One group wanted to find out whether the Board and the Exec agreed that there was a problem and what their joint commitment would look like.
- They questioned what the benchmark for metrics was – did demography provide the right baseline, possibly for local employment of professional and technical staff, but for academic staff was it more about reflecting the student population? In the end they were keen that the metrics were not abstract but rather related to the core purpose of their university and of the individual subject and discipline.

- There was agreement that they had to move diversity up the Board agenda and away from a last item of 'report' on (mainly) depressing data. Move it (through the risk register, for instance) to being seen as a significant risk which needed to be faced and mitigated with effective action.
- One group from one institution suggested that to create the change, the Board needed to appeal to the values of the university, that is, 'the pursuit of truth surrounded by friends' and what does being treated equally mean in that context?
- Whilst some bought into the idea that it would be effective in creating momentum to 'start somewhere' – some appreciated the philosophy of 'Think big – trial small'. For others it was a system-level change that they were advocating.
- All reflected on the need to communicate the intention with sensitivity and reflected that they would need help in this.
- They expressed a clear rationale that diversity was crucial to improving ability to enhance performance in relation to core HEI functions (teach, research and support and develop researchers, create great student experience and influence the city, region, country or world.

Session Five: The Regulator's Intention

This final session provided participants with a view from the newly established Office for Students. An overview of the new regulatory framework was provided as well as an insight into the priorities of OfS in reducing the gaps in access, success and progression for under-represented groups. Participants were asked to think about how such a focus on student attainment gaps might feed into wider discussions about EDI policy and practice.

Conclusions

The retreat was a useful vessel for those setting off purposefully on a journey that most recognize will require resources and resourcing especially in austere times. There was a recognition that this vision needs to be an organizational priority and one which is articulated by those in the most senior of leadership positions.

Conclusions

In reviewing the various interventions delivered by LFHE with the higher education sector, it is clear that some progress has been made to raise awareness, to explore what positive actions can achieve and to engage the higher education system as well as individual HEIs. Learning about the experiences of BME academics from LFHE activities tends to mirror what has come out of existing research studies.

However, this means that the pressing work is to establish and embed BME equality as an organizational priority across the sector, and that Advance HE continues to employ, alongside institutions and other sector bodies, a range of strategies to support progress in different ways and at different levels. The sector needs to be joined up and take into account how the personal experiences of BME staff in seeking leadership roles can be supported and enhanced by systemic policies and practice that enable success. Critical to this is sharing what works as well in terms of reporting the issues. More systematic reporting functions to benchmark and also set norms of achievement which can raise the game in workplace cultures.

A joined up, ongoing and holistic approach should impact more effectively to provide an environment and culture which ultimately enables leaders to succeed throughout the HE system, including at the most senior levels. This approach also needs to address a key challenge identified through the interventions reviewed here in that to really expedite change and show commitment, there is an essential need to obtain senior staff buy-in, for them to be visible advocates for change and that their vision for change needs to be communicated and championed across the whole organization.

Notes

1 BME is the term used in this chapter as this was the preferred term used by the Leadership Foundation for Higher Education (LFHE).
2 Please note that since all of these initiatives discussed here were undertaken, the Leadership Foundation for higher Education (LFHE) has amalgamated with the equality Challenge Unit and the Higher Education Academy to become Advance HE.

References

Alexander, C. and J. Arday (eds) (2015), *Aiming Higher: Race, Inequality and Diversity in the Academy*, London: The Runnymede Trust.

Andrews, M., C. Squire and M. Tamboukou (2013), *Doing Narrative Research*, 2nd edn, London: SAGE.

Aouad, G., L. Madabuko, D. Bebbington and K. Perera (2012), 'Self-Assessment Toolkit', London: The Leadership Foundation for Higher Education.

Balter, R., J. Chow and Y. Jin (2014), What Diversity Metrics Are Best Used to Track and Improve Employee Diversity? ILR School, Cornell University. Last accessed 10 May 2018: http://digitalcommons.ilr.cornell.edu/student/68.

Bebbington, D. (2009), *Diversity in Higher Education: Leadership Responsibility and Challenges*, London: Leadership Foundation for Higher Education.

Bhopal, K. and H. Brown (2016), *Black and Minority Ethnic Leaders: Support Networks and Strategies for Success in Higher Education*, London: Leadership Foundation for Higher Education.

Davidson, M. (1997), *The Black and Ethnic Minority Manager: Cracking the Concrete Ceiling*, London: Paul Chapman Publishing.

Delgado, R. and J. Stefancic (2017), *Critical Race Theory: An Introduction,* 3rd edn, New York: New York University Press.

Denscombe, M. (2008), 'Communities of Practice: A Research Paradigm for the Mixed Methods Approach', *Journal of Mixed Methods Research*, 2 (3): 270–83.

Equality Challenge Unit (2015), *Equality in Higher Education: Statistical Report*, London: ECU.

Equality Challenge Unit (2017), *Equality in Higher Education: Statistical Report*. London: ECU.

Fenton, S., J. Carter and T. Modood (2000), 'Ethnicity and Academia: Closure Models, Racism Models and Market Models', *Sociological Research Online*, 5 (2). Last accessed 10 May 2018: http://www.socresonline.org.uk/5/2/fenton.html.

Gooden, M. (2012), 'What Does Racism Have to Do with Leadership?' *Educational Foundations*, 26 (1–2): 67–84.

Ibarra, H., N. M. Carter and C. Silva (2010), 'Why Men Still Get More Promotions Than Women', *Harvard Business Review,* September: 80–4.

Ladson-Billings, G. (2004), 'What Is Critical Race Theory', in G. Ladson-Billings and G. Gillborn (eds), *The Routledge Falmer Reader in Multicultural Education*, 7–24, London and New York: Routledge.

Liu, H. and C. Baker (2014), 'White Knights: Leadership and the Heroicisation of Whiteness', *Leadership*, 12 (4): 420–48.

Manfredi, S., I. Vickers. and E. Cousens (2017) *Increasing the Diversity of Leaders in Higher Education: The Role of Executive Search Firms*, London: The Leadership Foundation for Higher Education.

Meers, N. (2014), *Key Concepts in Race and Ethnicity*, London: SAGE.

Miller, P. (2016), ' "White Sanction", Institutional, Group and Individual Interaction in the Promotion and Progression of Black and Minority Ethnic Academics and Teachers In England', *Power and Education*, 8 (3): 205–21.

Morely, L. (2013), *Women and Higher Education Leadership: Absences and Aspirations*, London: Leadership Foundation for Higher Education.

Morris, L. (2017), 'Reverse Mentoring: Untapped Resource in the Academy?' *Innovative Higher Education*, 42 (4): 285–87.

Morrow, E. (2015), *Why Does Ethnicity Matter in Higher Education Leadership?* Leadership Foundation for Higher Education (LFHE) Leadership Insights, June, London: Leadership Foundation for Higher Education.

Moses, Y. (1989), *Black Women and Academe: Issues and Strategies*, Project on the Status and Education of Women, New York: Association of American Colleges.

National Health Service (NHS) (2017), *NHS Workforce Race Equality Standard (WRES)*. Last accessed 7 June 2018: https://www.england.nhs.uk/publication/workforce-race-equality-standard-data-reporting-december-2017/] Accessed 7 June 2018.

Ogunbawo, D. (2012), 'Developing Black and Minority Ethnic Leaders: The Case for Customized Programmes', *Educational Management Administration & Leadership*, 40 (2): 158–74.

Singh, G. and J. Kwhali (2015), 'How Can We Make Not Break Black and Ethnic Minority Leaders in Higher Education?' Stimulus Paper. The Leadership Foundation for Higher Education, London.

Squire, C., M. Andrews, M. Davis, C. Esin, B. Harrison, L.-C. Hyden and M. Hyden (2014), *What Is Narrative Research?* London: Bloomsbury.

Tharenou, P. (2001), 'Going Up: Do Traits and Informed Social Processes Predict Advancement in Management?' *Academy of Management Journal*, 44 (5): 1005–17.

Universities and Colleges Union (2012), 'The Position of Women and BME Staff in Professorial Roles in UK HEIs', London: Universities and College Union.

Part Three

Race and intersectionality

10

Race, religion and school leadership: The experience of Muslim-Pakistani head teachers

Asima Iqbal

Introduction

While many of us were engaged with racial justice, religion crept up on us as a new dimension: the new race, the point of difference, the characteristic to fear [. . .]
(Warsi, 2017)

Taken from the polemic Baroness Warsi's book, *The Enemy Within: A Tale of Muslim Britain,* the above excerpt provides insight into the experiences of a British Muslim of Pakistani heritage related to the challenges she faced by virtue of her multiple identities. Drawing on her unique place in the British sphere as a child of Pakistani immigrants who became the United Kingdom's first Muslim Cabinet minister, Warsi questions (within the British context), the cultural differences, issues of integration, 'British values', terrorism and her affiliation with her faith and her community. While Warsi's account of her 'British [Pakistani] Muslim' experiences is a recent one, Tariq Modood, with a similar immigrant background, has been advocating the importance of recognizing minorities' sense of inclusion and well-being for over three decades.

Modood's intellectual work on issues of racism and equality is a reflection of his personal experience (as a South Asian) and knowledge of the misrecognition of ethnic minorities, which he describes as 'neglected victims and voices' (Modood, 2005: 5). In an attempt to move away from the conceptualization of race and racism as a biological concept where people of a particular race receive differential treatment on the basis of their colour, Modood (2005) argues that more than the physical appearance, the racialized image of Asians is rooted in their cultural heritage including language, religion and family structures. According to Modood, South Asians not only suffer from 'colour racism' as they clearly belong to a non-white group but also are victims of 'cultural racism' owing to the specific cultural traits associated with this particular group. To understand and propose ways to counter disadvantage and racial discrimination in Britain, it is therefore imperative to find out if the 'Paki-bashing', a kind of 'racialized bullying' that Asian Muslims experienced in the 1960s and 1970s has taken a new form today. Whereas, historically the concept of 'race' was more commonly associated with culture, subsequent developments in the field have acknowledged the importance of religion, Islam in particular, in the genealogy of race (Rana, 2007). This chapter thus arises in a context where religion has a key role in racial dynamics; hence, the cultural and religious dimensions of racial discrimination need to be recognized.

The accommodation of post-immigration ethno-religious minorities, a phenomenon which Modood (2015, 2013) calls 'multiculturalism', is subject to controversy. This is especially so since global events, such as 9/11 and 7/7, led British Muslims to regard themselves as the 'subject of public debate and focus for social security policy in British society' (Gilliat-Ray, 2010: 262). Apart from these international events, the Trojan Horse Controversy (THC) was a national incident which led to increased suspicion of and hostility towards Muslims and played a pivotal role in marking Muslims as problematic. The controversy was based on an anonymous letter released in March 2014, which claimed that schools in Birmingham were targeted by Muslims working as school governors in an effort to replace school leaders with head teachers who wanted to adopt a more Islamic agenda (Clarke, 2014; Kershaw, 2014; Gardner et al., 2015). Further claims of the letter included an agenda of 'taking over' state schools and forcing them to adopt a more Islamic culture. Following the controversy, a specific form of hatred, like Islamophobia, was triggered which arguably focused on school governors, most of whom were British males of Pakistani origin (Miah, 2017).

Thus, if some religious and ethnic groups were stigmatized, to what extent would minorities in question feel able to value the religious aspect of their identity (Modood, 2010), especially when for most of them, 'religion has assumed a primacy or at least a salience' (Modood, 2015: 9)? Such perpetual debates about how to accommodate 'racial groups', which are endangered by different forms of racism and exclusion that have prevailed in Britain for centuries, suggest that further consideration needs to be given to issues of 'racism' as perceived and experienced by racial and cultural groups in general and Asian Muslims in particular. This chapter offers just such evidence by drawing on the findings of an empirical study that offers valuable insights into how race and religion, as aspects of their personal identity, influence the leadership practices of British Muslim head teachers of a Pakistani origin.

The current study was a cross-cultural research conducted in England and Pakistan to compare the manifestation of religion in a professional role in two religiously and culturally diverse countries. While cross-cultural studies in educational leadership have received considerable scholarly attention in recent years (Miller, 2016; 2017), not many writers have been able to draw on systematic research into the impact of religion, as an aspect of culture, on educational leadership. This chapter uses the narratives of five British [Pakistani] Muslim head teachers working in state schools in Birmingham and London to understand how the close intertwining of the two social constructs, race and religion, impacts the educational leaders themselves and those being led. In this chapter, I present a theoretical review of the terms 'race', 'ethnicity' and 'religion' and how they intersect. This is followed by the methodology adopted for the current study. Next, the analysis of the findings draws on the narrative accounts of the selected head teachers and is integrated with the relevant literature. In the concluding section, I summarize the discussion in the chapter while highlighting the contributions of the current study.

The issue in context – The intersectionality of race, ethnicity and religion

Research into understanding of the terms 'race' and 'racism' has a long history. Earlier conceptions of race regarded the term as a biological concept whereby 'human populations were divided into sub-species mainly on the basis of visible physical characteristics' (Bhopal, 2004: 442). However, such a conceptualization remained dominant from early nineteenth century to the end of the Second World War, after which the topography of race shifted between biological characteristics, historical commonality, basic identity and the inaccurate categorization of people based on their traits (Lee, 1994; Morris-Reich and Rupnow, 2017). Regardless of the shift, Lee argued that little consideration was given to the changes in racial conceptions over time, that is, to defining race 'not by its inherent meaning but by the social contexts through which it is constructed' (1994: 751).

Regarding race as a 'social category', Hall (1996) views race as a social and cultural feature of one's identity formation. Thus, a shift from 'biological racism' to 'cultural racism' has resulted in the disarticulation of the concept of 'race', as race and racism are replaced by 'cultural prejudice and religion-based discrimination' (Rana, 2007: 149). This, according to Rana (2007), has led to the profiling of Muslims as a racialized category while simultaneously opening up the debate regarding whether Islamophobia, as a fear and hatred of Islam and Muslims, should be regarded as racism. The inclusion of religion, and Islam in particular, in the category of race, and the resulting equation between Islamophobia and racism is considered problematic. Rattansi (2007) argues that Muslims all over the world are different owing to their skin colours and their ethnic and national backgrounds. Therefore, even if Islamophobia is proven to exist, it is not easy to link it directly with racism.

According to Bhopal (2004), 'ethnicity is a multi-faceted quality that refers to the group to which people belong, and/or are perceived to belong, as a result of certain shared characteristics, including geographical and ancestral origins, but particularly cultural traditions and languages' (442). Such shared characteristics, according to Rattansi (2007), can include subjective elements of identity construction which people form as a consequence of their association with particular groups. However, in the context of Britain, the measurement of these characteristics is quite problematic since Britain is home to people from many different groups, interests and identities, and more and more people have multiple identities (Parekh, 2000). Thus, a group of people may associate themselves with their ancestral origins, yet by virtue of migrating to a different geographical location, they may assimilate the cultural traditions of the host country.

Having defined the terms 'race' and 'ethnicity', I will now move on to discuss how religion integrates with and intersects the previous two terms. I will broadly refer to religion as a set of values and beliefs that shape the experience, knowledge and practices of people who belong to a particular religious tradition. However, more than the definition, I intend to emphasize on 'religion as an identity aspect', to assess the extent to which the close intertwining between race and religion influences the way people belonging to a particular 'race' and/or 'ethnicity', and 'religion' perceive themselves and/or are perceived by others. In a study to assess evidence of religious discrimination in England and Wales, the authors found that religion and ethnicity were highly complex phenomena which were 'both difficult to define, and yet both shape people's experiences and form part of their identity' (Weller, Feldman and Purdam, 2001: 11). The findings of this study further revealed that very often the ethnic, cultural and religious aspects of the participants' identities were closely related and visibly ostensible, thus making the relationship between these forms of identity even more complicated and contested.

While arguing for the need to systematically review discrimination based on religion and belief, Heasman (2002) asserts that religious discrimination, in twentieth-century Britain, was viewed as a corollary of racial discrimination, as a result of which the Race Relations Act 1976 declared Sikhs and Jews as ethnic groups but not Hindus and Muslims. However, an extension of this Act was the Race and Relations (Amendment) Act 2000 which, in addition to covering 'incitement to racial hatred' also included 'incitement to religious hatred'. A host of academic literature and reports have been written to investigate why religious discrimination should be regarded as seriously as any other form of discrimination, namely racial. For example, the *Swann Report* (1985) proposed that members of all ethnic groups, majority as well as minority, should participate actively within a framework of commonly accepted shared values and practices. In particular, the report advocated for the integration of ethnic minority communities in British society, such that they were able to maintain the most essential elements of their ethnic identity, for example, adherence to a specific religious faith.

Apart from the abundant academic literature on religion in Britain, a host of commissioned reports have been published on this subject, which shows that the whole question of religion and belief in British society is being debated and investigated widely (see Spencer, 2008; Butler-Sloss, 2015). In a more recent report requested by government officials to review integration and opportunity in isolated and deprived communities, Dame Louise Casey highlighted the religious and cultural practices of certain communities that not only contributed to their social and economic isolation but also threatened their commitment to British values and laws (Louise, 2016). Although *The Casey Review* (TCR) affirmed the value of religion in society and recognized the importance of interfaith work in improving social cohesion and equality, its disproportionate focus on Muslims was somewhat alarming. Members of the Christian Muslim Forum expressed their frustration over the singling out of Muslims as being the main problem with regards to integration and felt that the unnecessary conflation of Asian and Muslim identities did not provide a solution to the issue of integration (Hakim, 2017). According to Modood (2015), the transmutation of identities, where colour identities (such as black) evolved into ethnic identities (e.g. Pakistani) and finally into religious identities (such as Muslims) has made religion more prominent in the British public sphere. Hence, it is worth exploring whether challenges faced by Christianity in the United Kingdom in terms of justifying and legitimizing 'a role for the Christian faith in the public sphere' (Davie, 2015) have any similarities with the challenges faced by Islam and Muslims in England.

A study conducted in England to investigate the views of Christian Religious Education (RE) teachers regarding a faith-based teacher identity, highlighted the problematic relationship between faith and professional role (Bryan and Revell, 2011). Teachers who participated in this study were reluctant to associate their professional practices with their faith. A number of explanations were proposed by the authors for the marginalization of faith by the teachers. These included adhering to the 'secular' norms of the society, the hegemonic discourse of British society leading the teachers to use value-neutral terms and the assumption that 'exposure to faith in a variety of educational settings can lead to indoctrination' (Bryan and Revell, 2011: 147). Parallel to Christian professionals, Bryan and Revell's (2011) study thus provides a basis for exploring the discourses used by Muslim professionals in public institutions in England, a field which is scarcely researched.

In the particular context of school leadership, research on the impact of values and beliefs of Muslims on education and educational leadership is very limited (Shah, 2016). Owing to the increasing diasporas of Muslims in the United Kingdom, Shah and colleagues (2006b, 2009, 2010, 2013; Shah and Conchar, 2009; Shah and Iqbal, 2011; Shah and Shaikh, 2010) emphasized the need to recognize the diversity in the ideological perspectives of British Muslims and the resulting impact on educational leadership. According to Shah (2006b: 216), 'the effect of leadership values, perceptions and practices' on the learning experiences of Muslim students is crucial to address issues of Muslim youth's identity in multi-ethnic schools. Considering the growing number of Muslim pupils in British schools, school leaders are expected to understand and acknowledge this group of pupils in a way that they 'feel like equal and valued members of the student community' (Shah, 2016a: 127). This, according to Shah (2016a), adds a 'value dimension' to the leadership role of head teachers (Shah, 2016: 127), which might or might not be influenced by the head teachers' religion. Elsewhere, Shah (2006a, 2016) argued that leaders' ethics, particularly those attributed to a religion, shaped the worldviews that underpinned their actions. While the theoretical conceptualization of Islamic beliefs and values are somewhat similar for Muslims in different parts of the world, their practical manifestation can vary to a large extent.

Although the new public discourse on religion treats Islam as an 'archetypal religion', which is misrepresented as being associated with radicalization, social disintegration, extremism and an affront to Britishness (Revell, 2012; Stringer, 2013), religious affiliation is becoming increasingly significant for Muslims in Britain owing to the fact that they form the largest faith group in the country after Christians (Shah and Shaikh, 2010). One consequence of the dominant negative discourse on Islam and the increasing affiliation of Muslims with their religion is reflected in the growing number of Islamic faith schools whose underlying objective is to protect the Muslim identity, which is perceived to be 'under threat or attack' (Tinker and Smart, 2012). However, leaders of these schools face significant challenges while operating in a secular British society such as diverse expectations of Muslim parents, lack of support from the Muslim community, lack of qualified Muslim teachers and negative perceptions of Muslim faith schools (Hammad and Shah, 2018). Whether these challenges are school-specific or Muslim-specific calls for an interpretive frame of inquiry that investigates how Muslim professionals construct the meaning of religion in a multicultural society regardless if they are leading Islamic faith schools or schools without a religious character.

To conclude this section, the literature reviewed suggests that while 'race', 'ethnicity' and 'religion' can all be regarded as a perceived form/s of identity for individuals, the interplay between them is quite complicated. While remaining alert to the complexity of the interplay, I will focus on the empirical evidence provided by the current study to show that any particular form/s of identity can lead to both institutionalized practices of preference and discrimination. In the section that follows, I will outline the methodology used for this research project.

The study

The current study aimed to explore how religion was perceived, interpreted and experienced by Muslim head teachers working in state schools in England and Pakistan. To fulfil the objective of this research, the social phenomenon for this project was described as 'the place of religion in a professional role'. The reality of the social phenomenon depended on how the Muslim head teachers constructed and interpreted it. Aiming to 'grasp the subjective meaning' of the social phenomenon (Bryman, 2012: 712), the research followed a constructivist-interpretive paradigm to explore the Muslim head teachers' understanding of the social phenomenon, and how as part of a social world, their ideas about it were reviewed and reworked (Matthews and Ross, 2010) as they reflected on their interaction with other people (staff, pupils, parents and community).

The selection of the research approach was a pragmatic decision based on the research questions and the overall aim of this project. I adopted elements of (a) multiple case study and (b) phenomenology, with the intention to understand the social phenomenon in meaningfully contrasting cases or situations (Bryman, 2012: 72). Since the head teachers and the phenomenon were inseparable, I adopted Stake's definition of a case study in which he says that a [case study] is '*not* a methodological choice but a choice of *what* is to be studied' (2005: 443; italics in original). In particular, I regarded my 'cases' as 'instrumental', that is, the 'case' was of secondary interest. More importantly, the case(s) facilitated my understanding of the social phenomenon (Stake, 2005: 445). Acknowledging the importance of understanding (*Verstehen*) the 'lived experiences' of Muslim head teachers (Creswell, 2013: 76), I used 'hermeneutic phenomenology' to gain access to the meanings attributed by Muslim head teachers to their actions and then to 'interpret their actions and their social world from their point of view' (Bryman, 2012: 30).

While using a hermeneutic phenomenological approach for the present study, I reflected on my own position in the research process as an 'insider' to the faith tradition. Regarding this position as crucial in interpreting and reporting the head teachers' interpretation of their religion in a leadership role, I focused on their experiences while bracketing out my personal experiences as a Muslim (Creswell, 2013: 78). However, there were some advantages as well of having a similar faith *and* ethnic background as the selected head teachers. This called for 'researcher reflexivity', where I had to continuously reflect on my personal interpretation of religion as well as the phenomenon under study in order to 'move beyond the partiality of [our] previous understandings' (Finlay, 2003: 108).

I used a 'purposive' sampling method as it matched the objective of my research and allowed me to answer the questions formed for this study. Under the umbrella of purposive sampling, I used 'criterion sampling' (Patton, 1990) since the selected head teachers had to match a particular criterion, that is being Muslims of Pakistani origin. Finding these head teachers was a challenging task since Muslims are a minority in England and not many of them are working at higher levels in state schools. From the ten to twelve introductory emails sent to Muslim head teachers (with a Pakistani name), only five responded. Hence these five self-selected head teachers formed the sample in England and comprised three male head teachers and two female head teachers (see Appendix). The fact that the head teachers subscribed to the Islamic faith was a sufficient criterion for them to be included in the sample. Whether they practised elements of their faith was not important for my research study. Therefore, questions regarding the head teachers' religion focused on investigating how they perceived religion in a professional role only.

The data collection process of the current study involved semi-structured interviews with the head teachers and focus group interviews with teachers and pupils. The head teachers were interviewed in two phases to allow events and patterns to unfold over time (Bryman, 2012: 402). This kind of interviewing injected 'a sense of process' in the research as the head teachers had the opportunity to reflect on their responses while preparing themselves for the second-phase interviews. Considering the sensitivity associated with probing about religion, the first-phase interviews aimed towards understanding the leadership practices of Muslim head teachers in the two countries. The second-phase interview guide was designed after conducting a preliminary analysis of the first-phase interviews with the ten head teachers. While the head teachers were given the opportunity to reflect on their leadership practices in the first-phase interviews, in the second phase, they were asked to relate their leadership actions to their own faith, Islam. The focus group interviews with teachers and pupils aimed to obtain multiple perspectives about the selected head teachers' leadership actions, the principles that underpinned these actions and how religion influenced the Muslim head teachers in a leadership role. By conducting the focus groups in a relatively unstructured way, I provided the teachers and pupils an opportunity to share their experiences of the head teachers' leadership and their perceptions of the head teachers' religion in a leadership role.

Findings

The data for this chapter was drawn from the narratives of the five head teachers in England only. In particular, those findings are presented which provide insight into the duality of identity the selected head teachers experienced while being a Muslim *and* a British Pakistani. In this section, I will illustrate, based on the head teachers' experiences, how each of them perceived the advantages and disadvantages of their dual identities in a leadership role.

Perceived advantages of being a British Pakistani Muslim

Contrary to their childhood experiences, where almost all the selected head teachers faced some sort of bullying and racism, there were a number of positives related to the identity aspect of the head teachers' 'Muslimness' on their professionalism in relation to (a) the community they served in their schools and (b) ethnic minority students. The two key perceived advantages that all five head teachers experienced by virtue of their Asian Muslim identity were

1. understanding the needs of Muslim pupils and parents and
2. removing stereotypes against Muslims.

Understanding the needs of Muslim pupils and parents

The narratives of the five head teachers as well as the focus group interviews with teachers and pupils affirmed that there was a certain 'value' aspect of the head teachers' faith identity in relation to the multicultural and multi-ethnic environment in their schools. Although the head teachers did not explicitly acknowledge this 'value' aspect, they made subtle references to the fact that they had a good understanding of the culture of the school, especially where majority pupils were Muslims. Out of the five head teachers, only one (Sajjad) confidently claimed that his Muslim identity actually helped him move to a leadership position:

> they recognized that if they could get somebody who's a good teacher, but was also Muslim, and was also from the same background as the kids, actually that could be a very positive mix in order to provide a positive role model for the youngsters and to get the best out of the children in terms of that real link with the community. (Sajjad)

Other head teachers, in an effort to keep their religious identity separate from their leadership role, grappled with the idea of how to portray their Muslim identity as positive. For example according to Ahmad,

> My identity has been positive and negative but within myself, I'm fairly clear of who I am and the work that I do. But religious beliefs and identity, from my own [...] is nothing more than a positive rather than a hindrance [...] (Ahmad)

The pupils, especially Muslim pupils (in some schools) felt 'proud' to share the faith identity of their head teacher as it meant that they could be accommodated for their special needs, such as halal food.

If he was English, he wouldn't have done the halal food and most of the children here would have been English [. . .] if he wasn't a Muslim, how would he know all these facts about the Muslim faith?[. . .] he knows a lot about English [faith] but he knows more about Muslims because he's born as a Muslim. (Pupils)

Whereas the Muslim pupils correlated such an accommodation with the shared Muslim identity, the head teachers considered it as a normal leadership practice since they felt responsible for all pupils in their schools, including Muslim pupils. Without 'imposing' anything on the Muslim pupils, the head teachers tried to accommodate them for their 'religious' needs as they wanted them to feel part of the school. According to Ahmad,

it's about absorbing them but not making it compulsory [. . .] If they want to do it, we will support it, if they don't want to, we're not going to force them to do because that I believe is their own personal aspect of it. (Ahmad)

Removing stereotypes against Muslims

Another form of perceived advantage experienced by the selected head teachers was when they acted as ambassadors of their faith to remove some typical stereotypes against Islam and Muslims. For instance, with the THC in perspective, Khalid was determined to engage in discussions and simultaneously reflect on what went wrong and where.

the actions of a group of individuals are not representative of the whole society'[. . .] particularly with TH, I think a lot of people were 'is this against Muslims and everything else?' and to me it was, if there is a major concern, and there is extremism out there, we need to look at ourselves and what we are doing. (Khalid)

Similarly, Ahmad, was determined to respond to people's apprehensions and answer their queries regarding the THC.

I think that's still good practice that you are questioned about what is it that you are doing. And there we create that understanding of what is happening rather than just the expectation. (Ahmad)

On another occasion, Khalid was questioned by a member of the Office for Standards in Education, Children's Services and Skills (Ofsted) team about why Muslims had to conduct their ritual prayers in Arabic instead of English. To this, Khalid replied that

> sometimes it's that lack of knowledge of how the prayer is conducted, or aspects of the prayer that sometimes, it's that one sweep of brush to say it must be extremist [. . .] that's not where extremism comes in; that's actually the balanced bit of religion [Islam]. (Khalid)

Another aspect of using their Muslim identity as a positive in a leadership position was the head teachers' acknowledgement of and commitment to their multiple identities, that is, a professional, a British citizen *and* a Muslim. Sajjad explained,

> I can openly and confidently be a practising Muslim in my professional role and be a highly successful head teacher and lead a group of people, many of them aren't Muslims and for them to see those qualities in me and for them to believe in me and follow me. (Sajjad)

And Laiba asserted,

> I think wherever you live, you have a duty for not only yourself but the people you represent to show that you are capable of being a citizen of that nation [. . .] you may look different but you have to accept and do some of the things they [the society] do but that shouldn't compromise your beliefs and what you do [. . .] (Laiba)

Thus, the head teachers felt confident to use their Islamic knowledge to respond to people's misconceptions about Islam while simultaneously acting as ambassadors of their faith. Although, as stated previously, the head teachers preferred to keep their religious identity in the background, there were various occasions when they felt an obligation to counter the negative perceptions of people about Islam and Muslims.

Perceived disadvantages of being a British Pakistani Muslim

While the previous section highlighted the perceived advantages the Muslim head teachers experienced by virtue of their religious and ethnic identity, this section will illustrate how their dual identity led to various forms of disadvantages and discrimination. The two oft-cited disadvantages were

1. challenges posed by Muslim parents and
2. the THC.

Challenges posed by Muslim parents

The head teachers' narratives provided examples of a variety of challenges they faced, in particular from Asian Muslim (mostly Pakistani) parents. These challenges ranged from parents restricting their children to participate in sex-education classes or learn about LGBT issues, to prohibiting girls to attend school, to judging the head teachers' religiosity when they did not comply with the Muslim parents' requests. On such occasions, the head teachers felt the need to keep their faith identity separate from their professional identity.

> [. . .] that challenge remains with me because the parents' view is that 'you should know better'! And when I say, I think I do, you can see that the clash occurs in that moment in time [. . .] that's where I think particularly a Muslim head has to be able to differentiate between where the religious aspect of it is and what job you're here to do. (Ahmad)

As the head teachers explained, there was a fine line between not allowing their religion to compromise their professional duties, and compromising their religious beliefs altogether while acting professional. It is here that the community would judge the extent to which the head teachers adhered to their faith. Some teachers in a focus group observed that

> he gets a little bit flagged from the [Muslim] community about how much he practises his faith, whether he practises it enough or doesn't practise it and what impact that has upon the students. (Teachers)

In situations where the selected head teachers were challenged by Asian Muslim parents for their inability to accommodate them regarding aspects of the curriculum, the head teachers decided to separate the components of religion from those of culture, as a way to deal with such situations. Sajjad explained the fulfilment of such 'community' expectations in the following way:

> I understand that I serve a community where that's [accepting same-sex marriages] going to be very difficult for them. But equally I have to reinforce the fact that this is a requirement by law and actually we live in a society where they [pupils] are going to encounter people who are homosexual. You can't hide away from it, you can't deny it [. . .] I can't allow that [morality] to prevent me carry out my legal duties. And that is a compromise because the alternative is to walk away. (Sajjad)

By making a clear distinction between religion and culture, the head teachers took a strategic decision in order to deal with the tensions between the community they served and the educational norms of their institutions.

In addition to being judged for their personal religious inclination, some of the selected head teachers felt they were discriminated against by Pakistani Muslim parents who undermined their leadership abilities on the pretext that they were not 'white'. According to Sajjad,

> And for some people, the level of respect they would have for a non-Muslim head teacher is greater than the level of respect they have for me, unfortunately. And we do have a mentality within our own community where we have an inferiority complex and we think that the white host must be better than us [. . .] one of the things my deputy head often says is the way some people within the community talk to me, they would never talk to a white head teacher like that. (Sajjad)

Mona, a female head teacher, faced additional discrimination owing to her gender:

> our own people [Asians] were becoming very negative and that's really sad [. . .] but then it becomes more jealousy against the faith. And you find that the jealousy streak comes from your own kind, which is really sad [. . .] they won't make contact with me but my deputy who's white; they'll speak to him throughout the meeting even though I'm the one who's leading it but they won't look at me because you're an Asian woman, what do you know? It's the way they perceive me and 'apney' [an Urdu word for people of your own kind] are worse.

The above form of 'negative discrimination' as narrated by the selected Muslim head teachers was a unique one. Another atypical example of 'negative discrimination' or disadvantage the head teachers experienced resulted from the THC and is discussed in the next section.

The Trojan Horse Controversy (THC)

Though not formally investigated during the research interviews, the THC was mentioned a number of times by the selected Muslim head teachers, and their interpretation of it suggested that they became part of the controversy owing to their faith identity. However, in this particular instance, it was the media, the local authorities (LAs) and the Department for Education (DfE) who challenged their Muslim identity rather than the parents and/or pupils. The way the head teachers dealt with this controversy suggested that not only did they feel responsible for dealing with such allegations targeted at Muslim professionals in education, but also they were determined to remove any stereotypes against Muslims in general. According to Khalid:

> what is out there is a perception of people of Muslim background, Muslim head teachers. And I think what people forget is that actually I'm here as a professional. I was not appointed because of the colour of my skin or my race or my religion. I actually came to this position as a head teacher. I was appointed as somebody who'll be able to lead this school as a head teacher. (Khalid)

Regarding the role of media in overemphasizing the link between Islam, Muslims and the controversy, Ahmad explained,

> the media would have done their homework, they knew who I was, they knew where I had come from, they knew what I was doing, so in some of the media, they actually made a correlation[. . .] the only references they've made within the media is they've said, you know, 'when a Sikh head teacher left, a Muslim head teacher came in'; and that's what the media sometimes plays with the fine nuances. (Ahmad)

While the THC proved to be controversial in terms of challenging the leadership position of the Muslim head teachers, they successfully managed to deal with the apprehensions and allegations of the DfE, Ofsted and the media by taking a professional stance. All selected head teachers unanimously claimed that the THC did not undermine their leadership. Although this claim could be attributed to the head teachers' understanding that they were in a political position where they were not allowed to say certain things in certain ways, it is also possible that they were undaunted by the whole controversy.

Discussion

The duality of the selected head teachers' identity played out differently in relation to pupils, parents, community and the media. On the one hand, the value aspect of the selected head teachers' religious and ethnic identity was apparent when they showed awareness of the need to accommodate Muslim pupils and parents in their schools and to remove stereotypes against Islam and Muslims. On the other hand, there was evidence of racism that the Muslim head teachers experienced from the Muslim community and the media.

While dealing with Muslim pupils and parents, the selected head teachers were flexible in using their religious faith in a professional role. Although none of them regarded the relationship between their religion and profession as problematic, the way they chose to express their religion indicated that they tried to keep their personal faith separate from their profession. Except for Sajjad, who did not like to segregate his personal faith from his profession, all the other head teachers emphasized 'profession' more than 'religion'. The segregation, as the narratives reflected, resulted from the head teachers' awareness of the cultural and religious mix of staff and pupils in their schools, owing to which they refrained from expressing their religion overtly. In an effort to show respect to the different cultures and religions that existed in their schools, the head teachers used a 'common-to-all-religions' discourse where they emphasized values that were common to all religions. Such a lack of inclination towards any one particular faith allowed the *Muslim* identity of the head teachers to coexist with their *professional* identity. The head teachers were aware that they were part of a society where Islam was not the dominant religion; therefore, their narratives implied that Islam was more of an identity signifier for them rather than a personal faith preference.

The examples of 'positive' discrimination, as experienced by the selected head teachers, were attributed to their religious and ethnic identity, and when these two facets of identity matched those of the pupils, it led to a 'perceived advantage' (Bush et al., 2005). According to Bush et al. (2005), 'where leaders are working in their own ethnic communities, they are often able to derive the support needed to persevere in the midst of perceived racism and discrimination' (2005: 68). Thus, the flexible ways in which the 'religious', the 'ethnic' and the 'professional' identities of the head teachers converged (in particular with the pupils) implies that any form of identity is subject to constant formation and re-formation in relation to the context in which it is constructed (Rattansi, 2007).

Although the selected head teachers felt capable of managing their multiple identities in a professional role, it was not clear if any one form of identity (religious or ethnic) influenced their working more than the other. However, in an effort 'to establish a kind of balance between their religious and secular convictions' (Habermas, 2006: 8), it is likely that the head teachers tried to be reflexive on their own faith position such that they did not have to 'split their identity into a public and a private part the moment they participate in public discourses' (ibid.: 10). Thus, findings from the current study provide useful empirical evidence about how Muslim head teachers in Muslim majority schools could be advantageous for the community in general, and Muslim pupils in particular. However, Sajjad's perception about the usefulness of his Muslim identity in progressing to a leadership position can be considered as a negative dimension too (Bush et al., 2006). That there is a possibility that black and minority ethnic head teachers (Pakistani Muslims in particular) may only be considered for positions concerned with ethnic issues rather than general leadership positions, cannot be ignored. Nevertheless, the findings support the case of increasing the participation of minority ethnic leaders in schools.

The challenges posed by Asian Muslim parents (and the wider society) towards these head teachers, which led to the perceived disadvantage of being a British [Pakistani] Muslim, highlighted a different form of 'racism', where the head teachers received differential treatment from Muslim parents by virtue of their affiliation with Pakistanis as an ethnic group and Muslims as a religious group. This form of 'new racism' or 'cultural racism' (Barker, 1981; Gilroy, 1987; Modood, 2005; Rattansi, 2007) was manifested in a manner which is quite different to the ways these terms have been described by the said authors. While Modood (2005) explained 'cultural racism' as a 'racism based on cultural differences' (27) and one which is most likely targeted towards non-whites, head teachers in the current study experienced this dimension of discrimination from people of their own kind. That is, while the head teachers were aware of their multiple identities owing to their multiple roles and subject positions (Rattansi, 2007), the Muslim parents and community they dealt with only viewed them as Pakistani Muslims who were expected to understand and accept the Muslim parents' needs for special provisions.

Such a community expectation, on the part of Asian Muslims, implied a form of refusal to assimilate to the host British culture, which according to Rattansi

(2007) is a form of racism towards Britons and British national culture (82). However, more than that, it appeared to be a form of cultural racism whereby the Pakistani Muslim parents, as part of a distinctive minority community, acted defensively in protecting the core elements of their religion, as far from denying the religious difference between them and the host society. They wanted to 'assert this difference in public and demand that they be respected just as they are' (Modood, 2005: 39). Thus, the findings of the current study add a new dimension to the idea of 'cultural racism' as in this particular case, the racism was initiated by and targeted towards members of the same minority community, that is, Pakistani Muslims.

The second form of perceived disadvantage that the selected head teachers experienced was in relation to the infamous 'Trojan Horse' affair in Birmingham. According to Miah (2017), Operation 'Trojan Horse' became pivotal in national educational and political debates in early 2014 as it was alleged that schools with majority Muslim pupils were being taken over with the intention of radicalizing young Muslims. The focus of the bulk of newspaper articles (867 in *The Mail* and 560 in the *Guardian*) and reports (Clarke, 2014; Kershaw, 2014; Gardner et al., 2015) published on the subject was to embed a security agenda in inner city schools while contributing to the racialized politics surrounding radicalization and Muslim youth. Miah (2017) links this agenda to 'racial politics', which was manifested through negative media discourse that attempted to stereotype all Muslims as possessing negative traits and being involved in an Islamic plot that posed a security threat at the national level (15). Although the focus of the current study was not to investigate the THC, the responses of the head teachers clearly indicate that they became part of it owing to (a) their Asian Muslim identity and (b) the fact that they were leading Muslim majority schools.

The investigations carried out to assess and evaluate the controversy could not specifically link the affair with extremism. However, it did question the idea of multiculturalism as the selected head teachers, though part of an ethno-religious community, did not believe in self-segregation. In fact, they showed a deep commitment to the 'British' values of democracy, rule of law and religious tolerance (Holmwood and O'Toole, 2018). Regarding the religious, ethnic and professional aspects of their identities as important, these head teachers strived to secure a leadership position to actively participate in the British public life. Hence their idea of multiculturalism was not an 'endorsement of multiple and separate differences, but an expression of how difference can be lived and respected through civic values' (Holmwood and O'Toole, 2018: 238). Nevertheless, the media discourse and commissioned reports portrayed Muslim communities as a security problem (Miah, 2017), and the social construction of the head teachers' Muslim identity, during the time of the controversy, was no exception.

Summing up the experiences of the head teachers, I would like to borrow a phrase from Holmwood and O'Toole's work on the THC, that 'religion is not a problem' (2018: 239), to understand how the Muslim head teachers dealt with the perceived advantages and disadvantages of their British Pakistani identity.

Implications

Given the numerous studies on cross-cultural educational leadership which proposed various models to explain school leaders' behaviours and actions (Dimmock and Walker, 1998a, 1998b; Hallinger and Heck, 1998; Cheong, 2000; Walker and Dimmock, 2002; Hallinger, 2003; Miller, 2016), this research contributes to increasing the understanding of religion as a variable of culture. With a particular focus on the 'Muslim' identity of the head teachers, the findings of the study draw attention to a scarcely researched area in school leadership, that is, the impact of faith identity on the head teachers' professionalism in relation to (a) the community they serve in the schools, (b) the ethnic minority students of which Muslim students are a majority and (c) the perceived advantages and disadvantages they experience in their professional role of their Asian Muslim identity.

The experiences of the selected head teachers indicated a very different form of 'cultural racism', where they felt discriminated from people of their own kind, that is, Asian Muslim parents. Remaining alert to their sense of belonging to a religious as well as a racial group, these head teachers valued their professional identity as much (or more) as their religious identity. The way they responded to the aforementioned situations reflected their determination to use the concept of 'multiculturalism' as 'a rebuttal to entrenched institutional racism, a slapdown of advocates of racial superiority, a sign of a comfortable global citizen, one who can be different and a part of the whole at the same time' (Warsi, 2017: 39). Taking their Asian Muslim identity as a positive, the head teachers' narratives reflected a strong resolve to act strong and resilient in the face of the institutionalized practices of preference and discrimination.

The findings of the current study contribute to the existing debates on race and religion in many useful ways. Although the terms race and racism have a history of misuse and injustice associated with them, empirical evidence from the current study indicated that these concepts are not always associated with oppression and discrimination. The way in which the five Muslim head teachers experienced their 'race' and 'religion' in a professional role highlighted the social contexts in which these concepts were constructed and used as tools to understand broader concepts such as diversity, multiculturalism, interculturalism and the like. That the selected Muslim head teachers were perceived not only as a religious group but also as a racial group (Meer, 2013) can help improve our understanding of how multiple identities of people in a position of power play out in relation to the stakeholders involved.

With a particular focus on Muslims, this research expands existing literature on the concepts of 'new racism' and 'cultural racism' by introducing a new dimension of cultural racism in which Asian Muslims can feel discriminated against by members of their own minority community. This is particularly crucial in understanding how to make 'multiculturalism' work in a society where Pakistani Muslims are a significantly large, non-white, ethno-religious minority group who follow a distinctive and cohesive value system largely rooted in Islam (Modood, 2005). To counter the racism and racialized politics this ethnic minority group faces in today's Britain, acknowledging the new dimension of cultural racism is important, in order to improve unity within this fast-growing community, especially if for most of them, the religious aspect of their identity is common as well as important.

The strategic way in which the head teachers separated aspects of religion from culture reflected their intention to remain true to their faith while simultaneously conforming to the expectations of the Western school system. Thus, at the same time as Pakistani Muslims want to defend the basic elements of their religion and culture, the findings of the current study provide evidence that Muslim professionals do not necessarily have to face a conflict between abiding by the rule of law and the basic tenets of Islam. This lesson is particularly important since the need to accept the expression of religion in public life, including schools, is being widely recognized now (Butler-Sloss, 2015; Holmwood and O'Toole, 2018).

Finally, the findings of the current study have important implications for educational leadership as well. With all their multiple identities (Asian/Pakistani, Muslim, British and professional), the selected head teachers were very conscious of the 'multicultural' environment in which they led their schools. Hence their expression of their faith clearly tied their religious identity to that of the majority pupils in their schools. Although this does not demonstrate the necessity of having a Muslim head teacher for schools with majority Muslim children, it does highlight the value of head teachers and pupils sharing a similar religious background. Thus, the close identification between Muslim head teachers and

Muslim pupils, and the empirical evidence it provided of the benefits of this association, could contribute to the wider debate in the literature of increasing diversity in leadership (Morgan, 2016).

Appendix
Demographic facts about Muslim head teachers in England

Head teachers	Some demographic facts
Ahmad	*Gender:* Male *Years as head teacher in current school:* 8 *Age:* 46–50 *School level:* Secondary *Location:* West Midlands
Khalid	*Gender:* Male *Years as head teacher in current school:* 9 *Age:* 41–45 *School level:* All-through school *Location:* West Midlands
Sajjad	*Gender:* Male *Years as head teacher in current school:* 5 *Age:* 41–45 *School level:* Primary *Location:* West Midlands
Laiba	*Gender:* Female *Years as head teacher in current school:* 5 *Age:* 51–55 *School level:* Primary *Location:* North-East London
Mona	*Gender:* Female *Years as head teacher in current school:* 4 *Age:* 46–50 *School level:* Primary *Location:* West London

References

Barker, M. (1981), *The New Racism: Conservatives and the Ideology of the Tribe*, Frederick, MD: Junction Books.

Bhopal, R. (2004), 'Glossary of Terms Relating to Ethnicity and Race: For Reflection and Debate', *Journal of Epidemiology & Community Health*, 58 (6): 441–5.

Bryan, H. and L. Revell (2011), 'Performativity, Faith and Professional Identity: Student Religious Education Teachers and the Ambiguities of Objectivity', *British Journal of Educational Studies*, 59 (4): 403–19.

Bryman, A. (2012), *Social Research Methods*, Oxford: Oxford University Press.

Bush, T., D. Glover and K. Sood (2006), 'Black and Minority Ethnic Leaders in England: A Portrait', *School Leadership & Management*, 26 (3): 289–305.

Bush, T., D. Glover, K. Sood, C. Cardno, K. Moloi, G. Potgeiter and K. Tangie (2005a), *Black and Minority Ethnic Leaders*, Nottingham: National College of School Leadership.

Butler-Sloss, E. (2015), *Living with Difference: Community, Diversity and the Common Good*, Cambridge: The Woolfe Institute.

Cheong, C. Y. (2000), 'Cultural Factors In Educational Effectiveness: A Framework For Comparative Research', *School Leadership & Management*, 20 (2): 207–25.

Clarke, P. (2014), *Report into Allegations Concerning Birmingham Schools Arising from the 'Trojan Horse' Letter*. GOV.UK. Last accessed 3 May 2017: https://assets. publishing.service.gov.uk/government/uploads/system/uploads/attachment_data/ file/340526/HC_576_accessible_-.pdf.

Creswell, J. W. (2013), *Qualitative Inquiry and Research Design: Choosing among Five Approaches*. 3rd edn, Washington, DC: SAGE.

Davie, G. (2015), *Religion in Britain: A Persistent Paradox*, West Sussex: John Wiley & Sons.

Dimmock, C. and A. Walker (1998a), 'Comparative Educational Administration: Developing a Cross-Cultural Conceptual Framework', *Educational Administration Quarterly*, 34 (4): 558–95.

Dimmock, C. and A. Walker (1998b), 'Towards Comparative Educational Administration: Building the Case for a Cross-Cultural School-Based Approach', *Journal of Educational Administration*, 36 (4): 379–401.

Finlay, L. (2003), 'Through the Looking Glass: Intersubjectivity and Hermeneutic Reflection', in Finlay, L. and Gough, B. (eds), *Reflexivity: A Practical Guide for Researchers in Health and Social Sciences*, 105–19, Oxford: Blackwell Science.

Gardner, L., L. Owen, M. Smith, B.-J. Bonsu, A. Chudasama, S. Armitage and H. Pearce (2015), *Extremism in Schools: The Trojan Horse Affair*, London: House of Commons Education Committee.

Gilliat-Ray, S. (2010), *Muslims in Britain: An Introduction*, Cambridge: Cambridge University Press.

Gilroy, P. (1987), *There Ain't No Black in the Union Jack: The Cultural Politics of Race and Nation*, Oxford: Unwin Hyman.

Habermas, J. (2006), 'Religion in the Public Sphere', *European Journal of Philosophy*, 14 (1): 1–25.

Hakim, M. S. (2017), *CMF Response to Casey Review: Integration and Opportunity*, London: Christian Muslim Forum.

Hall, S. (1996), 'Race, Articulation, and Societies Structured in Dominance', in H. A. Baker, M. Diawara and R. H. Lindeborg (eds), *Black British Cultural Studies: A Reader*, 16–60, Chicago: University of Chicago Press.

Hallinger, P. (2003), 'Leading Educational Change: Reflections on the Practice of Instructional and Transformational Leadership', *Cambridge Journal of Education*, 33 (3): 329–52.

Hallinger, P. and R. H. Heck (1998), 'Exploring the Principal's Contribution to School Effectiveness: 1980–1995', *School Effectiveness and School Improvement*, 9 (2): 157–91.

Hammad, W. and S. Shah (2018), 'Leading Faith Schools in a Secular Society: Challenges Facing Head Teachers of Muslim Schools in the United Kingdom', *Educational Management Administration & Leadership*, 1–17.

Heasman, K. (2002), *Discrimination on the Grounds of Religion or Belief*, London: NATFHE.

Hofstede, G. and M. H. Bond (1984), 'Hofstede's Culture Dimensions: An Independent Validation Using Roackeach's Value Survey', *Journal of Cross-Cultural Psychology*, 15 (4): 417–33.

Holmwood, J. and T. O'Toole (2018), *Countering Extremism in British Schools? The Truth about the Birmingham Trojan Horse Affair*, Bristol: Policy Press.

Kershaw, I. (2014), *Investigation Report: Trojan Horse Letter*, London: EVERSHIELDS

Lee, J. C.-S. (1994), 'Navigating the Topology of Race', *Stanford Law Review*, 46 (3): 747–80.

Louise, C. (2016), *The Casey Review: A Review into Opportunity and Integration*, GOV.UK. Last accessed 20 May 2017: https://assets.publishing.service.gov.uk/government/uploads/system/uploads/attachment_data/file/575973/The_Casey_Review_Report.pdf.

Matthews, B. and L. Ross (2010), *Research Methods: A Practical Guide for the Social Sciences*, New York: Pearson Longman.

Meer, N. (2013), 'Racialization and Religion: Race, Culture and Difference in the Study of Antisemitism and Islamophobia', *Ethnic and Racial Studies*, 36 (3): 385–98.

Miah, S. (2017), *Muslims, Schooling and Security: Trojan Horse, Prevent and Racial Politics*, London: Palgrave Macmillan.

Miller, P. (2016), *Exploring School Leadership in England and the Caribbean: New Insights from a Comparative Approach*, London: Bloomsbury.

Miller, P. (2017), 'Cultures of Educational Leadership: Researching and Theorising Common Issues in Different World Contexts', in P. Miller (ed.), *Cultures of Educational Leadership: Global and Intercultural Perspectives*, 1–24, London: Palgrave Macmillan.

Modood, T. (2005), *Multicultural Politics: Racism, Ethnicity, and Muslims in Britain*, Minneapolis: University of Minnesota Press.

Modood, T. (2010), 'Moderate Secularism, Religion as Identity and Respect for Religion', *The Political Quarterly*, 81 (1): 4–14.

Modood, T. (2013), *Multiculturalism: A Civic Idea*, 2nd edn, Cambridge: Polity Press.

Modood, T. (2015), *'We Don't Do God'? The Changing Nature of Public Religion*, London: The Leadership Foundation.

Morgan, N. (2016), *Educational Excellence Everywhere*, London: Department for Education.

Morris-Reich, A. and D. Rupnow (2017), 'Introduction', in A. Morris-Reich and D. Rupnow (eds), *Ideas of 'Race' in the History of Humanities*, 1–32, London: Palgrave Macmillan.

Parekh, B. (2000), *The Future of Multi-Ethnic Britain: Report of the Commission on the Future of Multi-Ethnic Britain*, London: The Runnymede Trust.

Patton, M. Q. (1990), *Qualitative Evaluation and Research Methods.* 2nd edn, Thousand Oaks, CA: SAGE.

Rana, J. (2007) ,'The Story of Islamophobia', *Souls*, 9 (2): 148–61.

Rattansi, A. (2007), *Racism: A Very Short Introduction*, Oxford: Oxford University Press.

Revell, L. (2012), *Islam and Education: The Manipulation and Misrepresentation of a Religion*, Sterling: Trentham Books.

Shah, S. (2006a), 'Educational Leadership: An Islamic Perspective', *British Educational Research Journal*, 32 (3): 363–85.

Shah, S. (2006b), 'Leading Multiethnic Schools: A New Understanding of Muslim Youth Identity', *Educational Management Administration & Leadership*, 34 (2): 215–37.

Shah, S. (2009), 'Muslim Learners in English Schools: A Challenge for School Leaders', *Oxford Review of Education*, 35 (4): 523–40.

Shah, S. (2010), 'Re-thinking Educational Leadership: Exploring the Impact of Cultural and Belief Systems', *International Journal of Leadership in Education*, 13 (1): 27–44.

Shah, S. (2013), 'Islam, Education and Gender: Discourses and Practices among Pakistani Diaspora in the UK', in Z. Gross, L. Davies and A.-K. Diab (eds), *Gender, Religion and Education in a Chaotic Postmodern World*, 241–52.

Shah, S. (2016), *Education, Leadership and Islam: Theories, Discourses and Practices From An Islamic Perspective*, Oxon: Routledge.

Shah, S. and C. Conchar (2009), 'Why Single-Sex Schools? Discourses of Culture/Faith and Achievement', *Cambridge Journal of Education*, 39 (2): 191–204.

Shah, S. and M. Iqbal, (2011), 'Pakistani Diaspora in Britain: Intersections of Multi-Locationality and Girls' Education', *British Journal of Sociology of Education*, 32 (5): 763–83.

Shah, S. and J. Shaikh (2010), 'Leadership Progression of Muslim Male Teachers: Interplay of Ethnicity, Faith and Visibility', *School of Leadership and Management*, 30 (1): 19–33.

Spencer, N. (2008), *Neither Private Nor Privileged: The Role of Christianity in Britain Today*, London: Theos

Stake, R. E. (2005), 'Qualitative Case Studies', in N. K. Denzin and Y. S. Lincoln (eds), *The Sage Handbook of Qualitative Research*, 443–66, 3rd edn, Thousand Oaks, CA: SAGE.

Swann, Lord (1985), *The Swann Report: Education for All*, Lincolnshire: National Council for Mother Tongue Teaching.

Tinker, C. and A. Smart (2012), 'Constructions of Collective Muslim Identity by Advocates of Muslim Schools in Britain', *Ethnic and Racial Studies*, 35 (4): 643–63.

Walker, A. and C. Dimmock (2002), 'Cross-cultural and Comparative Insights into Educational Administration and Leadership', in A. Walker and C. Dimmock (eds), *School Leadership and Administration: Adopting a Cultural Perspective*, 13–32, London: RoutledgeFalmer.

Warsi, S. (2017), *The Enemy Within: A Tale of Muslim Britain*, London: Allen Lane, Penguin Books.

Weller, P., A. Feldman and K. Purdam (2001), *Religious Discrimination in England and Wales*, London: Home Office Research, Development and Statistics Directorate.

11

What does it mean to be 'successful'? Narratives of British South Asian head teachers and head girls

Deborah Jones and Geeta Ludhra

Introduction

This chapter explores the narratives of four academically and professionally 'successful' British South Asian girls and women originally from two studies. In this newly merged study, Ludhra draws upon two head girls from her research with twelve academically successful British South Asian adolescents (Ludhra, 2015) and Jones on two women from her research with twenty male and female head teachers (Jones, 2017). We focus on two key questions: First, 'what does it *mean* to be 'successful' in these roles?' Second, 'how is 'success' mediated across women's lived experiences?' As feminist researchers, we consider, in this merged study, 'behind the scenes' realities of becoming successful and how 'success' is performed.

Several studies of generations in relation to education have been undertaken, for example, longitudinal studies of teachers' lives (Hargreaves and Goodson, 2006) teachers and work styles (Edge, 2014; Stone-Jonson, 2016) and more recently of head teachers (Johnson, 2017). This is the first cross-generational study of 'success' in relation to British South Asian girls and women in differing educational contexts, across primary and secondary schools. Stone-Johnson (2016) notes that 'generations [. . .] share important milestones that inform their understanding of how the world operates' (cited in Johnson, 2017: 844). In her commentary on Mannheim (1952), Johnson notes that the point at which individuals are born can 'lead to a distinctive consciousness and influence their specific life chances as well as their perspective on history' (844). An aim of this chapter is to illuminate the differences or similarities that are evident across two generations of British South Asian girls and women.

We move beyond listing characteristics of 'success', towards a narrative of what 'success' means and how it is manifested. Challenges experienced across home and school contexts are explored, together with the ways in which family and cultural commitments are played out. In this study, we create a third space to think about 'success' narratives for minority ethnic girls and women, across time and experiences (Bhabha, 1990).

The category 'Asian' is a contested and broad one. In this chapter, the term 'British South Asian' is used to encompass diverse groups referring to girls and women whose parents or grandparents have migrated to the United Kingdom from the Indian subcontinent (Brown and Talbot, 2006) including India, Pakistan, Bangladesh and Sri Lanka. These incorporate East-African Asians, who came to the United Kingdom via Tanzania, Kenya or Uganda (Ghuman, 2011). Specifically, in this merged study of four participants, the girls and women were from Sikh and Muslim religious backgrounds.

Women and 'success'

The notion of 'success' is a contested one, being interpreted and experienced in various ways beyond academic and professional achievements. It can include practical intelligences, personality traits, and a demanding work ethic, and may take account of ways in which family, culture and emotional support can facilitate 'success' journeys (Gladwell, 2008).

There is a small but growing literature on 'success' in relation to different groups, for example, girls and women (Ringrose, 2013; Harris, 2004, 2010), white middle-class families (Ball, 2003), white middle-class girls (Walkerdine et al., 2001), women in the academy (Hoskins, 2012), minority ethnic pupils (Archer, 2012) and Muslim women (Ahmad, 2001). Research on success in relation to South Asian girls and women has been largely narrated through mainstream feminist research (Pomerantz et al., 2013), rather than black feminist studies on minority ethnic girls (Maylor and Williams, 2011; Marsh, 2013). As there is limited research which presents minority ethnic 'successful' women as active agents of change, there is a need to make South Asian women the starting point for research (Bhopal, 2010). This paper contributes to the literature, from both minority ethnic and cross-generational perspectives.

Within third-wave feminist literature, 'success' is constituted within the neo-liberal and meritocratic discourse of women can 'have it all', provided they work hard (Ringrose, 2013). Social media portrayals of 'girlpower' construct success as being achievable through hard work. Within the United Kingdom, 'managerialist regimes sideline equality issues and adopt [. . .] individualistic approaches that locate the responsibility for "success" or "failure" within the individuals' (Archer, 2009: 90). In the neo-liberal marketplace, women are seen to invest in the personal benefits of self-fulfilment, self-achievement and a 'belief that structural inequalities are personal problems' (Pomerantz and Raby, 2011: 549). Consequently, girls and women may experience psychological feelings of failure, shame or stigma (Goffman, 1990), resulting in feelings of inadequacy, whereby meritocracy becomes an illusion (Phillips, 2010; Pomerantz, Raby and Stefanik, 2013; Mirza, Meetoo and Litster, 2011). Therefore, neo-liberalism focuses on girls' and women's agency, freedom and 'choices' (Ringrose, 2013; Bauman, 2005).

Third-wave feminism is part of the 'gender equality illusion', whereby girls and women are constructed as 'entrepreneurs of their own lives' who 'engineer' their success journeys (Ringrose, 2013: 3). Such third-wave discourses of 'girlpower' fail to provide girls and women with tools to understand and challenge situations, where they experience sexism and other forms of 'oppression' (Taft, 2004: 73). Success discourses may trap girls and women 'between an idealized neoliberal girl subject' – one where she can 'run the world' and be anything that she wants to be – and the everyday realities of girls' and women's lives, which include experiences of inequality (Pomerantz, Raby and Stefanik (2013: 187) frequently compounded by the weight of intersectionalities (Yuval-Davis, 2006). The neo-liberal notion of 'girlpower' fails to acknowledge the structural, social and cultural dimensions experienced by women of colour (Crawford, 2017; Mirza, 2013).

Within the academic literature and media, cultural differences and supposed oppressions faced by British South Asian women, alongside their perceived 'compliant' nature are highlighted (Ahmad, 2001; Dale et al., 2002). Stereotypes fuel narrow depictions where South Asian girls and women are typified and exoticized through superficial and aesthetic aspects of 'culture' (Zagumny and Richey, 2013). Other discourses may depict them as victims of cultural practices, where they have limited 'choices', and lack independence, or agency (challenged by Martino and Rezai-Rashti, 2009). What it therefore means to be a twenty-first-century, British South Asian girl or woman, and academically or professionally 'successful', is layered and 'weighted' within a configuration of physical, psychosocial, cultural, religious, historical, economic and sociopolitical factors (Brah, 1996; Mirza, 2013).

In this merged study, 'success' (and perceptions of 'failure') refers to various dimensions of British South Asian Asian women's lives, where academic and professional achievements depict only part of their success journeys. Although there may appear a veneer of 'effortlessness', women may undertake a significant amount of 'invisible hard work' behind the scenes as part of developing their holistic 'success' identities (Mendick and Francis, 2012; Ringrose and Walkerdine, 2007). 'Success' journeys are viewed as complex, unfolding processes, whereby becoming, securing, performing and sustaining success are all integral to undertaking a leadership role effectively.

Black feminist thought

We draw on black feminist thought as it offers girls and women of colour valuable space for their voices to be centred, rather than marginalized, as in early first- and second-wave feminist movements. These were homogeneous and Anglocentric, focusing on the collective struggles of women (hooks, 1989; Brah and Phoenix, 2004; Ahmed, 2012). In prioritizing the experiences of white, middle-class women, first-wave feminists effectively excluded the voices of women from minority-ethnic backgrounds (Collins, 2000), first- and second-wave feminists tending to locate women's experiences within notions of patriarchy and capitalism (Beechey, 1979; Bhopal, 1997; Wilson, 1978).

We acknowledge that inequalities and power operations work in more complex, nuanced and intersecting ways for women of colour (Brah, 1996; Collins, 2000). This recognition underpins the emergence of black feminism (Crenshaw, 1998; Davis, 1981; Mirza, 1997; Brah, 2012), which offers space to discuss black women's lived experiences and narratives of struggle, from historical, religious, cultural and political perspectives, alongside other differences in experience relating to gender, class, religion, sexuality, caste and race, for example. We also recognize psychological influences may further compound how social differences are experienced within daily life (Brah, 1996; Phillips, 2010). So, for women of colour, everyday 'choices' are framed differently depending on how these lines of difference intersect.

Caution should be exercised, however, in relation to overemphasizing women's agency and the 'choices' available to them (Phillips, 2010; Narayan and Purkayastha, 2009). Third-wave feminist thinking may lead to complacency about structures of domination, where some girls and women perceive themselves as having more 'freedom' and 'choices' than in reality. Social and cultural processes that organize and regulate their lives may become so implicitly embedded that these are taken for granted in hegemonic ways (Phillips, 2010; Collins, 2000). However, individuals are not simply positioned through discourses of language or social structures, but

> everyone has agency, even though some clearly have more options than others. We should, in other words, recognise the agency of women even under conditions of severe oppression and exploitation, and not ignore the choices they make. (Phillips, 2010: 11)

Women's 'choices' (particularly girls and women of colour) are therefore mediated through dimensions and intersecting differences as highlighted above.

In this merged study, black feminist thought offers a critical framework to acknowledge the psychosocial dimensions of women's success journeys (Mirza, 2013), provides space for minority ethnic voices, encourages researcher reflexivity and enables the centring of participants' voices. It enables an analysis of multiple dimensions of difference and the ways in which they can be seen as troubling and constraining in some spaces, but positive in others (Mirza and Meetoo, 2018). For example, culture and religion may offer safety and confidence in the home context, yet be constraining within the school. Intersectionality facilitates a discussion of the realities of British South Asian women's lived experiences, and their perceived strength, power and survival abilities, grounded within historical narratives (Brah, 2007).

The study

This cross-generational study adopts a qualitative, interpretivist epistemology. A narrative approach was used (Goodson and Sikes, 2001) and three in-depth, unstructured interviews of up to ninety minutes were undertaken with each participant. Akin to 'research conversations' (Marsh, 2013), these allowed us to gain rich insights. Within each interaction, complex psychological factors emerged, moving beyond the interview encounter (Walkerdine et al., 2001). Each interview was 'situated and accomplished with audience in mind' (Riessman, 2008: 106).

Analysis was undertaken using repeated thematic, inductive coding. Requiring multiple readings of the data, major and minor themes emerged through a process of 'constant comparison' (Glaser and Strauss, 1967). Line-by-line coding was used to focus on the data itself and to safeguard against imposing inappropriate theories (Charmaz, 2008), sensitizing concepts whilst forming starting points for analysis. Data was segmented and colour-coded in relation to themes, ensuring participant responses remained complete and centring individual women's voices. This enabled segments to be read within the context of the whole narrative in order to avoid misinterpretation. The British Educational Research Association (BERA) Ethical Guidelines (2011) were adhered to throughout, where pseudonyms were used, and an ethics-as-process approach was followed (Liamputtong, 2010), where every research interaction included a reminder of the participant's rights in relation to their data (Rogers and Ludhra, 2011).

Positionality

As researchers, we come from different cultural, religious and classed backgrounds. As a British South Asian woman and a white British woman, we acknowledge the concept of cultural 'outsiders' and 'insiders' (Laimputtong, 2010), whilst recognizing the complexities of such binary terms. Our research conversations, often involving challenge and discomfort, over time led us to view our different backgrounds as adding a rich dimension to our analysis. We reject the notion that 'a single dimension of identity [. . .] is a barrier to cross-cultural research' (Crawford, 2017: 27) and adopt critically reflexive and interpretative positions in this project (Alvesson and Skoldberg, 2009; Hollway, 2012).

Participants

In this merged study, two head teachers and two head girls have been selected because of their shared ethnicity, leadership characteristics and success journeys.

Head girl 1 – Arti

Arti is 17, has one younger sister, and parents who work in administrative roles. She belongs to a Sikh family, but maintains a loose relationship with religion through her parents and grandparents. She speaks Punjabi and German, and studies English literature, biology and German in a state-funded, non-selective school. She will be the first in her family to attend university and begin teacher training.

Head girl 2 – Sara

Sara is from a Muslim family, and speaks Tamil, Sinhalese and Arabic. She is seventeen and has one younger brother. Her father works in a hotel and her mother in a caring role. Sara narrates a strong religious Muslim identity and studies chemistry, biology and psychology at a state-funded selective-entry school. She will be the first in her family to attend university and study medicine.

Head teacher 1 – Simran

Simran's Indian born parents came to the United Kingdom as young adults where she and her two siblings were born. Her parents were factory workers, and she was the first in her family to attend university. A Hindi speaker, she is a practising Sikh and married with two sons. Simran is head of an infant nursery school with 350 four-to seven-year-old children on roll. Aged forty-three and a graduate, she has undertaken this role for six years.

Head teacher 2 – Rani

Born in Kenya to Indian parents, Rani, a Punjabi speaker, came to the United Kingdom as a one-year-old with two elder siblings. First to attend university, her father was a civil servant and her mother a factory worker. Married with three children, she identifies as 'spiritual but not particularly religious'. Rani is head teacher of a school for children aged seven to eleven years, with 600 children on roll. She is a graduate, aged forty-seven and has been a head for nine years.

The evidence

Our participants' narratives illuminated what it *meant* for the girls and women to be 'successful' and how this was mediated across their lived experiences. Key markers of success included

- securing the role- gaining respect;
- leaving a legacy;

- enabling and nurturing others;
- juggling demands; and
- being a role model.

Securing the role – gaining respect

The roles of head girl and head teacher are synonymous with success. Tough journeys, 'grafting' en route and a range of drivers were discernible across all narratives. The girls and women had been inspired by their herstories, and a key impetus was to make their families and communities proud:

> [His] aspirations – that relentless blueprint from my father has made me – as the daughter of an immigrant – want to succeed and help others. (Simran)

Fathers functioned as role models for all women and girls who actively worked to emulate their practices.

Additionally, these girls and women were driven by a sense of fulfilling their own aspirations, linking to self-esteem and respect. They all described highly competitive selection processes, and aspired to the roles from early ages, making heavy sacrifices to secure their positions as head girl and head teacher. Rani, for example, describes working throughout the night to gain her headship qualification – 'sometimes not giving enough time to my family – success has come at a cost'. This 'cost' was construed in terms of women offering less emotional and practical support to family members than they felt necessary.

The issue of identities being subsumed within the role became common to all four of our participants, with Arti commenting, 'people now call me head girl, not my actual name [. . .] it does not mean that I am a different person'. She acknowledged how the role of head girl created a new formality and distance between her and her girlfriends. Similarly, Rani stated, 'I am the school', revealing how her identity had become heavily subsumed by her role, indicating a fusion of the personal and professional. This 'embodiment' of the role brought with it, status, power and personal fulfilment, along with a strong sense of social purpose.

The girls and women invested heavily in their professional identities from emotional, moral and professional perspectives (Mirza, 2013). Securing these roles made them conscious of prospective failure, increasing their vulnerability to shame and stigma within professional and community contexts: 'I feel I'm representing women – particularly women in my community. There are only three Asian heads out of sixty-nine, so if I mess up, people will think we're all like this' (Rani). Due in part to their heightened visibility as minority ethnic leaders within their spaces, their sense of fulfilment and success in securing the role is paralleled by a fear of losing the role, and in turn, self-respect.

Leaving a legacy

A key marker of 'success' was leaving a legacy and making a positive difference to the school environment. Their appointments made a significant impact on the communities they inhabited, which had high expectations of the differences that these girls and women could make. They were aware of the benefits of the legacy to the school community, but also to themselves in the furtherance of their continued education and careers. Although the meaning of 'legacy' was nuanced, key focal points included celebrating diversity and promoting mutual respect. Head girls initiated whole-school projects and coordinated ethnically diverse student events as part of their vision. This was linked to that of the head teacher, from whom they received guidance and a sense of security. Head teachers did not experience this same sense of security from other individuals and so, for them, the weight was greater. Arti perceived herself to be a role model to other pupils in the school, wanting to 'make a mark in the school'. Her assembly speeches encouraged peers to emulate her success:

> Universities are looking for students who have pushed themselves to the maximum [. . .] Nominate yourself to become form rep, work with the school council, lead a book club [. . .] challenge yourself to be the best!

Similarly, head teachers worked to create utopian microcosms, whereby the ethnic mix of staff reflected that of the children, and where there was respect for all cultures:

> Over time – I want the best people but I've tried to replicate the community [. . .] by making sure that my staff reflect the community, I'm on the way to making sure that the interface between home and school is amazing. (Simran)

Changing the face of the school according to their different spheres and power was a shared goal for all, demanding high levels of emotional intelligence and integrity, yet reflecting both altruism and self-promotion.

The head girls invested their time and effort in leaving a legacy that would support the head teacher's vision, and other students', as well as enhancing their own curriculum vitae (CV) in preparation for university. However, for the head teachers, their legacy was in part framed within accountability structures and school governance targets. Their vision was, however, much wider than this, as it extended to impacting the local community, accompanied by a strong sense of wanting to 'give back'.

Enabling and nurturing others

Success involved coaching and nurturing success in others through encouragement and practical support. For example, the two head girls offered other pupils counselling-style services, advising pupils on the completion of university application forms and revision techniques. Sara was sacrificial in supporting other students applying for medical school, despite her own heavy workload. She saw a key part of her role as supporting others, and she did this very well. Her assembly speeches were motivational:

> Try to grab all [. . .] opportunities [. . .] and don't just sit back! Not only will it help you develop skills for school, but also for the future and your careers!

Sara encouraged other pupils to embrace a 'can do' positive mentality, where there were no perceived barriers to 'success' in line with the neo-liberal discourse that success is determined by individual motivation and effort. However, the reality of this is very different, and the head teachers' narratives as older women revealed an alternative picture through their professional and family lives.

Similarly, head teachers supported their staff (and pupils) with career progression advice and counselled parent communities. The impact of their background was a key motivating factor in this:

> Part of my thing is empowering women staff and parents. I'm sure my white counterparts do this [. . .] but I think of how things have happened in my life [. . .] all of us are coloured by our background – we can either reinvent ourselves or we can use it – I'm using it. (Rani)

Rani was aware of the struggle experienced by herself, her mother and other British South Asian women during her formative years. She describes a lack of privilege, support networks and access to people who can 'get things done'. Consequently, she determined to provide support, for example, drop-in sessions for mothers of her schoolchildren, involving advice on many aspects of their lives. She understood the complexities of their cultural and gendered contexts, which made her empathetic, approachable and able to provide guidance.

These were altruistic women, all of whom cited their historical family narratives of struggle as a driver for success. All communicated a desire to help others, linking it to notions of class, gender and ethnicity:

> I owe my drive to my father he's been pushy and demanding – it was non-negotiable that you'd have a degree. If he could do that for me – I can do that – I can help those in my community. (Simran)

The impact of their family, specifically older generations, on their impetus to enable others was highly significant. They admired the hard work and qualities inherent within their fathers in particular, who had earned and sacrificed in order to send them to university. They acknowledged their own success was built on that of their fathers, and so the need to 'pay back' informed the ways in which they operated. Appreciative of their positions of relative power, they now saw it as their privilege to help others achieve success.

Juggling competing demands

The four participants desired to be successful in all aspects of their lives. They had high expectations of themselves and were organizationally strategic through the 'choices' they made and how they invested their time. They articulated their lives as a constant 'juggling' act, managing to maintain a certain level of success across a variety domains. They all juggled school and home commitments, expressing the need to be successful as wives, daughters, friends, sisters and mothers. Each participant had significant demands placed upon her by immediate and extended family members. They were skilled at 'operating in different worlds':

> I step into my house (I might change into an Indian suit) [...] I adopt a different persona [...] I'm speaking a different language, cooking different food, picking up different issues – no one cares I'm a head teacher [...] because I'm their mum or their daughter in law or I'm someone's wife [...] it means I understand what the children in school are going through. (Simran)

Juggling had been developed within the extended family and cultural networks. All participants highlighted how skills of code-switching and using different social registers translated to their professional and home lives. The family could be both a source of support and of stress. Living with in-laws was described by Rani as 'the worst four years' of her life, because of the expectations that she would spend long hours cooking, undertaking domestic chores and submitting to the authority of her elders on a range of issues. Nevertheless, she notes, 'I don't feel I could have been successful without the support of my extended family.' This was largely due to help with childcare.

The intense 'juggling' act of head girl leadership (McClellan, 2012) was managed alongside the girls' priorities to achieve academic excellence in their A level examinations. Arti discussed multiple juggling stresses, such as meeting her university application deadline, doing revision for exams, leading school societies, engaging in voluntary and paid work, giving head girl speeches and so on. Although not running her own home, like the head teachers, her roles took up significant amounts of time, and to accomplish them successfully, she worked long hours. She invested heavily in the 'educational extras' (Ludhra, 2015) – those areas beyond exam grades, which added extra weight to a young person's developing CV.

Being a good role model

Although the need for good role models is embedded within the public discourse, what exactly constitutes being a 'good' role model lacks transparency. Reflecting on the lack of minority ethnic role models for themselves, the head teachers determined to be effective role models for younger women:

> I hadn't got any role models from the Asian community who were heads – because that would have made a difference. If it was someone you knew, you'd think – yes, she did it with her family and her complex home life, you know, I can do it. (Rani)

Both head teachers visited different schools to 'talk to the girls', acknowledging the need to become role models for British South Asian girls in particular. They cited the importance of empathy, borne out of an understanding of the girls' cultural contexts, as key to making a positive impact and noted a 'real connection and bonding' with these young women.

Both head teachers recognized that, whereas they had suffered from a lack of British South Asian role models for most of their lives, there had been occasions they had selected white role models over Asian later in their careers, emphasizing it was insufficient for Asian women to inhabit authority roles – they also needed to demonstrate excellence in them. The head teachers had high expectations of themselves but also of others.

The two head girls saw themselves as role models to their peers and younger children within the school and their families, but also articulated a real need for Asian academic role models. 'X' as researcher, had a clear impact here:

I've never met an Asian woman get to the stage that you're at [. . .] you've got this thirst [. . .] to succeed, [. . .] you carried on studying after marriage and children. I was really inspired by you – I thought [. . .] I want to be like her one day, I want to do a PhD too.

The head girls discussed school careers talks and noted how invited speakers were usually white women with whom they could not connect. They wanted to see women who were from similar backgrounds and had 'made it' through struggles, without middle-class financial advantages, and cultural privileges. As a result of in-school experiences, they perceived themselves as minority ethnic role models for both younger students, and girls in their extended families. The effect of role models – or the lack of them – could not be underestimated.

Discussion

The narratives of the four participants have provided insights into what 'success' means across dimensions of their lives and have illustrated their various 'success journeys'. The two head girls were building their 'success' journeys in relation to achieving top examination grades to secure universities places, developing profiles as holistic citizens undertaking voluntary and community work, and participating in leadership activities in school and beyond. In this way, 'success' meant significantly more than achieving straight grades As. The two head teachers viewed themselves as successful not only in achieving the position of head teacher but also in making a difference in the community, supporting and nurturing upcoming staff, enabling minority ethnic parents in terms of language and general parenting and appointing staff to reflect the ethnic mix of their schools. In this way, the head teachers acted as cultural brokers between communities, adding further weight to their roles. Grounded in the historical experiences of their parents. these ways of operating were borne out of a sense of responsibility and duty of care towards the community and were integral to their perceptions of success.

Across the generations

There were similarities in the ways 'success' was experienced for all participants, as highlighted in the key markers in this chapter: securing the role – gaining respect; leaving a legacy; enabling and nurturing others; juggling demands; and being a role model.

Each narrative revealed a drive towards perfection in all areas, but in reality, sustaining success in every dimension was an impossibility. A key difference between the head teachers and head girls was that the girls narrated a wholly positive take on their aspirational futures, in relation to 'becoming successful' in their careers, degrees, partners and material possessions, for example. They did not appear to recognize the potential challenges that they might face in relation to ethnicity and workplace discrimination, and narrated the gender equality illusion (Ringrose, 2013) together with notions of meritocracy (Gonick, 2007; Mendick and Francis, 2012; Khoja-Moolji, 2014).

By contrast, the head teachers had experienced inequality and therefore recognized that meritocracy was a myth. They articulated the pressure of aiming for perfection and a 'regrettable relief' accompanying the realization they were unable to achieve success in all areas of life. Simran reflects:

> My ethnicity comes into my plate-spinning challenge of trying to be – [but] I'm not trying any more – the perfect daughter, wife [. . .] daughter-in-law [. . .] sister – everyone has roles for us whatever ethnic group we're from [. . .] mine are defined in a certain way [. . .] we all carry so much guilt.

This element of regret, or realism, did not appear in either of the younger women's narratives, suggesting life experience is accompanied by a greater understanding of structure and agency.

Success: Cages and keys

For all four participants in this merged study, becoming 'successful' offered keys for entry to new spaces – for example, for the head girls, high A level grades and excellent CVs, provided the key to a good university. Head teachers narrated how their position offered them status and respect within the educational community, and this brought with it power to effect change. For them, the role itself acted as the key for access to particular elite groups. Their respective leadership roles afforded them power, authority and respect.

However, the journey towards becoming 'successful' could also be viewed as a 'cage' where a sense of entrapment is felt and a fear of failure is experienced. On occasions, the same difference could present as both a key (to unlock or enable) or a cage (to restrict or paralyse), depending on the particular context and intersection. For example, the dimension of culture and religion in the home space might promote the furthering of a woman's education. At the same time, these, together with additional expectations, might promote the carrying out of typically gendered domestic chores (Coleman, 2002; Jones, 2017) and emotional support of the family, and these might hinder successful progression, whilst adding heavy psychological burdens.

In many ways a catalyst for high aspirations and supportive of academic and professional success, all four fathers (and in this sample, mothers to a lesser degree) had instilled in their daughters the need for hard work and 'to be better than' their white counterparts (Gladwell, 2008; Mendick and Francis, 2012), displaying values rooted in early migration experiences of struggle (Watson, 1977; Anwar, 1979; Brah, 1993). Parents' and grandparents' histories acted as a spur to 'move up' and 'out' of their current classed positions (Tinkler and Jackson, 2014; Reay et al., 2011). This functioned as a driver for success in achieving 'the whole package plus' – the constant, strategic striving to make themselves stand out, for example, in leading high-status projects. Success was not wholly a result of parental influence, however. All girls and women in this study conveyed high expectations regarding being successful across all areas of their lives due to self-motivation (Kehily and Nayak, 2009). Unable to draw upon the 'hot knowledge' of middle-class families (Archer, 2012), these girls and women were largely self-regulators of their success (Foucault, 1984; Rose, 1999).

Similar to their white counterparts, the head teachers had greater domestic responsibilities (Coleman, 2002; Jones, 2017) and competing personal and work-related expectations, resulting in relentless 'juggling', which on occasion caused anxiety, neglect of the self and an erosion of social life. All participants demonstrated high levels of self-regulation, but this came at a personal cost. Presenting an image of effortless success, all acknowledged private cages – stresses – kept hidden to maintain the successful 'superwoman role' which they embodied (Jackson, 2010).

Participants displayed a strong ethic of care within their families and communities, developing this alongside individual visions of success. Although potentially resulting in a suppression of their own well-being (Baumann, 2001), the need to support others in and outside of the home remained an integral part of the holistic success they deemed important. They acted as bridges between schools and communities 'enacting values focused leadership and serving as role models' for both British South Asians and other community members (Johnson, 2017: 857).

They experienced the pressure to be with more British South Asian people versus the pressure to connect with more white people:

> When I first came, people in the Education Authority would say – you'll really get on with 'X' Asian head and 'Y' Asian head – we're all lumped together but I wouldn't ring them if I had a problem – they're not my kind of people. It was done with good intent – but it's a bit racist really. (Simran)

This illustrates how British South Asian women may experience attempts to 'push them back' into a cage. Constrained by the prejudices or racism of others, these women were aware of marginalization despite gaining high-status roles. Yet both head teachers discussed their active pursuit of mentoring and the formation of networks with white women. Within these relationships, they found emotional support and strategic help, recognizing the importance of 'white sanction' (Miller, 2016) in their drive for success.

In describing the power she has in certain areas, Rani notes the same self-presentation may result in authority or a lack of it within different contexts:

> [If] I've worn a sari – some of my white parents have given me a look and I think if I wore this every day – would you come & talk to me? So [. . .] I don't wear it as much because of how I'd be perceived – because it's happened in other fields – the way I'm spoken to is very different than if I'm wearing western clothes [. . .] My own children don't want me to look like a 'Freshie', but my Muslim parents love it.

Opportunities granted by high-status roles may provide keys to greater respect from certain groups through identification, but may equally inhibit acceptance and communication with other groups.

All were in ethnically diverse contexts offering them relatively 'safe spaces' in which to operate. They articulated preferences for remaining within their own communities where they believed they could make the greatest difference as change agents. However, there is complexity in this. All expressed a reticence to move into predominantly white spaces for fear of being 'cultural outsiders' (Liamputtong, 2010). Ironically, the safe space which enabled success to flourish could also function as a cage, potentially limiting higher levels of success.

Culture and agency need to be rethought beyond the binary model of women being 'caught between the poles of oppressive patriarchal structures of subordination' and 'the promise afforded by feminism of liberation' (Martino and Rezai-Rashti, 2009: 115). A more nuanced analysis is required. Far from experiencing a lack of agency, alongside a respect for cultural values, women used small micrologies of power (Plummer, 2010), directing their own success in ways not known to their families. For all the women, education and qualifications provided negotiating power, enabling them to achieve success in their work. Head girls noted that staff would facilitate their projects, and that head teachers recognized the power of the role to effect change in community groups and local authority working parties. Foundational to this was their psychological capital, resilience and ability to code switch across audiences and spaces, accommodating multiple ways of being and performing womanhood (Marsh, 2013).

Notions of cultural hybridity (Ballard, 1994) link to those of South Asian women as 'cultural navigators'. Because of their marginalized position, they become skilled at navigating between different classed, gendered and ethnic worlds. In exercising control over their circumstances, they formed bridges between past family traditions and contemporary British society (Bagguley and Hussain, 2016). In so doing, they 'reflexively select, suppress and supplement family traditions' (Archer, 2007: 48, cited in Bagguley and Hussein, 2016: 47). The women displayed 'meta-reflexivity', challenging and working within structural constraints where they 'actively scrutinise their own aspirations, opportunities and community to make a way forward for themselves' (ibid.: 53). Fuelled by a commitment to their values, this process, which may involve conflict, is integral to how the participants in this study achieved success.

Conclusion

In this chapter we have discussed what notions of 'success' look like for our four participants, who are leaders in their own right in primary and secondary schools. The head girls and head teachers, although from different generations, displayed similar characteristics, attitudes and values through their success journeys. The differences were apparent in relation to their ages and differing lived experiences, head teachers having encountered university, career, marriage, the raising of children and cultural commitments. These differences impacted on the ways the women and girls viewed the world and the achievement of success.

All four participants were from working-class backgrounds and the first in their families to attend university. In our particular study, these factors did not hinder their progress, but, along with other differences, they added additional weight to their navigation of success. The head girls were not necessarily aware of potential barriers due to their, as yet, limited life experience. None of the four were privileged to have 'hot knowledge' (Archer, 2009) derived from their parents' education and professional careers or networks; however, they drew upon on their own psychological desires to drive their success stories, grounded in and inspired by the narratives of struggle from parents and grandparents (Mirza, 2013). Our participants performed their agency to navigate markers of difference across their lives, and their personal strength and resilience were manifest in their survival abilities and desire to persevere to achieve success at a personal cost (hooks, 1989). For the minority ethnic girls and women in this study, this involved little social life or personal care, long hours of work, the prioritization of others over themselves, surveillance and the fear of public failure within extended families and their own ethnic community. In this way the weight of surveillance and public failure was magnified for them, over their white counterparts. They had 'more' to prove as they were 'the first' British South Asian girls and women to occupy these roles, and as such, the drive to succeed and bring esteem to their own ethnic group was paramount in their thinking.

Although on the surface, our participants performed success in a seemingly effortless way, the reality was far from this. They employed discipline and drew on sophisticated mechanisms to cope with stress, in order to maintain the 'Superwoman' status that they embodied and performed (Jackson, 2010; Machin and Thornborrow, 2006). Acknowledging that parents were limited in the help they could offer, the women and girls were strategic in networking, rigorous in planning and independent in the ways they aimed for success – 'I'm different because I make and find my own way – I don't look at barriers – I look at the positive to make it work.'

Based on this research, several recommendations can be made. A strategic approach to support is required. First, 'identity-safe spaces' (Showunmi et al., 2016) could be created for British South Asian girls and women to explore and discuss how multiple intersections impact their success journeys, for example, the ways in which religion, culture and gender impact educational and professional progression. Although there is merit in exclusive 'safe spaces', equally there is a strong need for uncomfortable conversations to take place, where women across age groups and backgrounds develop mentoring and support mechanisms, which take account of privileged positions to enable and facilitate success in progression.

Whilst we recognize that there are several mentoring programmes nationally, some of which the head teachers in this study had participated in, these women did not narrate a sense of having positive British South Asian role models with whom they could wholly identify (Maylor, 2009). We advocate a more sophisticated approach towards the matching of girls and women within mentoring schemes which takes account of various intersections, including ethnicity. The establishment of intergenerational fora and mentoring systems, whereby British Asian and white professionals could work both together and separately across various educational contexts to mentor and be mentored, could facilitate a growth in knowledge, understanding and confidence, so impacting on career progression.

Further, critical, open dialogue and continuous professional development involving schools with differing ethnic compositions could promote intercultural communication and mobility, exploring ways in which white privilege and notions of 'colour-blindness' (Lander, 2014) may play out in nuanced ways. In this study, gender, race and meritocracy illusions have been explored, highlighting the need for critical feminist education to be on the school curriculum and addressed within a range of contexts for educational professionals. There is also a necessity to develop understandings around the constructs of race and ethnicity, and how 'whiteness' may be perpetuated to marginalize, exclude and prevent or hinder success in various spheres of life (Lander, 2014; Gilborn, 2008).

To move forward, there needs to be a willingness to take risks through uncomfortable conversations where women across differing backgrounds, together engage in dialogue, developing understandings of how women and girls who have experienced particular intersectionalities may be marginalized or hindered in their journeys to success and equally how they have succeeded despite these barriers.

Success is complex as women move in and out of comfort zones. For a successful British South Asian head teacher or head girl, being 'in the minority' brings visibility, the weight of responsibility and a sense that failure will impact on their entire community. 'Holistic' success is difficult, if not impossible, to achieve, but though psychological resilience and moral commitment the girls and women in this study were, nevertheless, resolute in striving for it.

References

Ahmad, F. (2001), 'Modern Traditions? British Muslim Women and Academic Achievement', *Gender and Education*, 13 (2): 137–52.

Ahmed, S. (2012), 'Feminist Genealogies', Intersectionality Panel Conference, Goldsmith University, 11 May 2012, London.

Alvesson, M. and K. Sköldberg (2009), *Reflexive Methodology: New Vistas For Qualitative Research*, Los Angeles: SAGE.

Anwar, M. (1979), *The Myth of Return: Pakistanis in Britain*, London: Heinemann Educational.

Archer, L. (2009), 'The Impossibility of Minority Ethnic Educational "Success"? An Examination of the Discourses of Teachers and Pupils in British Secondary Schools', *European Educational Research Journal*, 7 (1): 89–107.

Archer, L. (2012), ' "Between Authenticity and Pretension": Parents', Pupils' and Young Professionals' Negotiations of Minority Ethnic Middle-Class Identity', *The Sociological Review*, 60 (1): 129–48.

Bagguley, P. and Y. Hussain (2016), 'Negotiating Mobility: South-Asian Women and Higher Education', *Sociology*, 50 (1): 43–59.

Ball, S. J. (2003), *Class Strategies and the Education Market*, London: RoutledgeFalmer.

Ballard, R. (1994), 'The Emergence of Desh Pardesh', in R. Ballard (ed.), *Desh Pardesh: The South-Asian Presence in Britain*, 1–34, London: Hurst.

Bauman, Z. (2001), *Community: Seeking Safety in an Insecure World*, Malden, MA: Polity.

Bauman, Z. (2005), *Work, Consumerism and the New Poor*, 2nd edn, Maidenhead: Open University Press.

Beechey, V. (1979), 'On Patriarchy', *Feminist Review*, 3: 66–82.

BERA (British Education Research Association) (2011), 'Revised Ethical Guidelines for Educational Research', British Education Research Association. Last accessed 6 January 2017: https://www.bera.ac.uk/[. . .]/bera-ethical-guidelines-for-educational-research-2011.

Bhabha, H. K. (1990), 'The Third Space: Interview with Homi Bhabha', in J. Rutherford (ed.), *Identity: Community, Culture, Difference*, 201–13, London: Lawrence & Wishart.

Bhopal, K. (1997), *Gender, 'Race' and Patriarchy: A Study of South Asian Women*, Aldershot, Hants, England: Ashgate.

Bhopal, K. (2010), *Asian Women in Higher Education: Shared Communities*, Sterling: Trentham.

Brah, A. (1993), ' "Race" and Culture" in the Gendering of Labour Markets: South-Asian Young Muslim Women and the Labour Market', *New Community*, 29: 441–58.

Brah, A. (1996), *Cartographies of Diaspora: Contesting Identities*, New York: Routledge.

Brah, A. (2007), 'Non-Binarized Identities of Similarity and Difference', in M. Wetherall, M. Laflèche and R. Berkeley (eds), *Identity, Ethnic Diversity and Community Cohesion*, 136–45, Thousand Oaks, CA: SAGE.

Brah, A. and A. Phoenix (2004), 'Ain't I a Woman? Revisiting Intersectionality', *Journal of International Women's Studies*, 5 (3): 75–86.

Brown, J. and I. Talbot (2006), 'Making a New Home in the Diaspora: Opportunities and Dilemmas in the British South Asian Experience', *Contemporary South Asia*, 15 (2): 125–31.

Chappell, A. (2014), 'Explorations in Knowing: Thinking Psychosocially about Legitimacy', *Pedagogy, Culture and Society*, 22 (1): 137–56.

Charmaz, K. (2008), 'Views from the Margins: Voices, Silences, and Suffering', *Qualitative Research in Psychology*, 5 (1): 7–18.

Charmaz, K. (2006), *Constructing Grounded Theory: A Practical Guide through Qualitative Analysis*, Thousand Oaks, CA: SAGE.

Coleman, M. (2002), *Women as Head Teachers: Striking the Balance*, Stoke-on-Trent: Trentham Books.

Collins, P. H. (2000), *Black Feminist Thought: Knowledge, Consciousness, and the Politics of Empowerment*, New York: Routledge.

Collins, P. H. (2016), 'Black Feminist Thought as Oppositional Knowledge', *Departures in Critical Qualitative Research*, 5 (3): 133–44.

Crawford, C. (2017), 'Researching Race and Racism in Education during a Whitelash', *Research Intelligence BERA*, 132: 26–27.

Crenshaw, K. (1998), 'Demarginalizing the Intersection of Race and Sex: A Black Feminist Critique of Antidiscrimination Doctrine, Feminist Theory, and Antiracist Politics', in A. Phillips (eds), *Feminism and Politics*, 314–43, Oxford: Oxford University Press.

Dale, A., N. Shaheen, E. Fieldhouse and V. Kalra (2002), 'Routes into Education and Employment for Young Bangladeshi and Pakistani Women in the UK', *Ethnic and Racial Studies*, 25 (6): 942–68.

Edge, K. (2014), 'A Review of the Empirical Generations at Work Research: Implications for School Leaders and Future Research', *School Leadership and Management*, 34 (2): 136–55.

Foucault, M. (1984), *The History of Sexuality, vol. 1: An Introduction*, London: Penguin.

Foucault, M. (1988), 'The Ethic of Care for the Self as a Practice of Freedom (interview)', trans. J. D. Gauthier, S. J., in J. Bernauer and D. Rasmussen (eds), *The Final Foucault*, 1–20, Cambridge, MA: MIT Press.

Ghuman, P. A. S. (2011), *British Untouchables: A Study of Dalit Identity and Education*, Burlington, VT: Ashgate.

Gilborn, D. (2008), *Racism and Education Coincidence or Conspiracy?* Abingdon: Routledge.

Gladwell, M. (2008), *Outliers – The Story of Success*, New York, Boston, London: Little, Brown and Company.

Glaser, B. G. and A. L. Strauss (1967), *The Discovery of Grounded Theory: Strategies for Qualitative Research*, Chicago: Aldine Publishing Company.

Goodson, I. F. and P. J. Sikes (2001), *Life History Research in Educational Settings: Learning from Lives*, Philadelphia: Open University.

Goffman, E. (1990), *The Presentation of Self in Everyday Life*, Harmondsworth, UK: Penguin.

Gonick, M. (2007), 'Girl Number 20 Revisited: Feminist Literacies in New Hard Times', *Gender and Education*, 19 (4): 433–54.

Harris, A. (2004), *Future Girl: Young Women in the Twenty-First Century*, New York, London: Routledge.

Harris, A. (2010), 'Mind the Gap', *Australian Feminist Studies*, 25 (66): 475–84.

Hargreaves, A. and I. Goodson (2006), 'Educational Change Over Time? The Sustainability and Nonsustainability of Three Decades of Secondary School Change and Continuity', *Educational Administration Quarterly*, 42 (1): 3–41.

Hollway, W. (2012), 'Psychoanalysis as Epistemology: Developments in Psycho-Social Method', Conference held at Birkbeck University as part of a seminar series. Birkbeck, 22 November 2012.

hooks, B. (1989), *Talking Back: Thinking Feminist, Thinking Black*, Boston: South End Press.

Hoskins, K. (2012), *Women and Success: Professors in the UK Academy*, Stoke-on-Trent: Tretham Books.

Jackson, C. (2010), 'Demanding Time: Balancing School and Out-of-School Demands', in C. Jackson, C. F. Paechter and E. Renold (eds), *Girls and Education 3–16: Continuing Concerns, New Agendas*, 157–69, Maidenhead: McGraw-Hill/Open University Press.

Johnson, L. (2017), 'The Lives and Identities of UK Black and South-Asian Head Teachers: Metaphors of Leadership', *Educational Management, Administration and Leadership*, 45 (5): 842–62.

Jones, D. (2017), 'Constructing Identities: Female Head Teachers' Perceptions and Experiences in the Primary Sector', *Educational Management Administration and Leadership*, 45 (6): 907–28.

Kehily, M. J. and A. Nayak (2009), 'Global Femininities: Consumption, Culture and the Significance of Place', in J. A. Dillabough, J. McLeod and M. Mills (eds), *Troubling Gender in Education*, 24–41, London: Routledge.

Khoja-Moolji, S. (2014), 'Producing Neoliberal Citizens: Critical Reflections on Human Rights Education in Pakistan', *Gender and Education*, 26 (2): 103–18.

Lander, V. (2011), 'Race, Culture and All That: An Exploration of the Perspectives of White Secondary Student Teachers about Race Equality Issues in Their Initial Teacher Education', *Race, Ethnicity and Education*, 14 (3): 351–64.

Lander, V. (2014), 'Initial Teacher Education: The Practice of Whiteness', in R. Race and V. Lander (eds), *Advancing Race and Ethnicity in Education*, 93–110, Basingstoke: Palgrave Macmillan.

Liamputtong, P. (2010), *Researching the Vulnerable: A Guide to Sensitive Research Methods*, London: SAGE.

Ludhra, G. (2015), 'A Black Feminist Exploration of the Cultural Experiences and Identities of Academically "Successful" British South-Asian Girls', PhD diss., Brunel University London.

Machin, D. and J. Thornborrow (2006), 'Lifestyle and the Depoliticisation of Agency: Sex as Power in Women's Magazines', *Social Semiotics*, 16 (1): 173–88.

Mannheim, K. (1952), 'The Problem of Generations', in P. Kecskemet (ed.), *Essays on the Sociology of Knowledge*, 267–320, London: Routledge and Kegan Paul.

Marsh, K. (2013), ' "Staying Black": The Demonstration of Racial Identity and Womanhood among a Group of Young High-Achieving Black Women', *International Journal of Qualitative Studies in Education (QSE)*, 26 (10): 1213–37.

Martino, W. and G. M. Rezai-Rashti (2009), 'The Politics of Veiling, Gender and The Muslim Subject: On the Limits and Possibilities of Anti-Racist Education in the Aftermath of September 11', in J. Dillabough, J. McLeod and M. Mills (eds), *Troubling Gender in Education*, 111–25, London: Routledge.

Martino, W. and G. M. Rezai-Rashti (2012), *Gender, Race and the Politics of Role Modelling: The Influence of Male Teachers*, Abingdon: Routledge.

Maylor, U. (2009), 'They Do Not Relate to Black People Like Us': Black Teachers as Role Models for Black Pupils', *Journal of Education Policy*, 24 (1): 1–21.

Maylor, U. and K. Williams (2011), 'Challenges in Theorising "Black Middle-Class" Women: Education, Experience and Authenticity', *Gender and Education*, 23 (3): 345–56.

McClellan, P. (2012), 'Race, Gender, and Leadership Identity: An Autoethnography of Reconciliation', *International Journal of Qualitative Studies in Education*, 25 (1): 89–100.

Mendick, H. and B. Francis (2012), 'Boffin and Geek Identities: Abject or Privileged?', *Gender and Education*, 24 (1): 15–24.

Miller, P. (2016), ' "White Sanction", Institutional, Group and Individual Interaction in the Promotion and Progression of Black and Minority Ethnic Academics and Teachers in England', *Power and Education*, 8 (3): 205–21.

Mirza, H. (2013), ' "A Second Skin": Embodied Intersectionality, Transnationalism and Narratives of Identity and Belonging among Muslim British Women in Britain', *Women's Studies International Forum*, 36: 5–15.

Mirza, H., V. Meetoo and J. Litster (2011), 'Young, Female and Migrant: Gender, Class and Racial Identity in Multicultural Britain', in The Mediterranean Institute of Gender Studies (MIGS), *Young Migrant Women in Secondary Education: Promoting Integration and Mutual Understanding through Dialogue and Exchange*, 143–82, Nicosia, Cyprus: University of Nicosia Press, Last accessed 7 October 2013: http://www.medinstgenderstudies.org/wpcontent/uploads/Integration_of_young_migrant_women_2011.pdf-.

Mirza, H. and V. Meetoo (2018), 'Empowering Muslim Girls? Post-Feminism, Multiculturalism and the Production of the 'Model' Muslim Female Student In British Schools', *British Journal of Sociology of Education*, 39 (2): 227–41.

Narayan, A. and B. Purkayastha (2009), *Living Our Religions: Hindu and Muslim South Asian-American Women Narrate Their Experiences*. Bouder, CO: Kumarian Press.

Phillips, A. (2010), *Gender and Culture*, Cambridge: Polity Press.

Plummer, K. (2010), *Sociology: The Basics*, New York: Routledge.

Pomerantz, S. and R. Raby (2011), ' "Oh, She's So Smart": Girls' Complex Engagements with Post/Feminist Narratives of Academic Success', Gender and Education, 23 (5): 549–64.

Pomerantz, S., R. Raby and A. Stefanik (2013), 'Girls Run the World? Caught between Sexism and Postfeminism in School', *Gender and Society*, 27 (2): 185–207.

Reay, D., G. Crozier and D. James (2011), *White Middle-Class Identities and Urban Schooling*. Basingstoke, Hampshire: Palgrave Macmillan.

Riessman, C. K. (2008), *Narrative Methods for the Human Sciences*, London: SAGE.

Ringrose, J. (2013), *Postfeminist Education? Girls and the Sexual Politics of Schooling*, London, New York: Routledge.

Ringrose, J. and V. Walkerdine (2007), 'Exploring Some Contemporary Dilemmas of Femininity and Girlhood in the West', in C. A. Mitchell and J. Reid-Walsh (eds), *Girl Culture – An Encyclopedia*, 6–16, Westwood, CT: Greenwood Publishing Group.

Rogers, C. and G. Ludhra (2011), 'Research Ethics: Participation, Social Difference and Informed Consent', in S. Bradford and F. Cullen (eds), *Research Methods for Youth Practitioners*, 43–65, Oxford: Routledge.

Rose, N. (1999), *Governing the Soul: The Shaping of the Private Self*, London: Free Association.

Showunmi, V., D. Atewologun and D. Bebbington (2016), 'Ethnic, Gender and Class Intersections in British Women's Leadership Experiences', *Educational Management Administration & Leadership*, 44 (10): 917–35.

Stone-Johnson, C. (2016), *Generational Identity, Educational Change and School Leadership*, New York. Routledge.

Taft, J. K. (2004), 'Girl Power Politics: Pop-Culture Barriers and Organizational Resistance', in A. Harris (ed.), *All about the Girl: Culture, Power and Identity*, 69–78, New York: Routledge.

Tinkler, P. and C. Jackson (2014), 'The Past in the Present: Historicising Contemporary Debates about Gender and Education', *Gender and Education,* 26 (1): 70–86.

Walkerdine, V., H. Lucey and J. Melody (2001), *Growing Up Girl: Psychosocial Explorations of Gender and Class*, Basingstoke: Palgrave.

Watson, J. (1977), *Between Two Cultures*, Oxford: Basil Blackwell.

Wilson, A. (1978), *Finding a Voice: Asian Women in Britain*, London: Virago.

Yuval-Davis, N. (2006), 'Intersectionality and Feminist Politics', *European Journal of Women's Studies*, 13 (3): 193–209.

Zagumny, L. and A. B. Richey (2013), 'Orientalism(s), World Geography Textbooks, and Temporal Paradox: Questioning Representations of Southwest Asia and North Africa', *International Journal of Qualitative Studies in Education (QSE)*, 26 (10): 1330–48.

12

Black women leaders: Intersectional and present in the field of education 'hear our voice'

Sharon Curtis and Victoria Showunmi

Introduction

Whilst the volume of work on leadership continues to grow, leadership theory still generally fails to address issues of social justice and diversity, leaving unchallenged the current model of leadership, which was largely devised within a homogeneous, North American, Westernized, male-oriented paradigm (Lumby, 2007). Leadership has been practised without consideration of race, culture, ethnic background or linguistic abilities (Lumby and Coleman, 2007; Santamaria, 2012, 2013). The dominant discourse contained in the wider body of management and educational research presents a patriarchal view of leadership, and this partial view is recognized by the silence of women's voices in research as well as those who are marginalized and excluded as the 'other' (Lorde, 1984). Those who work towards eradicating oppression and inequality have developed a shared understanding of marginalization and have been seen to adopt a race-centred approach to their leadership (Gillborn and Mirza, 2000; Santamaria, 2013).

Tracing the history of educational leadership theory, Blackmore (2006) concludes that mainstream theory does not include conceptual frameworks that could address the educational oppression of some groups. Others, including critical race theorists, have noted the inadequacy of many leadership perspectives and the exclusion of the experiences and voices of minority ethnic people (Gillborn 2005; Ostler 2006). Ostler has argued for a move away from colonial concepts of leadership, while others have argued that it is a question of 'theory and practice becoming more democratic and therefore inclusive of all' (Lumby, 2007: 69).

The theoretical framework used in the research undertaken by Curtis (2014) challenges inequitable racialized systems and applies critical race theory (CRT). The use of CRT centralizes 'race' and racism, opening up wider debates on the intersections that affect black women's lives, and setting a context in which history informs our present-day understanding of being racialized and gendered (King, 1988; Crenshaw, 1989). Culturally relevant theories are needed that address the needs of black women and their lived experiences (Moseley-Smith, 2008). Further complexities exist in their bicultural lives, in which they pass between the dominant culture and the culture which they identify as their own. Examining issues of race and gender as potential outcomes of marginalization has given depth to this research, by examining their histories and policy development, including further potential barriers to the success of black women. Black feminism introduced in the research of Collins (2000) embraces these differences, together with a multiplicity of voices that allows black women to express their individuality and their lived experiences (Collins, 1990; Harding, 1991; Hartsock, 2004). Curtis (2014) focused on eight black women leaders in the early years sector. Using an intersectional frame in this research created opportunities to explore, through the methodological design and the analytical framework, how cultural and social categories overlap (Crenshaw, 1988). The individuals in both research projects did not represent a homogeneous group. In both studies the black women leaders in Curtis (2014) and Showunmi (2016) closely identified with the research criteria, as the following:

- Level of experience – the majority of candidates have over ten years' experience of educational leadership.
- Roles – working as children's centre leaders, deputies or curriculum leaders.
- Settings – including community childcare nursery classes and nursery schools.
- Location – not all located in the same geographical area.
- Qualifications and training – was examined within health, education, social services backgrounds related to leadership positions.

Although the researchers asked for women to come forward who identified themselves as black, the term 'black women' has been used in this research to include women from African, Asian, the Caribbean and mixed ethnic backgrounds. Although both research studies had different approaches, the research questions differed. The research questions in Curtis (2014) asked the following:

1) What experiences are black women leaders encountering in achieving leadership roles in the early years sector?
2) What factors support or constrain black women leaders in England?
3) What contribution are black women leaders making to their early years communities?

The research questions asked in the Showunmi (2012) study focused on the sociological aspects, which included questions such as:

1) perceptions of leadership, 2) the women's own identity an the impact on their leadership style, 3) barriers to leadership 4) perceptions held by others in relation to black women leaders by those in white spaces.

Education, therefore, as one system symptomatic of racialized relations, is an arena for exploring how race defines opportunity and outcomes in leadership. The triangulated methodological approach described later in this chapter has included the use of interviews, focus groups and the walk-and-talk methods of research. The lack of available research surrounding black women's experiences in leadership also extends to the production of statistical information including the number of black women in educational leadership (Tillman and Cochran, 2000). The dominant paradigm of leadership theory privileging Western, white, male identity and behaviour is reflected in practice. Acker (2006) observes that organizational hierarchies are usually racialized, classed and gendered, particularly at the echelons of leadership:

Top hierarchical class positions are almost always occupied by white men in the United States and European countries. This is particularly true in large and influential organizations. The images of the successful organization and the successful leader have many of the same characteristics, such as strength, aggressiveness and competitiveness. (445)

For those who live on the margins, the discussion within academia must move research forward by exploring the multiple dimensions of the effects of race and gender rather than presenting a reductionist view.

The issue in context

The history of black women's leadership in the United Kingdom is one that supports the experience of those dealing with day-to-day oppression through building their strengths to survive these systems through their resilience (Collins, 1990). CRT sets the context in this research to incorporate the history of black feminism and the understanding of the various forms of oppression experienced by black women. Women who have learned to deal with daily microaggression (Sue, 2010) have developed ways of coping while leading and understanding the effects on their psyche. The benefits of understanding these complexities and of centralizing their world alongside their experiences of leadership are supported by Gaetane et al. (2009), who claim,

> Drawing from these women's lived experiences through a critical race theory framework their epistemological orientations capture their cultural knowledge and self-defining standpoint, and their experiences have much to offer the field of education. (18)

Their lived experiences and the use of counternarratives to legitimize and centralize black history dismantles the distortions presented by dominant beliefs and assumptions. Sanchez-Hucles and Davis (2010: 176) suggest that 'consideration of the intersection of multiple aspects of identities provides a richer, more nuanced understanding of diverse leadership'.

The literature reveals an abundance of leadership models, most of which have some form of related structure of hierarchy that looks at social mobility from a patriarchal view. A socially constructed norm has been the dominance of male educational practice through their leadership in politics and within educational institutions (Moosa, 2008). These barriers are sustained in recruitment procedures, support systems and mentoring.

Further exploration examines some of the commonalities black women share in their journeys into leadership. Lorde (1984) has written extensively on the authenticity of experience and the importance of having this experience acknowledged. Rather than making a judgement within the arena of white feminist academia, Lorde was a notable outsider. Black women's exclusion from the mainstream women's movement has led to hesitancy among some women to identify themselves as feminists. When a framework was being adopted for the Curtis and Showunmi studies, many issues with regard to the differences experienced by women were debated. Although feminists do share many commonalities, the fact remains that this framework has to support the visibility of race and reflect the researcher's ontological world view. Black feminists have asserted that self-determination is essential for black women in defining who they are through a rich history which includes their struggle (hooks, 1981; Lorde, 1984; Collins, 1998). Throughout history black women have been forced to work long hours in the fields, and have been represented as sexual objects, labourers and carers (Carby, 1982). However, King (2007) shares her belief that black feminists need to embrace a positive image of black women as powerful independent subjects not victimized by these oppressions. The significance and purpose of this study will be set in a context which examines the biographies of black women's experiences, breaking silences and allowing their voice to be heard in these spaces. These combined studies present a critical insight into black women's leadership through the lens of CRT and black feminism whilst seeking to transform racialized hierarchies in the educational field.

Researchers are now exploring intersectional frames to identify the interconnecting and interacting roots of exclusion, marginalization and poverty (Bunjun and Morris, 2007). The use of narrative-based research is described as a method that is not simply about telling stories (Connelly and Clandinin, 1990). The methodologies draw from an interpretive paradigm and relate a narrative analysis used through the lens of CRT. This blended theoretical framework will deepen the understanding of the multiple factors that influence and affect black women as leaders. These counter-stories uphold the work of those who continue to promote social justice as leaders in the field tenacious, spiritual and resilient.

The concept of intersectionality arose out of the interplay of black feminism, feminist theory and postcolonial theory in the late 1990s. These dominant structures have the power to exclude those on the margins from exclusive spaces (Mirza, 1999). Scholars from Western societies have developed most theories according to their own perspectives. Rather than looking at the majority culture, the concept of intersectionality reflects those in a minority culture. McCall (2005: 1771) states,

> One could even say that intersectionality is the most important theoretical contribution that women's studies in conjunction to related fields, has made so far.

An intersectional framework explores women's natural, multiple identities in terms of the intersection of their ages, sexual orientations, faiths and beliefs, class, abilities and cultural differences (Crenshaw, 1991). This intersection is seen and accepted as a reality in the field of feminism and women's studies (McCall, 2005; Phoenix and Pattynama, 2006; Yuval-Davis, 2006). To all intents, silence still remains with regard to acknowledging the various intersections in black women's lives (Curtis, 2017). The term 'intersectionality', introduced by Crenshaw (1990), encompasses a broad range of oppressions faced by black women. Collins (2000: 227) is clearly in support of Crenshaw's work when she argues,

> An intersectional paradigm is important to further the understanding of multiple forms of oppressions that can exist. First, this paradigm can spark new interpretations of black women's experience.

An example of this is the complexities that remain within feminism when it focuses on gender. These inequalities have led to gender and racial imbalances in which black women have lower incomes and lower educational attainment and hold fewer prestigious positions than do those dominant in society who hold significant power (McCall, 2005). Issues pertaining to certain identifying factors, such as a leader's accent, choice of dress, how she chooses to wear her hair and her choice of food, are areas that identify black women leaders as having a different identity from those dominant within society. King (1998, 2007) is clear in her work that black feminist ideology should be included in research, as it creates visibility for black women by acknowledging their race and gender. The invisibility and visibility of race is dominated by powers of the different levels of hierarchies that select normative discourses positioned as one of white privilege. Williams (1997) believes that choosing to see or not see race is part of a political act. In support of this, hooks (1990) states that the first knowledge of racism for black women is as institutionalized oppression, and that it is used as a political tool against them. Race affects educational outcomes, employment and representation in powerful positions in institutions such as the police, the justice system, politics and law enforcement. Waring (2003) expresses the need for support from wider society to fully understand the impact of these oppressions, both overt and covert.

Black women are racialized and gendered as outsiders who have not benefited from the privileges of the inner circle of power; their absence remains invisible to those empowered (Catalyst, 2004). Miller and Vaughn (1997: 179) highlight that 'the twin disguises of racism and sexism still impose great restraints on the utilization of the competencies and talents of black women in these sectors'.

Studies on race are emerging slowly within the literature, whilst researchers highlight the complexities of researching race (Gunaratnam, 2003; Tuhiwai Smith, 2006; Hylton, 2012). Dominant mainstream researchers choose to ignore issues regarding race because it does not impact on their daily lives (Bonner, 1992,). A CRT lens depicts the systemic effects on race and identity in the context of ahistoricism created by the dominant discourse (Solórzano and Yosso (2002). Within research in education, the absence of race through history continues to cause controversies. Goldstein states that 'race related research needs to balance clarity of focus on race that interlink these experiences and the ability to develop support in order to be translated into policy' (2006: 32). CRT's position in relation to black women's experiences of racial bias is to see it not as an exception but as a norm within society (Crenshaw, 1991; Ladson-Billings and Tate, 1995). Racial ideology is a significant factor in race inequality and raises an ongoing debate in which several researchers from various disciplines highlight the importance of race relations (Bonilla-Silva, 2010; Feagin, 2001; Ferber, 1998, 2012). Adding to these discussions are those who have the power to choose to talk about this issue or to ignore the presence of race as a contentious issue in the twenty-first century.

In support of this leadership, scholars have argued for the inclusion of multiple perspectives and leadership that supports transformation for communities (Jean-Marie, 2006; Normore, 2008; Santamaria, 2011). This takes into account the variety of languages spoken, cultural values and norms, and a common understanding of equality (Jean-Marie, 2006; Normore, 2008; Santamaria, 2012). CRT in this research supports the deconstruction of dominant educational epistemology by opening new ways, new thoughts and the opportunity for educational inquiry to include new training practices. This includes research and analysis that supports cultural competence reflecting other races (Campbell-Stephens, 2009).

The research studies

This section presents the underpinning principles that have informed the methodology and the analysis whilst using a qualitative approach. Parker and Lynn (2002) in their work posit that CRT has important implications for qualitative research, particularly in the field of education. This framework supports ethnographic techniques as useful tools that incorporate and place important values on storytelling, reflexivity and voice (Delgado, 1989). CRT is applicable globally as an accepted view that black people across the world experience oppression (Delgado and Stefancic, 2000). The use of qualitative research allows the researcher to explore those socially constructed meanings by not adding the constraints of having to ascribe to a set of categories or labels predetermined for analysis (Patton, 2002). Primary research methods have now focused on listening to women and hearing about their experiences. Landman (2006) advocated a feminist research approach, which identifies the use of a variety of methods including interviews, the use of drama, diaries, autobiographies and other methods. The literature highlights discussions around feminism that have remained monologic according to the assumption that the experiences of all women remain the same. Ramazanoglu and Holland (2002: 3) believed 'that feminist research is imbued with particular theoretical, political and ethical concerns that make these varied approaches to social research distinctive'. Ethical concerns are an essential aspect in this research. The close interaction and sensitive information exchanged by the researcher and participants are bound by ethics. Confidentiality is an important aspect of the research, as is maintaining the ethic of care.

In order to clarify any further distinctions that are generalized amongst women and which support this study, the use of CRT and black feminism is the lens used to analyse the experience of the women in this research, utilizing the ideas drawn from critical race feminism. Solórzano and Yosso (2002) described critical race methodology as a theoretically grounded approach to research. This framework does represent methods and theories that will help to produce a more culturally enriched study, which will add to the literature within the United Kingdom (Tillman, 2002). Within the research of Curtis (2014), intersectionality has been used as an analytical tool that critically examines the intersections of race, gender and class with other identities, the ways in which these intersections affect those who are oppressed, and the influence they have on the privileges of others (Crenshaw, 1988; Perry, 2005). The development of a field of study that explores the complexities of black women's voices requires the application of a culturally sensitive research approach, whilst acting as a catalyst for change (Tillman, 2002).

Black women, therefore, have to make sense of their experiences and the impact of negative portrayals and the effects on their personal identities. These behaviours affect the lives of young people and of family structures. Williams and Nichols (2012) argue that black women's experiences of racial discrimination and everyday microaggressions should be analysed through an intersectional lens, specifically to examine the interlocking nature of race and gender. Brown (2012) emphasized that race is important, as it frames and informs institutional practices impacting on lived experiences in society. The women in the Showunmi (2014) study also shared issues of inferiority, with comments that related to the abnormality of cultural norms and values, and they reported that they were still subject to rigid stereotyping. UK academics Chakrabarty, Preston and Roberts (2013) and Gillborn (2008) have used CRT in their work to analyse and dismantle racism in various fields, including that of education. Furthermore, CRT addresses the experiences of being 'raced' and encountering racism as experienced by these women, and provides both the social and historical context for examining their journeys of leadership, promoting social justice and giving voice to their experiences (hooks, 1990; Collins, 1991; Lorde, 2007). Furthermore, Tillman (2002) drew attention to the importance of examining frameworks that have a cultural bias. These frameworks have traditionally ignored differences, imposing understandings of one culture (taken from Western theories) onto another. Brown (2011) emphasized that race is important, as it frames and informs institutional practices impacting on lived experiences in society. It is important to acknowledge that all research requires sensitivity across the board, and that it is imperative that the researchers built good alliances with black women leaders. Within the research study there are clear illustrations that demonstrate how the structure of CRT provides a critical framework that clearly intersects with race and with black women's feminist standpoints. Essed (1991) used the term 'everyday racism' in her work in order to look more closely at racist behaviour and ideas as part of institutionalized cultures. Tillman (2002: 3) described the use of a culturally sensitive research approach that recognizes difference and ethnicity, and indicated that culture is viewed as being central, taking into account a framework that includes culturally sensitive data interpretations.

Cultural sensitivity promotes communication of the experiences of black women that is facilitated by reciprocal interactions. The exchange between researchers and study participants recasts the identities of all involved, promotes critiquing of the research questions and stimulates ongoing reassessment of the research process (Jackson, 2002: 31).

The reassessment in this research process was devised according to five phases and was then analysed in two stages. Stage *one* comprised the individual experiences of black women leaders and stage *two* was a collective analysis of the data collected from the two focus groups. This facilitates a deeper analysis through the triangulation of the data and the use of the collective data in stage two (Curtis, 2014 and Showunmi, 2016). This did increase the research validity, innovation and authenticity. These accounts were fundamental to the approach to data collection. Both studies interconnect through the emphasis on analysing the data through a gendered and racialized lens (Showunmi, 2016). The work fits into the narrative discourse with its use of autobiographical accounts from the women leaders. These accounts were fundamental to the collection of data. The use of these accounts has been explored and examined employing their experiences inclusive of their varying professional contexts, which was critical to the methodology (Showunwi, 2016).

As researchers, we choose to engage with traditional methods used by black feminists to conduct the data collection, breaking black women's silence, thus centralizing their experiences and increasing the trust amongst the black women leaders and with the researchers. The strength of the research has been the evolving bond developed with these leaders by listening attentively to their stories.

This blended theoretical framework deepens the understanding of the multiple factors that influence and affect black women's experiences as leaders. These theories supported the analysis of their progression and contributions within the educational system. Evans-Winters and Esposito (2010) shared their support of theories that combat racial and gender oppression from multiple standpoints. The research therefore seeks to address the gaps within the wider discourse presented in the literature on leadership, through the work of Nkomo (1993):

> Until we expand our knowledge towards fully understanding how both race and gender affect the experience of women as managers in our organisations, we cannot hope to offer prescriptions for removing these ceilings and advancing their careers. (Bell, Denton and Nkomo, 1993: 107)

The inclusion of black women leaders within the wider educational literature is critical. Highlighting their abilities to make influential decisions that affect communities, including their roles as social change agents within the educational system (Santamaria, 2013), creates the space for alternative leadership that demonstrates a commitment to social justice and shows how avoiding issues of race through privilege affects the diversity of services. Sharing the narratives of the black women leaders and giving voice to their experiences presents new challenges to the dominant discourse. The study also challenges educational researchers to move beyond more traditional topics towards including voices from those at the margins of society by providing a space in academia that presents the opportunity to understand and relate the ideas and understandings of CRT and black feminism, and to make challenges to dominant discourses. The effectiveness of this framework in disrupting these issues has been described by Curtis (2014), whose research clearly demonstrates the design, the selection data transcripts and the analysis and coding that highlighted a rigorous and reliable approach taken in order to minimize claims of bias.

Education, therefore, as one system symptomatic of racialized relations, is an arena for exploring how race defines opportunity and outcomes in leadership. The triangulated methodological approach used in the study has included the use of interviews, focus groups and the walk-and-talk methods of research.

Although the researchers' studies were similar by nature, the approaches taken in gathering the data were different. Showunmi's research study (2012) was theoretically supported by grounded theory, whilst Curtis focused on the use of Critical Race Theory. Both researchers identified five phases of data collection with a focus on the experiences of the black women leaders.

Showunmi – (2012)

Step one –The autobiographical account

Step two – Discussion on lived leadership experience with other BME leaders

Step three – Recognition that the real lived experience connects with both the personal and the professional, and the implications this may have regarding others' perceptions about what leadership is and who a leader is perceived to be.

Step four – Reflect on own autobiographical account

Step five – Review literature on identity and leadership and develop the key question

The five phases of data collection used in the research are seen below:

Curtis – (2014)

1. initial one-to-one interview
2. walk-and-talk interview
3. initial focus group – (development of leadership quilt)
4. one-to-one – final interview
5. final focus group – (presentation of the quilt)

These were subsequently subjected to two stages of analysis, both individually transcribed from the individual interviews and collectively from the two focus groups. Finally, twelve themes emerged from the transcripts taken from the first stage of the interviews. Further analysis revealed three overarching themes, as follows:

1. *Echoes of their silentious presence* – have been described by the women in their journeys as one of representing a silent presence in which these women are represented as tokens or are completely invisible, silent, lone voices, isolated in the educational field.

2. *The drivers and their narrative journeys* – the women describe their personal drivers as their aspirations to stay in the field, overcoming barriers to meetings, panels and higher leadership positions, and how they create their own supportive networks.
3. *Communal kinship and collective identity* – the ability to work as social justice advocates and a commitment to the community using their cultural insights and cultural competence to provide services that deal with issues of race, and the importance of their strong sense of self

Primary methods of data analysis were applied after the transcripts had been manually coded (Strauss and Corbin, 1998). This coding was applied by linking key concepts and related experiences of leadership from black women through the literature review that related directly to the research questions. The research process also involved returning transcripts and discussing the narratives presented with the participants for their approval, as well as to seek further clarification.

These permeating threads connected the growth and experiences of these black women leaders, revealing critical insights that show their emerging strong sense of self-identity, and this overarching theme is presented in this chapter. It remains important in this research to capture women's lived experiences, as identified by Smith (1977), Collins (1991), Tyson (2003), Harding (2004) and Harstock (2004). This has been achieved by presenting a safe space for these women to voice their experiences of surviving and understanding their challenges and the assumptions, attitudes and drivers towards leadership and beyond. These women are conscious of the complexity of their personal and professional identities (Gaetane et al., 2009). This has been explored in order to show how this duality then impacts on their leadership and on their individual cultures.

Drawing from these women's lived experiences through a critical race theory framework, their epistemological orientations capture their cultural knowledge and self-defining standpoint, and their experiences have much to offer the field of education (Gaetane et al., 2009: 18).

The methods used in this research enrich our understanding of everyday events that support the context of these black women leaders' experiences. Collins (2000) advocates that black women cannot be studied outside of their experiences.

The evidence

Their strong sense of self

Jean-Marie, Williams and Sherman (2009) and Sanchez-Hucles and Davis (2010) have identified the need for research that critically identifies the ways in which these experiences differ. Findings showed that there are some clear issues around the ways in which society continues to identify black women which present the obstacle of race. Equally important is acknowledging what Copeland Carson (2006) describes as the integration of our dual identities. These women identify with the oral traditions that link to CRT and black feminism, and demonstrate the influences that strengthen their identity or sense of self by sharing their stories individually and collectively in this process (Solórzano and Yosso, 2002). They reveal their use of spiritual strength and their roles as nurturers in their families in developing a wider community approach. Their skills, knowledge and practices are shared through their cultural insights and the developed competences which are often described as part of their 'cultural wealth' (Yosso, 2005).

The data analysis revealed that the women within this research had taken many opportunities to talk about their own identities and sense of self (Collins 2000). When the women were asked to provide a workable definition for leadership, a variety of labels were discussed. Notably there was a mixture of culturally related illustrations that would not fit the normal discussion around leadership. In addition to this, many were able to discuss generic keywords as a way to describe leadership. This included supervising, being inspirational and providing aspirations for others (Showunmi, 2014).

This section presents and explores their voices and considers the effects of this dualistic identity as one of being black and female and their work as leaders (King, 1988). Empowerment as a social process supports black women in taking control of their own lives. Collins (2000) remains formidable in her own definitions, that black women's sense of self and their awareness of who they are will eventually become a vital component, which gives them the empowerment needed as a key to their own success. The women's use of collectivity, community and inclusion in their understanding of the overall vision was central. Shelby (2002) describes a black collective autonomy in which black people work together to discover their collective self-realization as people. This raised further questions in the group as the black women's account of their leadership style was not solely placed as a gendered approach. Collectively, empowerment supports progress and success in leadership, whilst supporting others in their communities and challenging inequalities in the wider society (Santamaria and Santamaria, 2012). As the researcher (Curtis, 2014), I heard succinct descriptions that reaffirmed these women's identities. These stories include the accounts of Eleanor, Aaliyah, Tallah and Esther, when they explain that *so on a personal level around the journey into leadership I think it is **I know myself well**.* (Eleanor).

Supporting this, Aaliyah in her first interview expresses, *I still have **my roots** and I think that is really clear.* (Aaliyah).

Esther further describes her development of her work by her sense of feeling:

> **I feel quite grounded** [. . .] and you know for me it's about instilling what I have into my children. I suppose being a leader is second nature. (Esther)
>
> Not everybody has got the right initiative to set things up but I think it's sort of in you [. . .] You have either got it or you haven't. (Tallah)

The use of their words expresses clearly their feelings of being in touch with themselves and of remembering those early aspirations and a desire to hold on to these descriptors and to remain grounded. Tallah explained that she needed to instil these roots, these values, into her own children, signifying that this was something she did not want to lose. Esther has strong beliefs around her developments and abilities, almost seeing it as a gift that is not possessed by everyone, something she feels is an integral part of her own identity. There was a common emphasis from the black women leaders on the importance of nurturing and the positive effects on change through their pastoral work and caring relationships that had developed. In most cases the leaders had a clear sense of their mission and were able to relate this directly to their teams and how they led the organizational work. Their stories revealed to me, as the researcher, confident and articulate women who identify their own self-definitions. Collins (1990) is clear that black women's own identified self-definition is key to their survival. These women's strong identities and their sense of knowing who they are increased their sense of striving towards success. The women continue in their interviews to explain that

> I've pushed and driven to be better than the rest because I believe that I can be better. (Estella)
>
> I take control of things. I don't know whether I was born like that or whether that's just because throughout my life it's been certain stages that I have had to do that. (Aaliyah)
>
> I'm not bothered if people can't accept me for who I am. (Amara)

So it hasn't been a traditional journey route through but I think it's mainly the person who I am, tenaciousness, nobody can tell me I can't do it, because we are pioneers and pioneers work hard, so yeah interesting journey. (Michaela)

I think this is actually a role or term that involves giving people a clear definition of where you are going, of what you do and how you get there and also particularly embedding your values and beliefs [. . .] (Senior Asian Woman)

The black women's descriptors of their various identities are as women who are driven and passionate, who can and have to take control when needed, who use their confidence to rebuild themselves, have the tenacity to continue to adapt in two different worlds, and have had experiences of rejection as drivers in their work (Curtis, 2014). Black women leaders have contained their sense of self-identity, which is essential to the rich descriptions used in the research (Curtis, 2014). This critical analysis has added to the findings that have identified what Turner (1985) and Santamaria (2012) describe as a rich and complex multifaceted leadership, cultivated into black women's own feminized identities, which are shown primarily within this research, unlocking for the reader their hidden, silent presence and experiences.

Discussion

Women's advances in leadership have fought the glass ceiling metaphor that is frequently used to suggest a transparent barrier that women face in their attempts to achieve promotion to the higher positions within organizations. Nicolson (1998) describes the glass ceiling as allowing women to see where they might go, but preventing them from ever getting there. Catalyst (2004: 3) in both studies state that it is clear that 'black women have to jackhammer the concrete ceiling of race and gender in order to move up the corporate ladder'. Black women have the additional burden of combating a unique set of historical stereotypes that can affect the way they view and achieve success (Davidson, 1997). For black women, the literature reveals a separate version of the glass ceiling, defined as the concrete wall. This, for many black women leaders, signifies the absence of real change when it comes to supporting and sustaining black women's advancement to senior positions (Davidson, 1997; Oakley, 2000). The concrete ceiling is also seen as being much more difficult to shatter, because black women leaders experience the world differently from the most dominant individuals in society.

Until we expand our knowledge towards fully understanding how both race and gender affect the experience of women as managers in our organizations, we cannot hope to offer prescriptions for removing these ceilings and advancing their careers (Bell, Denton and Nkomo, 1993: 107).

There are several anxieties associated with these barriers and obstacles which give rise to negative effects and associated stress. Despite a documented history of survival, black women face many social stresses (Beauboeuf-Lafontant 2009). Thomas (2011) suggests that the internalized historical representation of black women as having to be strong perpetuates anxieties that lead to irritation, frustration, anger and feelings of powerlessness. These anxieties were discussed by the black women leaders during one of the focus group activities, where they acknowledged how the impact of race and gender had created heightened emotional tensions for them. Individual expectation has demanded that black women remain strong, and some black women feel compelled to be the best, working harder than their white counterparts, and at times pushing themselves beyond their limits. Thomas (2011: 1) writes, 'The myth of the strong black woman can cause black women to push for unrealistic levels of self-sacrifice, self-denial and ensuing emotional distress.' Black women are active intellectuals promoting intellectual histories and challenging male-dominated research (Collins, 1991). Reclaiming black women's intellectual traditions involves examining the everyday ideas of black women who were not previously considered to be intellectuals (Collins, 1991: 5). Collins argues that this omission of validation of their knowledge maintains their position as one of subordination and oppression. Some black women identify themselves as womanists or humanists. However, Collins (1999, 2000) feels that black women need a label that is more political in order to make a stand against oppression. This is one in which CRT centralizes their race as one of visibility and provides a space for their voices to be heard in academia. Mirza (2009) states,

> The invisibility of black women speaks of the separate narrative construction of race, gender and class. In a racial discourse the subject matter is male, in a gendered discourse where the subject is white and female, in a class discourse where race has no place. (61)

This invisibility has kept black women's experiences absent in research, and their defined multiple oppressions and the effects of this in their leadership are not documented within the educational literature. The researcher has chosen to use theoretical underpinnings for black women leaders exploring the double jeopardy of being black and being a woman (Beal, 1969; King, 1988).

Further analysis revealed in the studies of Curtis (2014) and Showunmi (2012) used interviews and focus groups with black female students and leaders to look at their educational experience. The findings showed that these women encountered microaggressions, which they described as being unique to being black and to being female. These women encountered negative messages, stereotypes and challenges to their cultural values. When exploring these microaggressions, we can identify three categories, as follows:

1) Micro-assaults – These are explicit comments, often including derogatory remarks, which are made in relation to a person's racial identity.
2) Micro-insults – Much more subtle in nature, these highlight an individual's lack of awareness and racial and cultural insensitivity.
3) Micro-invalidations – These exclude the lived realities and experiences of black people through alienating their counternarratives and stories (Sue et al., 2007).

Micro-invalidations and insults are often seen as an unconsciously spoken form of racism that has a cumulative effect on health and a devastating impact on women's psyches. Comments such as 'I don't see colour', 'You are just the same as me' or 'You speak very good English' are ways in which those in positions of power maintain an unconscious racial name-calling (Solórzano, Ceja and Yosso, 2000; Sue et al., 2007).

Sue and Capodilupo et al. (2008) focus on gender microaggression, showing that invalidations, assaults and insults can be inferred in a way that suggests that women are inferior to men. However, the intersectional links between race and gender, and the impact of both gendered and racialized microaggressions on black women, are seen as an oversight (McCall, 2005). Williams and Nichols (2012) argue that black women's experiences of racial discrimination and everyday microaggression should be analysed through an intersectional lens, specifically to examine the interlocking nature of race and gender. Solórzano's use of CRT applied in the field of education recognized the subtleties of racial microaggressions (Solórzano and Yosso, 2000), and for those within the institutions their experiences are located on the outside of these spaces. Donovan et al. (2012), in their study on micro- and macroaggressions in which 187 self-identified black women took part, revealed that covert racism was still an issue for many of these women, although overt racism that includes microaggressions was a universal issue.

Implications

The significance of both studies is to add an important contribution to the field of educational leadership by exploring the journeys of experienced black women leaders. In particular, the avoidance of race as an ignored subject not presented or recognized in academia has traditionally caused contention for black feminists, creating invisibility in any analysis of their lives (Collin, 2000; Lorde, 1990; Maylor, 2009; Mirza, 2009). Taylor (2004) highlights her concerns in regards to the exclusion of black women from the educational literature. Similarly, Drake-Clarke (2009) describes black women's experiences as undertheorized and as existing on the margins of power structures, possessing neither race nor gender privilege. We know little of black women's experiences, as few studies have focused on race and gender and how these affect black women in their leadership roles (Stanley, 2009; Byrd, 2009; Davis, 2012).

The significance and purpose of these studies has been set in a context that examines the biographies of black women's experiences of leadership. The absence of these issues in the literature renders their contributions as black women leaders as one of absence and remains marginalized. The research shows that some of the factors enabling women leaders to build successful careers are found within their organizations, while others are external. The organizational structure, working environment, mentoring activities and leadership styles are all factors which can promote success, according to the women participants in the study. The examples given in this chapter demonstrate that, in order for women leaders to fulfil their full potential, it is crucial that the culture of the organization is one in which race and gender are recognized and supported. The study indicates the need for further work to be carried out in organizations to unlock the barriers that potentially stop women leaders moving ahead as fast as their male counterparts.

However, new challenges and perspectives will change assumptions associated with black women's lives if their voices are included within the dominant literature (Walker, 2005). Culturally sensitive research practice requires the researcher to avoid generalizations taken from the mainstream literature. It requires the researcher to highlight differences in the populations of black women and to have a deeper understanding of the subtle differences and diversity that occur within and between various cultural groups ((Solórzano and Yosso, 2000).

As agents of knowledge in this research, women have broken their silence and have shared their stories informed by their epistemological world views. Critical race theorists present an argument to break these silences and state that the use of CRT in educational research is recognized as a useful tool.

Therefore, the standpoint taken in making recommendations has to recognize the existence of difference. Intersectionality employed within the research does not suggest that we should abandon the use of categories as negative in the sense of labelling individuals; rather, it suggests that we should use the intersections as a means of bringing enrichment and enhancement to understanding complex lives, and use the experiences from this research to inform the changing world we now live in. This includes social justice and working towards the exclusion of racial oppression, recognizing that race is endemic and eliminating systems that remain colour-blind through claiming neutrality (Crenshaw, 1996; Harris, 2012; Matsuda, 1991; William, 1997; Wing, 2003). The issues of racialization presented through CRT and black feminism centralizing issues of race have presented a relevant framework in which to view these women's experiences and include my own. At the start of the research, I recognized the difficulties of researching race as a topic marginalized in academia. I share the fear of reprisal expressed by students and at times have struggled against conforming to the quiet tones of diversity and inequality (Lane, 2008). Black feminism has given me the lens and understanding as a black woman to define our own experiences and illuminate the absent female voice and the invisibility of black women in all spaces. Black feminists (Lorde, 1984; Collins, 2000; hooks, 1990; Bhavnani and Phoenix, 1994; Mirza, 1997) have all been critical in their work regarding the invisibility of black women's experiences in what they describe as the white feminist discourse. These feminists have challenged this discourse and proclaimed that black women can indeed define their own world views and realities through voicing their own experiences. We need to ensure that we no longer remain echoes of our silentious presence.

Conclusions

The women have shared their voices, experiences and knowledge to provide advice for academics and professionals. For new leaders, the message shared from the collective voice suggests how we psychologically prepare when facing isolation and marginalization in the educational field. As black women leaders, they recognize that progression and change are slow and tokenistic in these spaces. However, these women are clear that they feel that a new black female leader needs to be confident, aspiring, prepared to take some tough decisions and strive forward with undue strength *for enduring long battles!*

This research has illustrated black women's leadership, sharing their voice and knowledge and providing accounts of their journeys of leadership. Their stories have been rich, extensive, descriptive and heartfelt, but as such research studies are important, there is still space for more stories to come through. In conclusion, we contend that there is enormous cultural wealth invested in black women's experiences through their 'herstories' and present-day experiences of racialization. By promoting individual and collective marginalized voices to share these stories, it is possible to understand black professionals' experiences and approaches to leadership, to improve service delivery and to influence changes in policy direction. This will create services that acknowledge differences, improve the lives of our next generation of early years children and give black women leaders the opportunities to progress successfully.

References

Acker, J. (2006), 'Inequality Regimes', *Gender & Society,* 20 (4): 441–64.

Beal, F. (1969), 'Double Jeopardy: To Be Black and Female', in T. Bambara (ed.), *The Black Woman*, 90–100, New York: New American Library.

Beauboeuf-Lafontant, T. (2009), *Behind the Mask of the Strong Black Woman*, Philadelphia: Temple University Press.

Bell, E., T. Denton and S. Nkomo (1993), 'Women of Colour in Management: Toward an Inclusive Analysis', *Women in Management: Trends, Issues & Challenges in Managerial Diversity*, 4: 105–30.

Bhavnani, A. and K. Phoenix (1994), 'Shifting Identities: Shifting Racisms', *Feminist Psychology*, 4: 5–18.

Bhavnani, K. (2001), *Feminism and 'Race'*, Cary, NC: Oxford Readings in Feminism.

Blackmore, J. (2006), 'Deconstructing Diversity Discourses in the Field of Educational Management and Leadership', *Educational Management Administration & Leadership*, 34 (2): 181–99.

Bonilla-Silva, E. (2010), *Racism without Racists: Colour Blind Racism and the Perspective of Racial Inequality in the United States*, 3rd edn, Lanham, MD: Rowman and Littlefield.

Bonner, F. B. (1992), 'Needs Assessment of HBCU Faculty and Staff Women', University of Cincinnati [unpublished].

Bunjun, B. and M. Morris (2007), *Using Intersectional Feminist Frameworks in Research: A Research for Embracing the Complexities of Women's Lives*, Ottawa, Canada: Canadian Research Institute for the Advancement of Women.

Byrd, M. (2009), 'Theorising African American Women's Leadership Experience: Socio-Cultural Theoretical Alternatives'. *Advancing Women in Leadership*, 29 (1): 1–19. Last accessed 14 July 2018: http://advancingwomen.com/awl/awl_wordpress/theorizing-african-american-womens-leadership-experiences-socio-cultural-theoretical-alternatives/.

Carby, V. (1982), 'White Woman Listen: Black Feminism and the Boundaries of Sisterhood', in Centre for Contemporary Cultural Studiees, *Empire Strikes Back: Race and Racism on 70's Britain*, 212–35, London: Routledge.

Cassidy, W. and M. Jackson (2005), 'The Need for Equality in Education: An Intersectionality Examination of Labelling and Zero Tolerance Practices', *McGill Journal of Education*, 40 (3): 435–56.

Catalyst (2004), *Advancing African American Women in the Workplace: What Managers Need to Know*, New York: Catalyst.

Chakrabarty, N., L. Roberts and J. Preston (2013), 'Critical Race Theory in England', *Race, Ethnicity and Education*, 15 (1): 120–35.

Collins, P. (1998), *Fighting Words: Black Women and the Search for Justice*, Minneapolis: University of Minnesota Press.

Collins, P. (2000), *Black Feminist Thought: Knowledge, Consciousness and the Politics of Empowerment*, 2nd edn, New York: Routledge.

Collins, P. H. (1990), *Black Feminist Thought*, New York: Routledge.

Collins, P. H. (1991), *Black Feminist Thought*, reprint, New York: Routledge.

Connelly, M., and D. Clandinin (1990), *Stories of Experience and Narrative Inquiry*, Washington, DC: American Educational Research Association.

Copeland-Carson, J. (2006), 'Seeing Double. Special Issue: Making History at the Frontier: Women Creating Careers as Practicing Anthropologists', *NAPA Bulletin*, 26 (1): 55–81.

Crenshaw, K. (1988), 'Race, Reform, and Retrenchment: Transformation and Legitimation in Antidiscrimination Law', *Harvard Law Review*, 101: 1331–87.

Crenshaw, K. (1989), *Demarginalizing the Intersection of Race and Sex: A Black Feminist Critique of Antidiscrimination Doctrine, Feminist Theory and Antiracist Politics*, Chicago: University of Chicago Legal Forum, 139–67.

Crenshaw, K. (1990), 'Demarginalizing the Intersection of Race and Sex', in D. Kairys (ed.), *The Politics of Law: Progressive Critique*, 195–217, 2nd edn, New York: Pantheon.

Curtis, Sharon E. (2014), 'Black Women Leaders in Early Years Education', PhD diss., Leeds Beckett University, Leeds.

Curtis, Sharon E. (2017), 'Black Women's Intersectional Complexities: The Impact on Leadership', *Management in Education – BELMAS*, 31 (2): 94–102.

Davidson, M. (1997), *The Black and Ethnic Minority Woman Manager: Cracking the Concrete Ceiling*, London: SAGE.

Davis, R. (2012), *A Phenomenological Study of the Leadership Development of African American Women Executives in Academia and Business*, Las Vegas: University of Las Vegas.

Delgado, R. and J. Stefancic (2001, 2012), *Critical Race Theory: An Introduction*, New York: New York University Press.

Delgado, R. (1989), 'Storytelling for Oppositionists: A Plea for Narratives', *Michigan Law Review*, 87: 2411–41.

Donavan, A., J. Galban, R. Grace, J. Bennett and Z. Felicie (2012), 'Impact of Radical Macro and Microaggressions in Black Women's Lives: A Preliminary Analysis', *Journal of Black Psychology*, 39 (2): 185–96.

Drake-Clarke, D. (2009), 'Discrimination Happens without Effort: How Black Women Human Resources Mangers Negotiate Diversity Issues in a Corporation', PhD diss., University of Georgia, Athens.

Essed, P. (1991), *Understanding Everyday Racism: An Interdisciplinary Theory*, London: SAGE.

Evans-Winter, V. and J. Esposito (2010), 'Other People's Daughters: Critical Race Feminism and Black Girls' Education', *Educational Foundations*, 24 (1): 11–14.

Feagin, J. (2001), *Racist America: Roots, Current Realities and Future Reparations*, New York: Routledge.

Ferber, A. (1998), *White Man Falling: Race, Gender and White Supremacy*, Lanham, MD: Rowman & Littlefield.

Ferber, A. (2012), *Sex, Gender and Sexuality: The New Basics*, New York: Oxford University Press.

Gaetane et al. (2009), 'Leadership for Social Justice: Preparing 21st Century School Leaders for a New Social Order', *Journal of Research on Leadership Education*, 4 (1): 1–31.

Gillborn, D. (2005), 'Education Policy as an Act of White Supremacy: Whiteness, Critical Race Theory and Education Reform', *Journal of Education Policy*, 20 (4): 485–505.

Gillborn, D. (2008), *Racism and Education: Coincidence or Conspiracy?* Abingdon: Routledge.

Gillborn, D. and S. Mirza (2000), *Mapping Races, Class and Gender: A Synthesis of Research Evidence*, London: Institute of Education.

Goldstein, P. (2006), 'A Study of the Barriers in Translating "Race" Related Research into Policy', *Research Policy and Planning*, 24 (1): 24–38.

Gunarathnam, Y. (2003), *Researching Race and Ethnicity: Methods, Knowledge and Power*, London: SAGE.

Harding, S. (1991), *Whose Science? Whose Knowledge? Thinking from Women's Lives*, Ithaca, NY: Cornell University Press.

Harris, A. (2012), *New Wave Culture: Feminism, Subcultures, Activism*, London: Routledge.

Hartsock, N. (2004), 'The Feminist Standpoint: Developing the Ground for a Specifically Feminist Historical Materialism', in S. Harding (ed.), *The Feminist Standpoint Theory Reader: Intellectual and Political Controversies*, 35–54, New York: Routledge.

hooks, B. (1981), *Ain't I a Woman?* Boston: South End Press.

hooks, B. (1990), *Ain't I a Woman: Black Women and Feminism*, London: Pluto Press.

Jean-Marie, K. (2006), 'Welcoming the Unwelcomed: A Social Justice Imperative of African American Female Leaders at Historically Black Colleges and Universities', *Education Foundations*, 20 (1–2): 85–104.

Hylton, K. (2012) Talk the talk, walk the walk: defining Critical Race Theory in research, Race Ethnicity and Education, 15:1, 23-41, Doi: 10.1080/13613324.2012.638862

King, D. K. (1988), 'Multiple Jeopardy, Multiple Consciousness: The Context of a Black Feminist Ideology', *Journal of Women in Culture and Society*, 14 (1): 42–72.

Knapp, G. (2005), 'Race, Class, Gender: Reclaiming Baggage in Fast Travelling Theories', *European Journal of Women's Studies*, 12 (3): 249–65.

Landman, M. (2006), 'Getting Quality in Qualitative Research: A Short Introduction to Feminist Methodology and Methods', *Humanities, Languages and Social Science*, 65: 429–33.

Lane, J. (2008), *Young Children and Racial Justice*, London: National Children's Bureau.

Lorde, A. (1984), *Age, Race, Class and Sex – Women Redefining Differences: Essays and Speeches*, Berkeley, CA: The Crossing Press.

Lorde, A. (1984), *Sister Outsider: Essay and Speeches*, Berkeley, CA: The Crossing Press.

Lorde, A. (2007), *Sister Outsider: Essays and Speeches*, Berkeley, CA: The Crossing Press

Lumby, J. and M. Coleman (2007), *Leadership and Diversity: Challenging Theory and Practice in Education*, Stoke-on-Trent: Trentham Books.

Lynn, M. and L. Parker (2002), 'What's Race Got to Do with It? CRT's Conflicts With and Connections to Qualitative Research Methodology and Epistemology', *Qualitative Inquiry*, 8 (1): 7–22.

Maylor, U. (2009), 'Is It Because I'm Black? A Black Female Research Experience', *Race, Ethnicity and Education*, 12 (1): 53–64.

McCall, L. (2005), 'The Complexity of Intersectionality', *Journal of Women in Culture*, 30 (3): 1771–800.

Miller, J. and G. Vaughn (1997), 'African American Women Executives: Themes That Bind', in L. Benjamin (ed.), *Black Women in the Academy: Promises and Perils*, 179–189, Gainesville: University of Florida Press.

Mirza, H. (1997), *Black British Feminism: A Reader*, London: Routledge.

Mirza, H. (2009), *Race, Gender and Educational Desire: Why Black Women Succeed and Fail*, London, New York: Routledge.

Moosa, Z. (2008), *Seeing Double: Race and Gender in Ethnic Minority Women's Lives*, London: Fawcett Society.

Mosely Smith, A. (2008), 'Race and Gender in the Leadership Experiences of Three Female African American High School Principals: A Multiple Case Study', PhD diss., Georgia State University, Atlanta.

Nicholson, N. (1998), 'How Hardwired Is Human Behaviour?' *Harvard Business Review*, 76 (4): 134–47.

Normore, A. H. (2008), *Leadership for Social Justice*, Domiguez Hills, California State University. USA. New York: SAGE.

Oakley, J. (2000), 'Gender-Based Barriers To Senior Management Positions: Understanding the Scarcity of Female CEOs', *Journal of Business Ethics*, 27 (4): 3213–234.

Osler, A. (2006), 'Changing Leadership in Contexts of Diversity: Visibility, Invisibility and Democratic Ideals', *Policy Futures in Education*, 4: 128–44.

Patton, M. Q. (2002), *Qualitative Research and Evaluation Methods*, 3rd edn, Thousand Oaks, CA: SAGE.

Perry, G. K. (2005), 'Whose Job Is It? A Mixed Method Analysis of Occupational Stereotyping and Occupational Ranking in the New Economy', PhD diss., University of Nebraska, Lincoln.

Phoenix, A. and P. Pattnama (2006), 'Intersectionality', *European Journal of Women's Studies*, 13 (3): 187–92.

Ramazanoglu, J. and J. Holland (2002), *Feminist Methodology Challenges and Choices*, London: SAGE.

Sagebiel, F. and V. Showunmi (2012), *Organisational Culture and Successful Women Leadership*. Set WEPAN USA Conference proceedings.

Sanchez-Hucles, V. and D. Davis (2010), 'Women and Women of Colour in Leadership: Complexity, Identity and Intersectionality', *American Psychologists Association*, 65 (3): 171–81.

Santamaria, J. and A. Santamaria (2012), *Applied Critical Leadership in Education: Choosing Change*, New York: Routledge.

Santamaría, L. J. (2013), 'Critical Change for the Greater Good: Multicultural Dimensions of Educational Leadership toward Social Justice and Educational Equity', *Education Administration Quarterly*, 50 (3): 347–91.

Shelby, T. (2002), 'Foundations of Black Solidarity: Collective Identity or Common Oppression', *Ethics*, 112 (2): 231–66.

Showunmi, V., D. Atewologun and D. Bebbington (2015), 'Ethnic, Gender and Class Intersections in British Women's Leadership Experiences', *Educational Management Administration & Leadership*, 40 (5): 592–609.

Solorzano, D. and T. Yosso (2002), 'Critical Race Methodology: Counter-storytelling as an Analytical Framework for Education Research'. *Qualitative Inquiry*, 8 (1): 23–44.

Solorzano, D., M. Ceja and T. Yosso (2000), 'Critical Race Theory, Racial Microaggressions and Campus Racial Climate: The Experiences of African American College Students', *Journal of Education*, 69: 60–73.

Stanley, C. (2009), 'Gaining Voice from the Perspectives of African American Leaders', *Advances in Developing Human Resources*, 11 (5): 551–61.

Strauss, A. and J. Corbin (1998), *Basics of Qualitative Research: Techniques and procedures for Developing Grounded Theory*, 2nd edn. Thousand Oaks, CA: SAGE.

Sue, D. W. (2010), *Microaggressions in Everyday Life: Race, Gender and Sexual Orientation*, Hoboken, NJ: Wiley.

Sue, D. W., C. M. Capodilupo and A. Holder (2008), 'Racial Microaggressions in the Life Experience of Black Americans', *Professional Psychology Research and Practice*, 39: 329–36.

Taylor, C. (2004), 'An Inquiry into the Experience of the African American Principal: Critical Race Theory and Black Feminist Perspective', PhD diss, Georgia Southern University, Statesboro.

Thomas, S. (2011), 'Powerlessness and Anger in African American Women: The Intersection of Race and Gender', *International Journal of Humanities and Social Sciences*, 1 (7): 1–8.

Tillman, B. and L. Cochran (2000), 'Desegregating Urban School Administration: A Pursuit of Equity for Black Women Superintendents', *Education and Urban Society*, 33 (1): 44–59.

Tillman, L. (2002), 'Culturally Sensitive Research Approaches: An African American Perspective', *Educational Researcher*, 31 (9): 3–12.

Turner, C. (1985), *Psychosocial Barriers to Black Women's Career Development*, Wellesley: Stone Centre.

Walker, M. (2005), 'Race Is Nowhere and Race Is Everywhere: Narratives from Black and White South African University Students in Post-Apartheid South Africa', *British Journal of Sociology of Education*, 26 (1): 41–54.

Waring, A. (2003), 'African-American Female College Presidents: Self-conception of Leadership', *Journal of Leadership and Organisational Studies*, 9 (3): 31–44.

Williams, L. and M. Nichols (2012), 'Black Women's Experiences with Racial Micro-Aggressions in College: Making Meaning at the Crossroads of Race and Gender', *Diversity in Higher Education*, 12: 75–95.

Williams, P. (1997), *Seeing a Colour Blind Future: The Paradox of Race*, London: Virago Press.

Wing, A. K. (2003), *Critical Race Feminism: A Reader*, 2nd edn, New York: New York University Press.

Yosso, T. (2005), 'Whose Culture Has Capital? A Critical Race Theory Discussion of Community Cultural Wealth', *Race, Ethnicity and Education*, 8 (1): 69–91.

Concluding remarks: Agenda-setting research: Theory, practice

Paul Miller and Christine Callender

We have succeeded in bringing together researchers, practitioners and agencies working in the area of race discrimination/inequality in education in a single volume to examine and interrogate complex and multifaceted issues associated with race and educational leadership across the education sector in England. In doing so we have taken a three-pronged approach that debates and spotlights three areas: (i) attainment and pipeline issues (ii) talent development, management and career progression and (iii) intersections of religion, gender and ethnicity. Whilst this approach was partly dependent on the nature of the chapters selected for inclusion within the volume, the approach was also partly influenced by the issues examined by the contributors, which themselves represent important focal points. A starting point for understanding the educational experiences of individuals is to examine their experience of education, that is, ranging from the curriculum they are taught, to the classroom with peers and teachers, and to field interactions for those in teacher training. As have been reported in several research studies, a curriculum that is exclusive leads to disillusionment and isolation for those who do not see themselves within it, or who do not feel represented by it. Furthermore, where students, including those training to be teachers, do not feel welcome and/or adequately supported in educational institutions, this can result in interest impairment, leading to in underperformance and a lack of engagement.

A first step in expanding the pool or the stock of potential leaders of black, Asian and minority ethnic (BAME) heritage is the delivery of a curriculum, that promotes equality, and which places equal value and meaningful emphasis upon the cultural heritage and artefacts of all those studying such a curriculum and not just some students. A curriculum for all acknowledges racial, religious, cultural, social, political and other differences, and has the potential and power to equip learners and entire school communities with knowledge about 'the other' as well as the potential and power to transform stereotypical attitudes held by some learners and others within educational institutions and across the sector. The development and implementation of such a curriculum, however, requires *courage* and *activism* from policymakers and educational leaders who must, first, acknowledge that *British society is broken*, and, second, that a curriculum for all has an important role to play in mending and creating bridges between and among peoples and cultures. Consequently, the content of education itself and the practices of educational institutions must lead any process of social transformation or renewal for society as a whole. Thus, where teaching and leadership practices do not challenge racial stereotypes and biases (as well as other stereotypes and biases), these must be 'called out' in order to mitigate potential damage to the 'experience' of those individuals and groups already marginalized or at risk of such marginalization.

A second step, and an important principle, in expanding the stock or potential pool of leaders of BAME heritage is highlighting deliberate efforts by educational leaders and teachers to promote and foster race equality. Acknowledging where curricula have been changed and/or where steps have been taken by educational institutions to promote and deliver a positive experience for students and staff of BAME heritage is an important counterbalance to existing narratives of how individuals of BAME heritage 'experience' educational institutions, and a potential game changer in current debates and challenges concerning pipeline issues. Educational leaders and teachers who embark on deliberate steps to foster race equality are therefore called upon to publicize their efforts in order that these may come to the attention of those within and outside their institutions, and, importantly, within public consciousness and discourse. Accordingly, courage and activism are required from educational leaders and those who work in educational institutions, at all levels, to challenge and replace racially exclusive and racially neutral attitudes and practices with racially inclusive attitudes and practices that promote and foster respect and equality, and to devise and implement programmes, processes and systems towards uncorking or unclogging institutional and systemic blockages in the pipeline with the aim of growing the numbers of BAME leaders within their own institutions and across the sector.

This important volume has raised important issues on race and educational leadership in England, which we hope will contribute to policy and practice debates and lead to changes in policy and practices within institutions and across the sector. Nevertheless, whilst we have succeeded in showing awareness of the field, and have attempted to provide some 'balance' of content in terms of the variety and scope of the chapters presented, we are acutely aware that our work is not over. For, whilst we recognize the significance to the field of pulling this volume together, and whilst we acknowledge the potential of this volume to influence practices and policies within individual institutions and across the sector in current and future decades, we also recognize that this volume did not capture *important* policy and practice issues to do with (i) the early years, and (ii) perspectives and experiences from educational professionals from non-BAME heritage across the sector. We also acknowledge that *most* chapters have focused on institutional and/or systemic failures, and less on where policies and/or practices *may* have succeeded in bringing about change for individuals and/or groups. This, of course, was not deliberate but rather, a reflection of the pervasiveness of the negative experiences of individuals and groups, and the relative lack of evidence to suggest otherwise. Furthermore, we also note that nearly half of the chapters presented are (i) conceptual, or (ii) derived from studies that are small scale, and/or (iii) are qualitative in design. We highlight these issues not as limitations of individual chapters and/or of the volume as a whole, but rather to highlight (i) practice, (ii) policy, (iii) methodological and (iv) epistemological gaps in current research on race and educational leadership in England, and thus, where opportunities exists for further, urgent and different types of research.

Index